Visions of a New Land

Visions of a New Land

Soviet Film from the Revolution

to the Second World War

Emma Widdis

Yale University Press

New Haven & London

Printed in the United States of America.

Library of Congress Cataloging-in-Publication Data
Widdis, Emma, 1970–
    Visions of a new land : Soviet film from the Revolution to the Second World War /
Emma Widdis.
        p. cm.
Includes bibliographical references and index.
    ISBN 0-300-09291-1 (alk. paper)
    1. Motion pictures—Soviet Union—History.   2. Soviet Union—In motion
pictures.   I. Title.
    PN1993.5.R9 W53 2003
    791.43′0947—dc21

                                                                      2002012134

A catalogue record for this book is available from the British Library.

The paper in this book meets the guidelines for permanence and durability
of the Committee on Production Guidelines for Book Longevity of the Council
on Library Resources.

10 9 8 7 6 5 4 3 2 1

Y12427

Convinced that every innovation in the city influences the sky's pattern, before taking any decision they calculate the risks and advantages for themselves and for the city and for all worlds.
—*Italo Calvino*

Contents

Preface

When the Soviet Union went to war in 1941, it did so under the banner of a new identity and defended a new vision of its territory. In this book, I will explore the role of film in the creation of that identity—and that territory. I will examine how the Soviet space was represented in documentary and feature films made between 1917 and 1941, and trace the evolution of Russia's new "imaginary geography" under Lenin and Stalin.

To some extent, the dates that delimit my period of enquiry are inevitably artificial. I chose them, however, to mark out what I believe to be the long period during which models of spatial organization were tested and debated in cultural texts in Soviet Russia. I will focus in particular on the late 1920s and early to mid 1930s—on the period of the First Five-Year Plan and the beginnings of Stalinist consolidation. The scope of the book, however, is not and cannot be limited to this short period, and the broader time frame is vital to my argument. In the same way, this is a book about film, but in it I also draw extensively on a wide range of other materials and sources to illustrate and substantiate my broader claims. I hope, above all, to begin to answer two interrelated questions: First, how was the Soviet space imagined in cultural production? How did these "imaginary geographies" reflect real questions about the organization of the territory? And second, what kind of experience of the space was pictured? How did cultural texts offer models of a transformed relationship between Soviet man and woman and a transformed world? Film, then, can be only a part of the larger enquiry into the space and spaces of the Soviet utopia.

Many individuals and institutions have provided support and encouragement over the years during which this book has been written. I am grateful to the Slavonic Department of the University of Cambridge, to Peterhouse, to Fitzwilliam College, and to Trinity College, for vital financial and moral sustenance; I also thank the Kennedy Memorial Trust, and the Slavic Department of Harvard University, for the much appreciated opportunity to explore other spaces.

I cannot list all those who have helped in the preparation of this book. I owe a great debt to Julian Graffy, for his apparently endless generosity, both intellectual and material, and to Catherine Cooke, whose help in providing the illustrations was invaluable and whose advice and encouragement throughout the project were even more so. The following people read earlier versions of the manuscript and offered helpful suggestions: Svetlana Boym, Katerina Clark, Evgenii Dobrenko, Simon Franklin, Jana Howlett, and Richard Taylor. The book is greatly improved by their contributions. I have also gained much from discussions with Victor Listov, Maia Turovskaia, Naum Kleiman, Nikolai Izvolov, Neia Zorkaia, Katia Khokhlova, Romas Viesulas, and Valeri Bossenko in Moscow, and with Chris Ward, Susan Larsen, Amy Sargeant, Anne Henry, and Kate Tunstall. The staff of many libraries and archives in Moscow contributed to making my research easier and more productive, and Niamh O'Mahoney, Laura Cordy, and Adrian Newman offered vital help in the preparation of the manuscript and illustrations. I would also like to thank Jonathan Brent, Jessie Dolch, Mary Pasti, and Gretchen Rings for their invaluable support in the publication process.

I made a sincere attempt to identify the source of each illustration included in this book. In some cases, however, I was unable to locate an illustration's source. I therefore wish to apologize if I have inadvertently failed to credit any person or organization.

Finally, the writing of this book would not have been possible without the support of many others. In particular, I thank Anthony Cross, Robert Douglas-Fairhurst, Michael Newton, Suzanne Nicholas, Muriel Zagha, Mike Widdis, and Dianna Widdis and, of course, Jason Goddard, to whom I owe so much. I hope it's worth it.

Note on Transliteration and Translation

Transliteration of Russian is according to the Library of Congress system. Titles in the text are given in Russian and English at first mention, and thereafter in English. Titles in the notes are in Russian only. Although most citations are in English, key Russian terms used throughout the text are defined in the Glossary: in the text, they are given in Russian and English at first mention, and thereafter cited in Russian. All translations from the Russian are mine unless otherwise noted.

Introduction Projecting

This is a book about Soviet spaces. And about *Sovietness*. Through
film, it will trace the map—real and imaginary—of Sovietness. What,
then, is Sovietness? Its influence, malevolent or otherwise, on twentieth-
century history is indisputable; yet it remains a category about which
we understand little. The existence and essence of Sovietness have
been variously denied, disputed, and attacked over the past ninety
years. More recently, it has been politically dismantled by the collapse
of the Soviet Union in 1991. It should have disappeared. And yet in
contemporary Russia and the former Eastern bloc at the beginning of
the twenty-first century, for better or worse, something that we recognize as Sovietness remains very much alive: it is a way of understanding the world, and a way of living in it.

Such endurance seems to indicate that Sovietness was not merely a
construct of propaganda, a false identity imposed from above on oppressed peoples and easily discarded in 1991 together with almost a
century of history. It was, rather, a lived identity—and such it remains, as the lived heritage of post-Soviet Russia. Sovietness is, moreover, a unique historical phenomenon: an identity constructed anew

in the media age, in the course of a single century. Born in a dialogue between ideology and pragmatism, state and citizen, Sovietness was envisaged from its very beginnings as a revolutionary way of living in the world. It enlisted modern technology in its attempt to create a new space.

To understand the history and heritage of Sovietness is a vital task for us today. Its roots lie in the first two decades after the revolution of 1917, marked as they were by a search for the shape and contours of the new order. Spanning the transition from the revolutionary socialism of the civil war period, through the economic "retreat" of New Economic Policy, and into the Five-Year Plans that marked the beginnings of Stalinism and the command economy, these were the formative years of the new regime. They were the years during which the coordinates of Sovietness were defined.

Identifying these coordinates is the project of this book. Looking at feature and documentary film in particular, but also at popular journalism, avant-garde aesthetics, and architectural projects, I will examine how Soviet propaganda offered a new model of identity. Understanding Sovietness, I suggest, means understanding the space of Sovietness. In 1917, the revolution proclaimed a world remade, and the shape of that new world was a vital, and complex, question. The success of any social or political project depends on the provision of an imaginary "map" of the social and spatial totality within which the individual is to function: in the case of the Soviet Union, the sheer scale of the territory made this a monumental, and crucial, task.[1] Examining visions of the territory during this period is a means of examining competing visions of social organization. Social revolution demands spatial revolution: the new regime needed a new map.

"A COUNTRY WITH NEW BLOOD CIRCULATION"

Walking in Moscow in 1927, the German philosopher Walter Benjamin made an interesting observation: "Russia is beginning to take shape for the man of the people"; he wrote in a later essay: "On the street, in the snow, lie maps of the [R]SFSR piled up by street vendors who offer them for sale. . . . The map is almost as close to becoming the centre of the new Russian iconic cult as Lenin's portrait."[2] Four years later, in 1931, a Soviet adventure journal for children entitled *Vokrug sveta (All Around the World)* boasted of how many maps of itself Soviet Russia was now producing. One Leningrad factory, it claimed, produced only 800 maps per year before the revolution; now, by contrast, it was producing 125,000 globes and 28,000 geographical maps of the territory annually—although "for our boundless Union 125,000 globes is too little."[3]

These real maps indicated a much broader phenomenon. Between 1917 and 1935, a vast map-making process took place in Soviet Russia. The creation of a coherent "imaginary geography" for the enormous *neob"iatnyi prostor* (boundless space) of the Soviet Union was a vital task for the new regime, marking the boundaries of power.[4] Drawing the map—real and imaginary—of the new territory was a process of social and political consolidation. It was a means of positioning the citizen and individual within the nation, constructing relationships between centre and periphery, and associatively between private and public space.

This map-making process was not limited to cartography: it was a huge propaganda campaign involving the vast machinery of the Soviet cultural system. From the very first days after the revolution, the new state began an obsessive process of self-representation. In film, in print media, in literature, and in visual art, the task was to seek out and to propagate appropriate images of the new world—to reclothe the old world in revolutionary garments, or to reshape it in revolutionary form. The terms and shapes of this self-representation offer valuable insight into the ideological and pragmatic imperatives that underpinned the formation of the Soviet Union. Through the cultural texts that claimed to document the construction of socialism, we can trace the evolution of the imaginary national map of the Soviet Union through the 1920s and 1930s. The terms and images through which the territory was represented reveal how the new space was envisaged by the producers of culture, and how it was presented to a wider audience as a context for everyday life. Through film in particular, we can see how the new Soviet map was projected onto the vast, shared screen of the popular imagination.

In practical terms, of course, the exploration and mapping of the newly Soviet space were vital to the consolidation of the regime. The success of the new state depended on minimizing the vast distances that separated centre from periphery, creating an integrated social body. During the 1920s, projects for socialist reconstruction—such as electrification, the beginnings of industrialization, the expansion of rail networks, and radio installations—transformed the national map. They were, in a sense, acts of *surveying* the national space: the transformation of space (the unknown) into "territory" (the known and mapped). In 1928, the announcement of the First Five-Year Plan initiated an all-out drive for industrialization: the "Great Leap Forward" *(velikii perelom)* into modernization. During the First Plan (1928–32), industrialization and collectivization fundamentally altered the spatial organization of the nation.

Throughout the first two decades after the revolution, the structure of the new Soviet space was hotly debated: relations between centre and periphery were unfixed and contested. At stake, after all, was the materialization of utopia in real space, the construction of a revolutionary world. Underlying this reenvisaging of the national territory was the search for a revolution in spatial organization to mirror the revolution in social organization, mapping what the writer Isaak Babel' described as the "new blood circulation" of Soviet Russia.[5] The social body was to be mapped onto the spatial body. How would the Soviet space be different from the Imperial or the capitalist space?

The answer to this question seemed to lie in a rethinking of nationhood. A shared understanding of the national space is a crucial feature of national identity.[6] In the Soviet case, the picture is more complex. Describing the Soviet Union as a nation is fraught with difficulty, for both pragmatic and ideological reasons. Inheriting a vast and disparate empire, the Soviet leadership seemed to call for Sovietness as an explicitly non-national identity. The forthcoming world revolution, symbolized in the workers' "International," which was the official anthem of Soviet Russia from 1917 until 1943, would break down national boundaries, re-creating the world as a global order of proletariat rule. Pending that international revolution, however, Soviet Russia was faced with an urgent pragmatic imperative: to define a single, revolutionary space. Historians often see the years 1920–35 as marking the shift from the ideal of international revolution embraced by Vladimir Lenin and Leon Trotsky toward Joseph Stalin's "Socialism in One Country." It is my purpose here to examine how this transition was mapped in representations of the territory and how competing ideals and images of nationhood were tested in cultural production.[7] By the end of the 1930s, I suggest, the Stalinist "map" was drawn.

TO EXPLORE OR TO CONQUER?

Questions of space and territory are profoundly important in Soviet and Russian history. The vast expanses of the territory have played a key role in the historical development of nation and empire. In the words of the poet Aleksandr Blok in 1908, writing on the brink of a new era, "Our spaces are fated to play an elemental role in our history."[8] After 1917, those spaces continued to play their fateful roles. The sheer scale of the territory posed the same basic problems for the new Soviet state in the first decades after the revolution as it had for the Tsars: firm links between centre and periphery were a precondition for social and political control. And they were difficult to maintain.

Blok's statement of the "historical" and fateful role of space seamlessly blends the apparently practical with the clearly symbolic—a mix characteristic of descriptions of the Russian territory. The *neob"iatnyi prostor* is a powerful symbol of Russian national identity. In the early years of the twentieth century, Vasilii Kliuchevskii began his *Kurs russkoi istorii (Course of Russian History)* with a description of the uniqueness of the national space, describing how a Russian traveller arriving in the West feels restricted and hemmed in, recalling his native land where "he sees the level, empty fields, which seem to curve around the horizon, like a sea, with rare settlements and a black path around its edge."[9] Part of a tradition that includes such nineteenth-century writers as Nikolai Gogol' and Lev Tolstoi, Kliuchevskii defined the Russian national character according to this sense of boundless, empty space. Through the long history of Russian culture, *prostor* (wide, open space) and *prostranstvo* (space) have been complex signifiers. The territory is at once a metaphor of freedom (*volia*, describing a unique blend of "freedom" and "will," in contrast to the more straightforward *svoboda,* which indicates freedom from legal restraint) and of confusion, of success and of failure. The richness of the *rodnaia zemlia* (native land) is, symbolically and practically, untapped. Immeasurable, the territory is a symbol of the Russian soul itself.

In this tradition, Nikolai Berdiaev wrote in 1918 of the significance of the territory in the Russian spiritual and cultural imagination. The "Russian soul," he wrote in *The Fate of Russia,* "is oppressed by the boundless Russian fields."[10] In a later text, Berdiaev expanded this link between landscape and national identity: "The landscape of the Russian soul corresponds with the landscape of Russia, the same boundlessness, formlessness, reaching out into infinity, breadth."[11] The Russians, he suggested, "do not know the joy of form."[12] The formless, unknowable *prostor* shapes Russia's unique historic destiny, frequently evoked through the symbol of the folkloric *put',* or journey.[13] The famous *ptitsa-troika* appearing at the end of Book One of Gogol''s *Dead Souls,* envisages Russia as a troika flying headlong across the steppe into the future—but into a future that is undefined and unknown: "Rus', where are you heading? Answer us," the narrator begs. But the enigmatic Rus' gives no answer.[14]

This tendency, so marked through Russian history, to link real and imaginary landscapes and to view the territory as both symbol for and cause of national characteristics, demonstrates the importance of the present study. The formation of the Soviet state did not diminish the symbolic and practical effects of the territory. The revolutionary government inherited not only a vast, almost uncontrollable empire, but also a complex cultural mythology of the territory.[15] What they did with that mythology—how they tried to mould and alter it—was central to the success or failure of their project. The nature of Russia's new historic destiny, her revolutionary *put'*, was to be defined by a new vision of the territory. Shifts in attitudes to the *prostor* thus trace the evolution of the ideological and philosophical premises that underpinned the new state.

In real terms, of course, the inherited geography was not entirely unformed. Indeed, the image of the prerevolutionary territory as unmapped—and unmappable—ran parallel to the real project of mapping undertaken by successive Tsars from Peter the Great onward. An official atlas of the Imperial space, produced by the Academy of Sciences on Imperial command, had been published as early as 1745, comprising "nineteen special maps, presenting the All-Russian Empire and its Neighbouring Territories." During the nineteenth century in particular, when the Russian empire increased to its largest proportions, the project of mapping took place at a number of levels: in the literal sense of cartography, in the construction of infrastructure and networks of communication (the St. Petersburg—Moscow railway was built between 1842 and 1851), and in the development of related yet separate disciplines such as ethnography.[16]

The Russian Geographical Society was formed in 1845. By the beginning of the twentieth century, the "official" topography of Imperial Russia had clear shape, with the twin cities of Moscow and St. Petersburg anchoring its radial organization, as scientific expeditions into the vast territory gathered information for the centre. In cultural terms, however, the territory was still consistently evoked in terms of *neob"iatnost'* (un-boundedness/ungraspability). While the rapidly growing urban centres of Moscow and St. Petersburg acquired their own imaginary geography in cultural texts of the nineteenth century in particular, the *prostor* was evoked as at once unknowable and uncontrolled. The official topography of Imperial Russia was, in a sense, one of an elite; within it lurked the "inhabited" or "lived" spaces of rural (peasant) Russia that remained largely unmapped. In the apparently authoritative discourse of an encyclopaedia of 1895, for example, it was still possible to write that "vast tracts of the territory of the empire remain technically unmeasured *[sniatymi instrumental'no]*."[17]

Thus the uniqueness of the Soviet project was, in a sense, twofold. First, it was an attempt to link unofficial and official topography, to recruit the arts to the project of conveying images of a known and knowable territory. Second, it was a project of *remapping,* constructing a new Soviet geography that was to be explicitly differentiated from that of the Imperial regime. Even if the shape of the new Soviet empire might echo that of the prerevolutionary Imperial space, the organization of that space—and the experience of living in it—was to be radically reformulated. National and regional identities were to be sewn together into the single category of Sovietness.

The shifting rhetoric of expansion provides a useful prism through which to begin an analysis of the Soviet imaginary geography. *Osvoenie,* the mastery or conquest of space, is the term most frequently used to define both prerevolutionary and postrevolutionary attitudes to the uncharted vastness of the space.[18] It corresponds, apparently, to preferred models of Soviet history, in particular of the Stalin era, which emphasize centralized control.[19] Each Five-Year Plan throughout the Soviet period contained a section called *osvoenie prostranstva* (the mastery of space): the national space, unknown and untamed, is transformed by the extension of Soviet power into a territory both known and enlightened. The etymology of the term is complex. From the pronoun *svoi* (one's own) and the verb *osvoit',* *osvoenie* expresses both annexation, the "making one's own" in spatial terms (*osvoenie tselinnykh zemel'* [the cultivation of virgin lands]), and mastery, understood as the ability to *use* (*osvoenie russkogo iazyka* [mastering the Russian language]).[20] Thus the word embodies a duality of knowledge and control: through knowledge, one gains the ability to dominate. *Osvoenie* articulated a relationship of exploitation.

Osvoenie was associated with Imperial expansion and the opening up *(otkrytie)* of Siberia and was thus part of a colonizing process.[21] In the Soviet context, as we shall see, it assumed a still more defined form, consistently linked to the more aggressive *zavoevanie* (conquest [through battle]) in descriptions of the transformation of the territory. The space is "conquered"—that is, it is incorporated, contained within a clearly demarcated border.[22] The centre assimilates the periphery. This radial vision of space corresponds in many ways to Michel Foucault's famous description of Jeremy Bentham's Panopticon prison as encoding radial structures of visibility (surveillance) that guaranteed social control.[23] Foucault examined the ordering of space as a means of guaranteeing social discipline, stating that "space is fundamental in any exercise of power," and suggested that the model of the Panopticon could be applied to larger spatial organization, at a national level.[24] Its key feature, he claimed, was that it created "a state of conscious and permanent visibility that assures the automatic functioning of power."[25] Visibility ensures knowledge, and knowledge ensures the spread of the disciplinary mechanism through the social body. The extension of infrastructure across the national territory, Foucault suggests, is a development of the principle of organization that underpins the Panopticon.

This theory of space and power provides an interesting perspective on the radial model of Soviet space, characteristic of the High Stalinist period, in which the territory was symbolically subjugated by a dominant centre. *Osvoenie* was a process of illumination by which the space was made knowable. The imaginary map of High Stalinism pictured an immobile space, hierarchically organized around a dominant centre from which lines of influence extended radially, and the relationship between centre and periphery encoded relations of power. At the centre, Moscow functioned as the viewing position from which the whole territory could metaphorically be "seen," and hence controlled: Stalin, mythically, wrote through the night at his desk, a light glowing at his window, the epicentre of the Soviet space. A cult of visibility, internalized by the ordinary citizen and at its height during the purges, defined the organization of the regime. Events outside the capital found their justification in recognition from Moscow, and space—the vast *prostor*—was to be conquered and staked out, to cement control from the centre.

The French Marxist Henri Lefebvre, in his influential text *The Production of Space* (1974), posits a binary opposition of *domination* and *appropriation* through which to understand the social organization of space. These terms, rooted in the writings of Karl Marx himself, provide a useful perspective on the Soviet map. "Dominated space," Lefebvre suggests, is ideologically and politically constructed space, organized according to relations of power—"the realization of a master's project."[26] It is planned rather than lived, public rather than private. Technology facilitates the domination of space, permitting an extension of control. Lefebvre's notion of domination corresponds in important ways to *osvoenie*, as I have defined it, seeing infrastructure as a means of controlling the space. Furthermore, Lefebvre locates the emergence of dominated space in attempts to "master" nature—to transform rather than merely to experience.[27] In the imagery of Socialist Realism during the 1930s, the mastery of nature was a key theme, the banner under which many key industrial projects took place. Soviet man was to tame the natural world, inhabiting the uninhabitable spaces of the Arctic North, for example. Katerina Clark has shown how the opposition between "nature" and "culture" structured Stalinist representations of progress. The principal task was the transformation of the elemental forces of nature into the harmony and order of the new civilization.[28] Thus, implicitly, the Soviet project was one of dominating nature.

Although these analogies are useful, a narrow focus on the aesthetic of domination in Stalinist Russia risks oversimplifying the complex history of Soviet attitudes to the physical world. It is the central claim of this book that the "dominated," radial model of the Soviet space, consolidated during the second half of the 1930s, may be differentiated from that which predominated during the first decade of Soviet power and into the First Plan. It was, moreover, itself inflected by a fundamental ambiguity that characterized representations of space throughout the 1920s and 1930s. At its simplest, the rhetoric of *osvoenie* as conquest represented a rethinking of the revolutionary impetus: it reproduced, paradoxically, the centre-periphery relations that Marxist theory had identified as central to the capitalist system. In the *Communist Manifesto,* Marx and Friedrich Engels wrote that "the bourgeoisie has subjected the country to the rule of the towns." The centre subjects (conquers) the periphery as a precondition for the survival of state power.[29] The built and inhabited environment underpins social structures. A revolution in social organization thus demands a parallel revolution in spatial organization, and in particular the creation of a new kind of "equalized" territory, in which hierarchies of centre and periphery are eliminated: the building of utopia in real space. During the first decades of Soviet power, this need to create a different kind of space was recognized. Furthermore, "revolution" was envisaged as the creation of a new relationship between individual and space. The tensions produced by this social and political imperative are made manifest in the complex history of the early Soviet spatial imaginary, which this book seeks to reveal.

Visions of this changed relationship between individual and space provide a revealing index of the cultural and philosophical shifts that took place in Soviet Russia between the 1920s and the consolidation of Stalinism during the 1930s.[30] Vladimir Papernyi has defined the culture of the 1930s against that of the 1920s according to a binary opposition of "vertical" and "horizontal" structures.[31] "Culture One" (the 1920s), he suggests, was defined by horizontal spatial organization. The Stalinist 1930s ("Culture Two") were marked by centralization and hierarchy. Drawing on examples from architecture, film, and literature, Papernyi's structuralist account provides a valuable perspective on images of space but suggests a broadly schematic distinction between the implicitly "good" 1920s and "bad" 1930s. In fact, competing models of centrifugal and centripetal spatial organization coexisted and collided throughout the first two decades of Soviet power. They were underpinned, moreover, by competing models of *experience.* Expanding Papernyi's distinction, I will suggest that *osvoenie* is an inadequate term through which to describe the attitude to the Soviet space that was expressed in the culture of the 1920s and into the 1930s. A better understanding of the complex imaginary geography of the period may be obtained through the notion of *exploration*. "Exploration" was expressed in Russian by a number of different terms, most frequently *razvedka* (reconnaissance or prospecting) and *izuchenie* (study). Where *osvoenie* describes an assimilative, dominating attitude to the periphery, in which the region is subject to a structure of control from the centre, exploration describes a more decentred investigation of the region, which does not seek to conquer. The shifting boundaries between these two models of the relationship to the territory can be traced in descriptions of the Soviet space throughout the 1920s and 1930s.

In the imaginary map of the 1920s, then, the *prostor* was not a hostile, resistant natural force to be tamed by heroes or by a dominant centre. It was, rather, a land ripe with possibility, the material from which a new world was to be constructed. Borders were not protective divides that demarcated self from other, but rather represented the exciting spaces of transition into the workers' International, the global socialist space. Exploration, movement across the map, and the creation of new routes and networks of communication were clearly articulated and urgent tasks. Infrastructure was just the beginning. The territory was to be re-created as a decentred, nonhierarchical, and dynamic space, in which the periphery had more cultural and ideological value than the centre. Projected routes across the territory, lines of interconnection, proliferated on the imaginary map. Relationships between and across spaces shifted dramatically. During the First Five-Year Plan in particular, with the massive industrializing push of the *velikii perelom*, the entire nation was forced into flux, marked by what Katerina Clark describes as a "dash to the periphery."[32] During this period, then, the *neob"iatnyi prostor* was to be explored. Exploration, moreover, carried vital ideological significance. It was a means of remaking the "dominated" space of prerevolutionary Russia and creating a new relationship between Soviet man and woman and the world. The physical experience of movement through space was symbolically offered to everyone.

Here we may return to Lefebvre: in opposition to the *domination* of space, he situates *appropriation*. Space that is appropriated is modified to suit those who live in it, as it is experienced and inhabited. It is space produced by practice, constructed by movement. Lefebvre's terms are rooted in those of Marx, and it is this that justifies their relevance here. In the *Economic and Philosophical Manuscripts of 1844*, Marx wrote of Communism as the overcoming of "alienation," in terms that owed much to a reading of G. W. F. Hegel's *Phenomenology of Spirit*. Hegel's error, Marx suggested, lay in not recognizing that "alienation" was the result of the opposition between abstract thought and "sensuous reality."[33] This opposition, he suggested, brought about man's alienation *from himself*—that is, from his existence as a sentient being—and consequently from other men. For Hegel, the overcoming of alienation was the "supercession of objectivity." For Marx, by contrast, alienation could be overcome by the establishment of a new kind of relationship between man and the object world—not the "supercession" of objectivity, but the remaking of it. True Communism was "the genuine solution of the antagonism between man and nature, and between man and man."[34] It is the first half of this statement that interests us here, for it focuses on the relationship between man and the physical world. The overcoming of private property was to be brought about by the "sensuous appropriation by and for man of human essence and human life." The self-realization of the individual was a precondition for the establishment of collective society, and it was to be achieved through "the complete emancipation of all human senses and qualities."[35]

A "sensuous" rapprochement between man and the physical world lay, then, at the centre of Marx's vision of the end of alienation. In rediscovering the physical world, man would be able to "appropriate" that world and to establish a new kind of relationship with it. "Each of his human relationships to the world—seeing, hearing, smell, tasting, feeling, thinking, contemplating, feeling, willing, acting, loving—in short all the organs of his individuality," Marx wrote, "are in their objective action, or their relation to the object, the *appropriation* of this object."[36] This term, *appropriation,* later taken up by Lefebvre, was used frequently by Marx in these early writings and appears to underpin his vision of the rapprochement between man and the object world. The "emancipated" senses permit a relationship with the object world, which is not premised on the exercise of power—neither on the domination of man over the physical world nor vice versa. The *appropriative* relationship is envisaged as one of mutual benefit.[37]

Thus it is evident that a phenomenological emphasis underpinned at least these early writings of Marx and had certain influence on the philosophical and aesthetic preoccupations of the Soviet avant-garde. Influenced by Walter Benjamin's view of the experience of modernity, Susan Buck-Morss has suggested that the Soviet avant-garde were driven by what she calls a "utopics of sensuality"—the drive to recover the sensory experience of the world that had been lost to humanity through the conditions of modern technology.[38] The thrust of this sensory utopics was twofold. First, it sought to create a productive relationship between man and the object world of technology. The machine, enemy of man under conditions of capitalist labour, was to be reappropriated as comrade. Soviet technology was not oppressor, but liberator, and the task of man was to *appropriate* technology through and for the body. The machine aesthetic of avant-garde culture was driven by this imperative, seeking to eliminate the distinction between the human body and the machine. Second, the appropriative project sought to remake the world according to new principles, or more precisely, to remake the relationship between the new Soviet man and the natural world.

The present analysis will investigate how various "imaginary maps," presented through film, architecture, and journalism, mediated the physical world (space) and articulated this new experience of space. I will explore the imagined geography of the Soviet Union in terms of the schematic opposition between exploration and conquest. Both terms suggest broader world views: "exploration" *(razvedka)* describes a decentred, nonhierarchical vision of space in which difference is emphasized over sameness, and the quest for information is differentiated from control. It envisages a spatial organization that is not radial, but that corresponds more closely to the structure of a grid or network: the territory is equalized. The experience of movement is offered to everybody. The *put'* is a perpetual movement forward into the future, and the present moment is the key point of focus. The exploration of space is dynamic, a continual act of *appropriation* and creation. In contrast, under the heading of conquest (here *osvoenie*), I picture a radial model of space, controlled from the centre and hierarchically organized. Ultimately, I will show how these two models intersected and collided in cultural texts—and, in so doing, reveal the complexities of the Soviet imaginary geography.

Between 1920 and 1935, real and imaginary maps of the Soviet territory actively and creatively coexisted in cultural representations. This cannot be reduced to a simple dynamic of centrally produced propaganda and rhetoric, which distorted and misrepresented reality. The key to understanding the achievements of the Soviet propaganda machine is to appreciate the creative power of cultural imagery and the extent to which visions of utopia were a real, creative force in the construction of the new society.[39] Bolshevik society was continually representing itself, and the very process of *creating* the imaginary map functioned as a means of integration and consolidation. Examining diverse cultural phenomena and resources in order to trace the imaginary geography of the early Soviet Union, I will trace the intersection of reality and representation, aesthetics and ideology, in the creation of the new Soviet map. How did pragmatic imperatives shape the development of avant-garde aesthetics?

What were the parameters of identity established through visual and verbal media? Answers to these questions can be found, I believe, in an analysis of Soviet film. Film played a unique role in the creation of Soviet identity: it both represented the new national map and, perhaps more interestingly, was seen as a means of creating a new relationship between Soviet man and woman and the physical world. The visual frames that film places on the world offer models of experience. As Oksana Bulgakowa recognizes, temporal and spatial structures form the basis of narrative potential in any film.[40] More important still, they provide the raw material out of which the film is constructed. In Soviet Russia, the shaping of this raw material was tantamount to the shaping of the new world.

THE CINEMATIC NETWORK

The interest of cinema during this period lies not only in an analysis of its images and its stories, but also in the organization of the new cinematic industry as a paradigmatic *set'* (network) of communication in the new Soviet space. Cinema, as is well-known, was Lenin's "most important of all arts"—a powerful means of communicating with an illiterate population. It had an important role to play in the creation of a single ideological space, and the Soviet leadership were quick to recognize its potential as propaganda. The establishment of the cinematic propaganda machine was an important part of the broader project of mass education. Examining the structure of the emergent cinema industry and its network, therefore, provides us with a perspective on the structure of the propaganda network as a whole. Through cinema, moreover, we see the intersection of culture and politics almost at its most dramatic: filmmakers worked subject to the permission and funding of the regime. A brief history of the rhetoric that surrounded the building of a national cinema network enables an examination of the spatial organization of the Soviet propaganda machine.

In 1918, N. F. Preobrazhenskii (as chairman of the Moskinokomitet [Moscow Cinema Committee]) announced: "Our duty before history is to film everything that we can and preserve it for future generations; our duty to the people is to show them everything that is happening now."[41] This statement expresses the dual role of documentary film, which was to function as both historical document and integrational and educational weapon. It would "preserve" the present, granting it the historical significance that it deserved and, more important, provide a means of involving those at the periphery in the construction of socialism.[42]

In response to this imperative, the first *agit-poezd* (propaganda train)—containing a printing plant, a theatre company, and a film crew—travelled to the civil war front at Kazan' in the summer of 1918.[43] Footage shot at the front was sent back to Moscow (where it was processed and edited by volunteers, including a young Dziga Vertov (later to become an important figure in Soviet film history), and the material was then sent to other fronts and across the territory to incite popular support. This process continued after the civil war, and by 1925 there were one thousand "travelling cinemas" with mobile projectors *(kinoperedvizhniki)* active in the Soviet Union, travelling the nation showing Soviet (especially documentary) films.[44] Cinema brought national "news" to the village, seeking to transform peasants and workers into participants, or citizens, of the new state.

Kinofikatsiia (cinefication) aimed to cement ideological control over the periphery. Its central aim was assimilative, extending influence from the centre to the regions. In practice, however, during the 1920s, this dynamic was more complex. In January 1925, cinematic production and distribution were centralized through the creation of Sovkino, a national planning agency for cinema.[45] To ensure *kinofikatsiia,* Sovkino operated centrifugally: the formation of ODSK (the Society for Friends of Soviet Cinema) in July 1925 was an attempt, through the formation of local organizations, to provide a vanguard for the provision of cinematic equipment and the involvement of cinema in the everyday life of the regions.[46] The formation of ODSK grew out of the recognition that it was insufficient simply to bring cinema to the village. The creation of a cinematic "public" *(obshchestvennost')* was essential in order to make cinema a part of everyday life.[47] This cinematic public would depend on a network in villages and towns that would not be centrally directed but would rely instead on continual communication between local and regional committees. The goal of ODSK was to establish this network.[48]

Cinema was to function as an integrator—creating a unified Soviet space. Film was believed to be the most effective medium for "raising the cultural level of the peasant . . . taking him out of the confines of rural narrow-mindedness, bringing him by example closer to the town, to the worker."[49] After 1924, "Face to the Village" *(litsom k derevne)* became a powerful slogan, announcing a general propaganda campaign in which cinema was central. Between 1925 and 1929, all editions of *Sovetskoe kino (Soviet Cinema),* the official journal of the Narkompros (State Commission for Enlightenment) cinema section, contained an extensive section entitled *"litsom k derevne,"* claiming the *kinofikatsiia* of the village to be a key task for Soviet construction.[50] As a first step, ODSK was responsible for the organization and maintenance of the growing number of mobile projectors, with which activists travelled the region. The extent of ODSK's success in establishing an effective cinematic *set'* was the subject of on-going debate between 1925 and 1927.[51]

The First Party Conference on Cinema in March 1928 was a turning point in the ideological and political status of cinema, a clear statement that henceforward film must be a weapon in the socialist transformation of the country and the creation of a unified Soviet people. The enormous mobilization of the nation demanded by the First Five-Year Plan necessitated an intensified programme of *kinofikatsiia,* and during the first half of 1928 the number of travelling projectors (1,881) and new cinemas across the territory almost doubled.[52]

The resolutions of the conference called, moreover, for more truly "Soviet" films that would encourage popular support for state initiatives. From the mid-1920s, the production and distribution of newsreels had been identified as key ideological tasks.[53] Dziga Vertov's *Kinonedelia (Film Week),* the first of which was produced on 1 June 1918, and thereafter weekly for one year, and his later *Kinopravda (Film-Truth)* series are the best-known examples of the Soviet newsreel, but other examples abound. During the First Five-Year Plan in particular, documentary film "journals" multiplied.[54] The *Soiuzkinozhurnal (Union Film Journal),* coordinated by the Soiuzkinokhronika (Union of Film Chronicles), produced thirty-nine editions in 1926. By 1929, the figure had grown to eighty-four (silent) films and then did not drop to fewer than seventy films per year.[55] Between 1929 and 1938 the series *Za sotsialisticheskuiu derevniu (For a Socialist Village)* was produced to encourage local activists in the pursuit of collectivization and to "integrate" the peasant. *Nashi dostizheniia (Our Achievements),* made to accompany a printed journal edited by Maksim Gor'kii, was a series of filmed "journals" produced monthly in 1930 that aimed specifically at involving the periphery in the actions and achievements of the centre (the Soviet state). "The 'little people,'" a title in the series proclaimed, citing Gor'kii himself, "should know that their every labour is returned to them in the form of those achievements of which this journal tells." Filmed journals such as "Our Achievements" generally comprised news fragments taken by different cinematographers in different regions emphasizing the valuable contributions of the region to the great achievement of the state. In this way, cinematic images mapped a single Soviet space in which centre and periphery were interdependent, documenting the construction of socialism at the level of the region. The consolidation of the centre depended, rhetorically, on the actions of the periphery; the achievements of the "little man" were a source of national pride.

Making *kinofikatsiia* effective entailed an attention to everyday life, to the local space as these "little people" experienced and practised it. The "mass," filmmakers and ideologues proclaimed, would respond most to the familiar, to representations of their own lives. In 1925, an editorial in *Soviet Cinema* suggested that instead of concentrating on films of the centre, therefore, and on military parades and demonstrations, documentary film should "grasp the full scale of the authentic life of all the peoples inhabiting the USSR, their everyday life and daily events."[56] A sense of the urgency of this developed toward the end of the decade, and in 1929, a debate took place in the pages of the popular journal *Zhizn' iskusstva (Life of Art):* filmmakers (implicitly from the centre), one writer proclaimed, needed better to understand the lives of "ordinary" people: "We have to put our directors face to face with their audiences, in factories . . . and in villages."[57]

The "Face to the Village" campaign was an attempt to make films about subjects that would interest and be relevant to the peasant: "We must talk in his own sincere language about the cow that is sick with tuberculosis, about the dirty cowshed that must be transformed into one that is clean and bright."[58] Despite the obvious limitations of this view of "what the peasant wants," it appears clear that the centre did try to understand the particularities of the regions. Attempts to undertake viewer research were made in both city and country, often organized by ODSK, the Komsomol (the Union of Youth), or ARK (the Association of Revolutionary Cinema Workers): "To study the peasant viewer is to study the life, interests, and everyday practices of the village."[59] The question of viewers' preferences was at the centre of a larger debate about the ideological value of fiction or documentary film, entertainment or education. In an article of 1924, Vertov wrote of the experience of a "film screening in a village," describing the response of a peasant audience to "real" tractors as more positive than that evoked by actors and fiction. The newsreel, he claimed, was the means by which the peasant could be educated to become a cinema viewer, as it represented the familiar and the everyday on-screen.[60]

The search for an appropriate "Soviet" film genre continued through the 1920s. In practice, "revolutionary" films such as Sergei Eisenstein's *Bronenosets Potemkin (Battleship Potemkin)* were less popular among audiences than the foreign films that were imported through the 1920s.[61] From 1926, Sovkino initiated a campaign to create a truly Soviet picture that would correspond to viewers' preferences and tastes while remaining politically correct and effective as propaganda. Soviet cinema would combat the popularity of Western imports and popular comedies with its own popular genre. The conference in 1928 called for an eradication of "bourgeois" vestiges from Soviet cinema and the increased mobilization of cinema in the service of industrialization and modernization. No real success was achieved in this project, however, until the 1930s, with the advent of what is termed Socialist Realist cinema. In 1930, Boris Shumiatskii was appointed chairman of Soiuzkino, the newly centralized organization of Soviet film, and remained in that position until 1938. Shumiatskii was responsible for the "Hollywoodization" of Soviet cinema, urging directors to focus on popular genres.[62] The creation of a popular, ideologically sound Soviet cinema accompanied the consolidation of Socialist Realism in literature. In parallel, the decentred network of film organization was increasingly replaced by a centralized and controlling industry.

These changes were accompanied by a gradual shift in symbolic systems. The dynamic, decentred space pictured by documentary and feature film during the 1920s and the Five-Year Plan was superseded by the radially organized landscape of Stalinism. Why and how this happened is the subject of this book. Two interrelated projects thus structure this enquiry: first, to trace the emergent structures of the Soviet imaginary geography, and second, to explore the representation of the *relationship* between the new Soviet man or woman and his/her radically transformed space.

The first chapter will begin by examining the practical transformation of the Soviet space that occurred between approximately 1920 and 1935, showing how infrastructural projects such as electrification and industrialization changed the shape of the territory and how they were represented in propaganda. The historical context thus established, Chapter 2 locates the more specialized discourse on film within broader debates on the transformation of space. It examines how film was perceived to play a privileged role in the shared task of all the arts—not only to represent the transformed territory, but to shape and mould that territory through the very act of representation and to remodel the relationship between the space and its inhabitants. In the third chapter, the practical consequences of the self-assumed task of film are revealed: we see how urban and domestic spaces were reenvisaged during the 1920s, tracing the emergence of a new space of experience in Soviet film culture. In Chapter 4, our gaze shifts—together with that of the Soviet movie camera—from the city to the periphery, showing how the *prostor* was envisaged as a land ripe with possibility, the material from which a new world was to be constructed. The key task of Soviet man and woman was to explore the space, to travel across the territory.

Travel is also the theme of Chapter 5, which examines how different modes of transport—the train and the plane—encoded different relationships with the territory and how the shifting prominence of different ways of looking at (and experiencing) the territory tracks the shifting visual imagination of Soviet culture. Using this narrow focus, Chapter 5 traces the gradual shift from exploration toward conquest, which is the broader subject of Chapter 6. Through this blend of chronological and thematic focus, integrating a history of aesthetics with a broader cultural history, it is hoped that a revealing new picture of the period will emerge.

Chapter 1 Connecting

Скоре–е–е–е–е–е–е–е!
Скорейскорей
Эй-
губернии-
снимайтесь с якорей
За Тульской Астраханская-
за махиной махина-
Стоявшие неподвижимо
даже при Адаме-
двинулись
и на
другие
прут - погромыхивая
городами

(Fa-a-a-ster . . . / FasterFaster / Hey, provinces / Raise your anchors! /
Astrakhan, follow Tula / one *makhina* [large, bulky thing] after another /
Standing immobile /Even in Adam's day / have now moved / and are
shoving / others, rattling / their cities)
— *Vladimir Maiakovskii*

In the years between 1917 and 1930, the Soviet territory was a space under new management—and new ownership. The nationalization of land and property, in effect from 1917, entailed a conceptual transformation of the imagined national map: the capitalist space became a state-controlled space. The first *Dekret o zemle* (land decree) was passed on 26 October 1917, symbolically transferring the ownership of all land, earth, and water from private to state hands.[1] And these "state hands" were equated, significantly, with the hands of the people. Thus the territory became, symbolically at least, a whole—and a whole that "belonged" to the masses.

As such, the territory—its structures and its development—could be centrally planned. The first state committee for construction was formed by decree in 1918. Its tasks were defined as "the planning of towns and settlements and the construction of infrastructure *at a general-state level* [emphasis added]."[2] Lenin's famous plan for the electrification of "all Russia," presented to the Eighth Congress of Soviets in 1920, was the first national plan, and it was quickly followed by the creation of Gosplan (the State Planning Commission) in 1921.[3] Gosplan presented its first annual economic plan in August 1925, and by 1926 its remit had been expanded to include preparatory work on a general plan for future national development: the beginnings of unified planning. With the announcement of the First Five-Year Plan in 1928, central planning became the key axis upon which the development of Soviet economy and society turned. Full-scale industrialization began, as Stalin announced the urgent need for the Soviet Union to catch up with and overtake *(dognat' i peregnat')* the industrial nations of the capitalist West. Mass collectivization was initiated in the autumn of 1929.

In political terms, the years between 1921 and 1927 were dominated by the New Economic Policy (NEP), which sought to revive an economy decimated by civil war through a temporary concession to private enterprise. The NEP years are often seen to lie outside the trajectory of "revolution" and to constitute a brief interruption of the revolutionary impetus, resumed in 1928 by the First Five-Year Plan. In terms of the imaginary geography of the Soviet space, however, there is significant continuity between the mid-1920s and the years of the First Plan (1928–32). In particular, these years saw the progressive unification of the territory and the development of the ideal of national planning: the transformation of space into territory was central to the consolidation of power and crucial to the creation of a new kind of identity—Sovietness.

The Soviet obsession with planning is frequently evoked to demonstrate the desire of the centre to extend control across the society as a whole and to impose

large-scale solutions on a vast territory. The very term *plan* has become synony-
mous with Soviet monumental ambition, corresponding to historical accounts
that emphasize centralized control.[4] Certainly, the parallel projects of electrification, industrialization, and collectivization between 1920 and 1932 represented an unprecedented attempt to transform the Soviet space *in its entirety:* a
reconceptualization of the national map. An examination of the visual and verbal terms through which these projects were described, however, reveals a more
complex picture of their aims and ambitions. In particular, it reveals a rhetorical emphasis on the creation of new *connections* between centre and periphery
and the expressed intention to construct an alternative spatial organization: a
socialist space.

Visions of this socialist space were structured by the ideological imperative
to abolish the hierarchical division of space—to overcome the separation of
town and countryside, urban and rural spaces, through (in Engels's words) "the
unification of town and village in a single whole."[5] This was not merely a project of unification, however; it was also, rhetorically at least, one of *equalization.*
Throughout the 1920s and into the First Plan, the economic cooperation of
peasant and worker—consistently expressed as the joining *(smychka)* of village
and town—was a powerful ideological catchphrase that had wider implications than its economic definition initially allows. *Smychka* was slogan as well as
policy, metaphor as much as reality: villager and worker were to be united as
Soviet citizens; centre and periphery were to be reconfigured as *equal spaces* in a
nonhierarchical society. The success of this dual project of unification and
equalization depended, of course, on routes and means of communication and
on the *otkrytie* (opening up) of isolated areas of the vast *prostor*. It relied on the
development of infrastructure. According to propaganda, the development of
energy distribution, transport, and communication networks would bring
about a "victory over distance," creating new patterns of connection.[6] The vast
prostor would be re-created as a single network of interconnected spaces.
Within this model of interconnection, key questions about the structure of Soviet identity were raised. How, in practical terms, was the equalized space to be
organized? How would local and national identities intersect?

ELECTRIFICATION: ILLUMINATING
THE TERRITORY

From the beginning, the development of infrastructure carried both practical
and symbolic weight—providing a physical structure for development and, at

the same time, a structure for the new imaginary map of the *prostor*. Nowhere was this conflation of the practical and symbolic more clearly expressed than in the monumental *Plan elektrifikatsii (Plan for Electrification)* announced in 1920. The GOELRO (State Commission for Electrification) plan, which grew out of a proposal by Gleb Krzhizhanovskii (former Imperial civil servant), was an important turning point in the ideological remapping of the Soviet Union and represented the first unified, single plan for the reconstruction of the economy.[7] It was a response to both ideological and pragmatic imperatives. The problem of transporting fuel and resources across the vast *prostor* had long represented the principal obstacle to rapid industrialization, and discussion of how to create communications networks that would rationalize the developing Russian industry had been frequent in Tsarist Russia of the nineteenth century. Between 1906 and 1917, criticisms of the transportation system of the empire, and plans for improving the Dnepr waterway and developing electrical power, were common.[8] After the revolution, the Bolsheviks sought immediate solutions to the same practical problems.

Electrification offered more than this, however. Certainly, it would facilitate industrialization on an enormous scale; but it would also—and just as importantly—transform everyday life in every corner of the Soviet territory, providing a network that would integrate centre and periphery. Developed in conjunction with *radiofikatsiia* (radiofication), which sought to provide radio transmission across the territory, electrification was envisaged as part of a communicative infrastructure that would extend across the *prostor*, uniting disparate spaces. In both symbolic and practical terms, it would provide a new structure for the mapping of the Soviet territory—what Krzhizhanovskii called an "electrical skeleton" of power lines.[9]

The structure of this skeleton—of the electrical network—raised fundamental questions about the organization of the national space. As such, it provides a glimpse of the broader dilemma characterizing attitudes to the spatial organization of the Soviet Union during this period. In particular, debate in 1920 focused on the opposition between radial spatial organization (in which central power stations, with Moscow as nodal point, would distribute power across the territory) and more decentred, gridlike models for the power net.[10] The final plan, presented in 1921, divided the Russian Republic into eight economic regions, effectively marking the beginning of regional planning.[11] It initiated a "a revolutionary shift in the geographical distribution of production."[12] Much emphasis was placed on axes that traversed the territory, linking constituent parts and creating new "centres" that would, the plan proclaimed, "be linked to one another by electrical lines."[13] This did not mean, of course, a rejection of the central position of the capital: in fact, the main map of electrification showed a traditional radial structure that retained Moscow at its centre. It was also marked, however, by power lines running between smaller cities such as Tula, Riazan', Nizhnii Novgorod, and Tambov, independently of the capital. This corresponded with the stated intentions of the plan: smaller towns were to assume the role of local centres. Electrification thus *dispersed* the traditional radial structure of centre and periphery. As such, it maintained the dual models of radial (centripetal) and decentred (centrifugal) spatial organization—caught, one might suggest, between the ideal of decentralization and the pragmatic value and necessity of the centre (Figure 1).

This opposition between the grid and more radial patterns for the organization of the electrical network ran through the debate on electrification, just as it underpinned broader debates about the organization of the territory and relations between centre and periphery in the new Soviet geography. The actual organization of the electrical grid, however, was almost secondary to its meta-

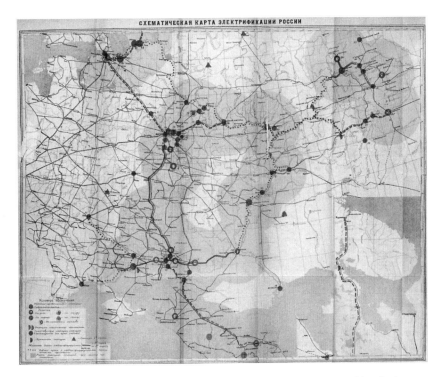

Figure 1. Map of the electrification of Russia. Moscow: Gosudarstvennoe tekhnicheskoe izdatel'stvo, 1921. Courtesy of the Russian State Library, Moscow.

phorical weight. As a symbol, the grid was broadly understood—and promoted—as a radical equalizer that made the periphery equal to the centre. Symbolically, there was no single centre in electrification. The provision of power across the nation would abolish the practical necessity for a centre, permitting industry and settlement at any point on the national map or network. Within the new network all areas—large industrial centres and small villages alike—would be symbolically equal: "even the smallest electric power stations would become local centres."[14]

As a unifying network, the power grid was to carry ideological as well as electrical energy. With electric light would come enlightenment (*prosveshchenie;* from *svet* [light], the term clearly expresses the association of light and knowledge): in Lenin's words, "the electrical education of the masses."[15] "Lenin's little light bulbs," the *lampochki Il'icha* of popular rhetoric, would light the dark corners of the Soviet state (Figures 2 and 3).[16] GOELRO was the primary weapon

Figure 2. "Lenin's little light begins to burn." From *Prozhektor.* Reprinted from *Oktiabr'skie Stranitsy (1917–1941),* compiled by V. S. Listov and G. A. Ambernadi, 158.

Figure 3. "A worker from an electrical factory with a two-kilowatt bulb." From *SSSR na stroike,* 1930, no. 3: 28.

in the battle against the remnants *(ostatki)* of capitalism and economic back-wardness in the countryside and the means of achieving the ideal of *smychka.* It would, Lenin proclaimed, "bring an end to the gulf between town and village, make it possible to raise the cultural level of the village, vanquish the remnants of backwardness, darkness, degradation, illness and poverty even in the most remote corners of the country."[17]

"Electrical education," moreover, was no mere metaphor: Lenin demanded that copies of the *Plan for Electrification* itself be kept at power stations and in schools as an inspirational instruction book for citizens.[18] The plan was to function as a symbolic and educational artefact, explicitly uniting centre and periphery, local and national spaces. As part of the propaganda and public-ity programme accompanying electrification, the journalist I. I. Skvortsov-Stepanov was commissioned to write a book that would popularize electrifica-tion and educate the masses as to its practical and ideological significance. The book's second edition in 1922 included a preface by Lenin himself, in which he recommended that the text be distributed and read by all members of the new Soviet state and that regular public readings should take place.[19] All of this con-spired to present the fulfilment of the plan as a national task, integrational and collective. All citizens would participate, symbolically and directly, in the achievements of the state. In the plan itself, the balance between huge-scale construction (the enormous hydroelectric plants to be built on the Volkhov

Figure 4. "Lenin and Electrification. Communism Is Soviet
Power Plus the Electrification of the Whole Country." 1925.
Private collection.

and Dnepr Rivers, for example) and smaller tasks (the electrification of individual villages) was carefully maintained: regional and national maps articulated this crucial balance.

The continual flux between macro and micro in descriptions of electrification was common to propaganda of the period and was mirrored at social and spatial levels. Lenin's famous pronouncement of 1920 that "Communism is Soviet power plus the electrification of the whole country" (Figure 4) reveals the complex relationship between control and empowerment that underpinned GOELRO.[20] On the one hand, electrification was represented as a vital means of extending Soviet power across the territory—a weapon in the project of state consolidation and homogenization; on the other hand, it was, rhetorically at least, a decentralizing project, which sought to enable, or empower, the regions (the "whole country") to play their own part in the creation of the new socialist world. Its implicit message was that every corner mattered: every corner deserved light. Referring to the plan, Lenin wrote, "this programme, every day, in every workshop, in every region, will be improved, developed, perfected and transformed."[21] This emphasis on progress and process defined the historical *put'* of the 1920s; Lenin's view of the plan as a symbolic document was part of a broader intention to create a sense of Soviet history in the making, in which "everyone" was involved.

The representation of the Soviet present as an historic present moment was fundamental to the Bolshevik propaganda campaign through the 1920s and into the 1930s, and film, of course, had a key role to play. As early as 1920, Lenin underlined the need to film the electrification process and to distribute the films widely.[22] Film was both agitation and education: its task was to spread the good news of electrification as an historic project and to educate the masses as to its practical significance in the here and now. Furthermore, films must encourage mass participation—as much symbolic as actual—in the process of transformation, showing how the grid had both national and *local* effect. Electricity was the primary enabler for the industrialization of the nation; at the same time, "Lenin's little light bulbs" would improve the lives of workers and peasants in all corners of the vast nation.

Two key images recurred in documentary films of electrification: the first showed the attachment of electrical cables to a village home (Figure 5); the second was a more intimate shot of a peasant family or individual inside the home, working by electric light. A section of Esfir Shub's famous documentary chronicle of the first decade of Soviet power, *Velikii put'* (*The Great Way*, 1927), carried the title "we are electrifying the Soviet village." The process was charted in a representative succession of images: from a panorama of the village (illuminated at night, as in many images of the period [Figure 6]), the camera moved successively closer, to street lamps, and then followed a cable running into an individual home and moved through a lighted window into the home itself. In the same way, Dziga Vertov's film of 1926, *Shagai, Sovet!* (*Forward March, Soviet!*) made explicit the multiple levels at which electrification was to function. It moved "from an oil lamp in the centre of the city" to "the electrification of the outskirts *[okrain]*" and thence "to the electrification of the village." The visual images of the film mapped this inclusive new network: wires and pylons appear

Figure 5. Electrifying the village. Film still from *Na Leninskom puti* (1932). Private collection.

first in a provincial town and then in a village, and finally the electrical life force enters an individual hut (Figure 7), illuminating (naturally) a portrait of the great leader, Lenin, father of electrification.

Thus the village—even the individual home—was symbolically connected to the greater Soviet space. The image of the home illuminated, and of the electric lamp, provided a consistent reference point for increased prosperity, and the motif of "electricity in the village" provided a key image in Soviet cultural production throughout the 1920s and into the 1930s (Figure 8). As a 1932 film, *Na Leninskom Puti (On the Leninist Journey)*, proclaimed, "across the nation . . . Lenin's light is starting to burn . . . we remember his testament, calling for *smychka*." In practice, however, the representation of electrification in documentary films made visible a more complex dialectic of homogeneity and difference in the representation of the relationship between local and national spaces. Sitting ambiguously between a drive for sameness and an emphasis on equality, the model of the grid raised important questions about the status of localness in Soviet imaginary geography. Illuminated, the village became a mark on the ideological map, woven into a national network. In parallel, how-

ЭЛЕКТРИФИКАЦИЯ СССР.

Figure 6. "Volkhovstroi at night." From *Prozhektor,* 15 May 1926, p. 8.

ever, the village was *identified,* and the coordinates of local identity were provided, and even encouraged.

THE FIVE-YEAR PLAN: INDUSTRIALIZATION
AND TRANSFORMATION

Electrification transformed the real and symbolic landscapes alike, providing
new points of orientation and new versions of the *put'* through the vast Russian
prostor. In a sense, it began the shift in conceptions of the Soviet territory from

Figure 7. "From electricity in the outskirts . . . to electricity in the home." Film stills from *Shagai, Sovet!* (Vertov, 1926). Private collection.

space (the vast and unmapped) into *place* (the known and mapped). The First Five-Year Plan accelerated this shift. In 1927, three major infrastructural projects were initiated: the Volga-Don Canal, the Dneprostroi hydroelectric power station, and the Turksib railway line, linking Turkestan cotton to Siberian grain and power. These were the cornerstones of early Soviet industrialization, and each rapidly became an important symbol of the Soviet historic present.

The targets for the First Five-Year Plan, placed before the Sixteenth Party Congress for approval (after the fact) in April 1929, were at best unrealistic, envisaging the doubling of Soviet industry's fixed capital stock between 1928–29 and 1932. Later versions of the Plan raised targets still further, and a decision to fulfil the Five-Year Plan in four years was taken in late 1929. Planning became, in a sense, a conceptual rather than practical or pragmatic activity, a process of imposing dreams on reality. This was the victory of "teleological" (target-orientated) planning over "genealogical" (pragmatic) planning, the resolution of a debate that was ongoing between 1925 and 1928.[23] It signalled the beginning of a shift in attitude toward the remodelling of the territory.

The drive for industrialization initiated by the First Plan effected a sudden transformation in the imaginary national map, accelerating the process of *otkrytie* (opening up) the territory that had begun through electrification. Through infrastructure, the space was to be transformed "from a field of conquest for brave pioneers, from neglected and isolated corners of the country, places of trial, of endurance, if not of punishment, into areas where genuine socialist society is being built."[24] Two hundred new industrial towns and one hundred agricultural towns were to be built as part of the Plan—many of them, such as Magnitogorsk, Avtostroi, and Kominternovsk, on virgin territory (Figure 9). Attention was focused on the vast expanses of the periphery (that which was "beyond Moscow") as land ripe for exploitation, and the Soviet space was seen as a provider of resources, of "inexhaustible riches" that, once tapped, would guarantee the successful industrialization of the nation.

By any standards, the achievements of the First Five-Year Plan were remarkable. In the space of the four years between 1928 and 1932, hundreds of new mining, engineering, and metallurgical enterprises appeared in the Urals, the Kuzbass, the Volga district, and the Ukraine (Figure 10). Two of the most significant achievements of early Stalinist industrialization—the enormous Magnitogorsk combine, part of the Ural-Kuznetsk iron and steel complex, and the giant hydroelectric power station on the lower Dnepr, Dneprostroi—were built from scratch. Dneprostroi began to function in 1932. These large projects shifted the national gaze away from the centre, from Moscow. They were, liter-

ЭЛЕКТРИФИКАЦИ

ВВОД ЭЛЕКТРОПРО
ВОДОВ В ИЗБУ

В. И. ЛЕНИН В 1921 г. НА ОПЫТНОЙ
ЭЛЕКТРОПАХОТЕ ПОД МОСКВОЙ

ЭЛЕКТРИФИЦИРОВАННОЕ СЕЛО (СЕЛО КОСТРОМА
КРЕМЕНЧУГСКОГО ОКРУГА УССР)

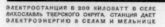

ЭЛЕКТРОСТАНЦИЯ В 200 КИЛОВАТТ В СЕЛЕ
ЛИХОСЛАВЛЬ ТВЕРСКОГО ОКРУГА. СТАНЦИЯ ДАЕТ
ЭЛЕКТРОЭНЕРГИЮ В СЕЛАМ И МЕЛЬНИЦЕ

ЧЛЕНЫ КОЛХОЗА «КРАСИВАЯ МЕЧЬ» ТУЛЬСКОГО ОКРУГА
ИСПОЛЬЗОВАЛИ ВОДЯНУЮ МЕЛЬНИЦУ ДЛЯ ЭЛЕКТРОСНАБ
ЖЕНИЯ СЕЛА И КОЛХОЗНОГО КРАХМАЛЬНОГО ЗАВОДА

Figure 8. "Electricity in the village." From *SSSR na stroike,* 1930, no. 3: 30–31.

ДЕРЕВНИ

ВОЗДУШНАЯ ПОД
СТАНЦИЯ—СТАНДАРТ
НАЯ СЕЛЬСКАЯ
ЭЛЕКТРОУСТАНОВКА

1917 г. В СЕЛЬСКИХ МЕСТНОСТЯХ РОССИИ БЫЛО ВСЕГО
... ЭЛЕКТРОСНАБЖАЮЩИХ УСТАНОВОК; В ЭТО ЧИСЛО
...ХОДИЛИ САМОСТОЯТЕЛЬНЫЕ МЕЛКИЕ ДЕРЕВЕНСКИЕ
...ЕКТРОСТАНЦИИ И ПОДСТАНЦИИ, ПОЛУЧАВШИЕ
...ЕРГИЮ ОТ СОСЕДНИХ КОММУНАЛЬНЫХ, ФАБРИЧНО-
...АВОДСКИХ И ДРУГИХ СТАНЦИЙ. ПОСЛЕ ОКТЯБРЯ
...ЕРЕВНЯ ПОТЯНУЛАСЬ ОТ ЛУЧИНЫ К КЕРОСИНУ
... ОТ КЕРОСИНА К «ГОРОДСКОМУ» ЭЛЕКТРИЧЕСТВУ.
...А ГОДЫ РЕВОЛЮЦИИ В ДЕРЕВНЯХ ВОЗНИКЛО МНОГО
...ОВЫХ ЭЛЕКТРОСТАНЦИЙ. К КОНЦУ ПРОШЛОГО ГОДА
...ЛЬСКИХ ЭЛЕКТРОСТАНЦИЙ БЫЛО УЖЕ 1100 С ОБЩЕЙ
...ОЩНОСТЬЮ ОКОЛО 35 ТЫСЯЧ КИЛОВАТТ ПРОТИВ
...00 КИЛОВАТТ В 1917 г. В КОММУНАХ И КОЛХОЗАХ ТЕПЕРЬ
...МЕЮТСЯ СВОИ ЭЛЕКТРОСТАНЦИИ, ГДЕ ЭЛЕКТРОЭНЕРГИЯ
...ДЕТ НЕ ТОЛЬКО НА ОСВЕЩЕНИЕ, НО И ДЛЯ НУЖД
...ОЗЯЙСТВА. ЭТО ТОЛЬКО СЛАБОЕ НАЧАЛО. МОЩНОЕ
...АЗВИТИЕ КОЛЛЕКТИВИЗАЦИИ СОВЕТСКОЙ ДЕРЕВНИ,
...ПЛОШНАЯ КОЛЛЕКТИВИЗАЦИЯ ГРОМАДНЫХ ОБЛАСТЕЙ
... МИЛЛИОНАМИ КРЕСТЬЯНСКОГО НАСЕЛЕНИЯ ПРИВЕДЕТ
...БЛИЖАЙШЕЕ ВРЕМЯ К НЕОБХОДИМОСТИ РАЗВИВАТЬ
...ЛЕКТРИФИКАЦИЮ СОВЕТСКОЙ ДЕРЕВНИ В КРУПНОМ
...АСШТАБЕ. НЕ ДЕСЯТКИ И ДАЖЕ НЕ СОТНИ, А ТЫСЯЧИ
...ДЕСЯТКИ ТЫСЯЧ КИЛОВАТТ—ТАКОВА МОЩНОСТЬ
...УДУЩИХ «ДЕРЕВЕНСКИХ» ЭЛЕКТРОСТАНЦИЙ
...ОВЕТСКОГО СОЮЗА, НАМЕЧЕННЫЕ ПРАВИТЕЛЬСТВОМ
...ЭТОМ ГОДУ ШИРОКИЕ ОПЫТЫ ЭЛЕКТРИФИКАЦИИ
...ЕЛЬСКОГО ХОЗЯЙСТВА (КАШИРСКИЙ РАЙОН
...ОСКОВСКОЙ ОБЛАСТИ), В ТОМ ЧИСЛЕ И ВВЕДЕНИЕ
...ЫТНОЙ ЭЛЕКТРОПАХОТЫ, К КОТОРОЙ ЕЩЕ В ПЕРВЫЕ
...ОДЫ РЕВОЛЮЦИИ ОТНОСИЛСЯ С БОЛЬШИМ ИНТЕРЕСОМ
... И. ЛЕНИН, ГОВОРЯ О ТОМ, ЧТО ЭЛЕКТРИФИКАЦИЯ
...ОВЕТСКОЙ ДЕРЕВНИ—НА ПРЯМОМ И ШИРОКОМ ПУТИ

ПЕРЕДВИЖНАЯ СЕЛЬСКАЯ ТРАНС
ФОРМАТОРНАЯ ПОДСТАНЦИЯ И МОТОР
НАЯ ТЕЛЕЖКА В 5 ЛОШАДИНЫХ СИЛ

ЭЛЕКТРОВЕЯЛКА «КРЕСТЬЯНКА»
ЗАВОДА ИМЕНИ ПЕТРОВСКОГО

ЭЛЕКТРИЧЕСКАЯ МЕЛЬНИЦА,
ПРИМЕНЯЕМАЯ В НЕКОТОРЫХ
КРУПНЫХ КОЛХОЗАХ

ГИДРОЭЛЕКТРИЧЕСКАЯ СТАНЦИЯ В СЕЛЕ «БОЛЬ
ШАЯ АЛЕКСАНДРОВКА» ХЕРСОНСКОГО ОКРУГА

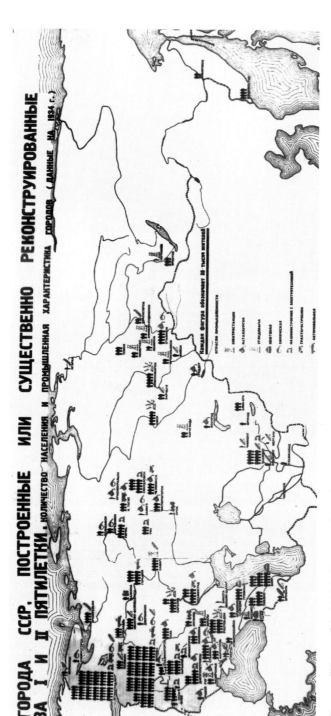

Figure 9. "Towns of the USSR, Constructed or Substantially Rebuilt During the First and Second Five-Year Plans." From *Soregor*, 1934, no. 5: n.p.

ally, new marks on the enormous new map of the Soviet Union that was being simultaneously constructed and drawn. In the words of an article in the popular press entitled "Routes on the Map of the USSR," "railways, hydroelectric stations, oil pipelines, plants and organizations are redrawing the map of the USSR."[25]

The launching of the First Five-Year Plan was accompanied by massive propaganda campaigns, in which cinema played a key role.[26] In the words of the left-wing critic and playwright Sergei Tret'iakov, film offered "a wide window, through which, with a propriatorial eye, we can watch our country constructing itself."[27] Documentary films charted the transformations that the Plan achieved: films dedicated to the construction of the vast steel plant at Magnitogorsk, for example, were produced through 1930–31.[28] One documentary film series, *Karta kapital'nogo stroitel'stva (The Map of Capital Construction)* produced from 1929, emphasized the extent to which the national map was transformed. Each episode opened with a large map of the entire Soviet territory, highlighting the newest *lampochki* of Soviet achievement, before focusing on individual projects, both large- and small-scale, which were transforming the territory. Everything was in the present tense; a new world was being created: "the country is building itself *(stroitsia)* . . . literally without end," an article declared in 1930.[29]

The trajectory of electrification, so crucial during the 1920s, continued into the First Plan and assumed appropriately grand proportions. The first large hydroelectric power station, Volkhovstroi (on the Volkhov River near Petrograd), opened in 1926, and the opening of Dneprostroi in 1932 was charted in numerous documentary films as a great achievement of the Soviet state. The role of film, and other propaganda, in this context was to invite the whole territory to share in its glory. One film, *Pusk Dneprostroiia (The Opening of Dneprostroi)*, was processed within three hours of the opening of the plant and sent to nearby cities for immediate screening in an attempt to create a symbolic simultaneity of experience.[30] In 1930, to celebrate the tenth anniversary of GOELRO, a special documentary film was produced.[31] In it, two maps were used to compare the Soviet territory with that of Imperial Russia, proclaiming that the Soviets had conquered the "vast distances" that hindered Tsarist industrial development. The film enumerated the mythical *"dalekie puti"* (long journeys) by which Tsarist Russia had moved coal and oil to central factories and plants (it is, for instance, 3,150 kilometres from Baku to St. Petersburg) and pictured trains crossing an empty steppe, a space representing the intransigence of the pre-Soviet territory. By contrast, the decentralization and reduction of distance made

Figure 10. Map of the Soviet Union in 1931. From M. Il'in, *New Russia's Primer: The*

OCEAN

Bering Sea

YAKUT A.S.S.
REPUBLIC

ARCTIC CIRCLE

Lena R.

Sea of Okhotsk

SOVIET REPUBLICS

LENA GOLD
FIELDS

...RIAN AREA

FAR EASTERN
AREA

KHABAROVSK

...CHITA

BURIAT
MONGOLIAN
A.S.S.REPUBLIC

IRKUTSK

MANCHURIA

Sea of Japan

MONGOLIA

VLADIVOSTOK

SYMBOLS

...ONAL ELEC. GENERATING PLANTS
...ready existing & being enlarged.
...der construction.

...METAL INDUSTRIES
...on & Steel works.
...ther Metals works.
...achine factories for Industrial purposes
...actories for Production of Agricultural
Machinery.
...emical Plants & Miscellaneous Chem. Wks.
...scellaneous Factories & Works.

FUEL
◆ Coal Mines
◆ Oil Refineries.
◇ Peat briquette plants.

⌐ Textile mills & factories.
⊐ Building material plants.
⊕ Paper Industry.
⊕ Saw mills & Lumber preparation
△ Location of *"sovhozes"* plants.
(state farms)

...IBET   CHINA

Yellow Sea

...tory of the Five Year Plan, frontispiece.

possible by electrification had, the film proclaimed, transformed the national space, rendering it knowable and discoverable. The key message of the film was that the centre (Moscow) was no longer the only nodal point; electrification, it suggested, *localized* production, enabling industrial processing at any point on the national map.

This film maintained a careful balance between grandeur and dynamism in its representation of construction. Although it emphasized the monumental force of power stations, taming the elements and harnessing the power of water, the visual focus of the film was on the dynamic process of construction. The energy of the film was provided by continual movement, underlining the dynamism of Soviet industrialization: power stations provide focal points for movement, which implicitly extends across the territory. This emphasis on movement was common to representations of industrialization through the 1920s and into the First Five-Year Plan. In Vertov's *Forward March, Soviet!* (1926), for example, the endless movement of the machine represented the ceaseless energy with which the new world was being built: "every machine," a title proclaimed, "continues the work of Lenin . . . the construction of a new world." Esfir Shub, in *Segodnia* (*Today,* 1930), visually deconstructed the machinery of factories, emphasizing the movement of turbines, the ceaseless labour of technology in service of the state. The movement of turbines echoed the energy of the revolutionary *put'.* The machine, moreover, was a visual metaphor of the new model of society, in which all elements—every cog—combined to create a functioning whole. In parallel, each citizen, and each space, was a vital part of the whole of the state.

COLLECTIVIZATION: REIMAGINING RURAL SPACE

This broad movement of incorporation underpinned the other key project of the Great Leap Forward: collectivization. In 1927, the Fifteenth Party Congress resolved that "the task of uniting and transforming small, individual peasant holdings into large collectives must become the principal task of the party in the villages."[32] There were pragmatic reasons for this dramatic decision. The explosive growth of urban centres and massive population movements occasioned by the rapid industrialization of the Plan required a considerable increase in agricultural output and distribution in order to feed the burgeoning workforce. State grain purchases in 1927, however, stood at 50 percent of their 1926 levels.[33] The *smychka,* originally billed as the economic alliance of peasant and worker, town and village, masked a relationship under strain: faced with the possibility of insufficient food to supply the required workforce, the state urgently needed to reorganize grain provision.

Full-scale implementation of "de-kulakization" (targeting supposedly wealthy peasants as saboteurs of the socialist ideal) and collectivization took place in 1929.[34] Like the rapid industrialization of the Plan, collectivization fundamentally transformed the geography of Soviet Russia. In conceptual terms, collectivization marked a privileging of urban "mapping" over the great rural "unknown" and the extension of control by the replication of urban organizational structures across the territory. As part of the Stalinist Great Leap Forward, it was a key aspect of the totalizing process of social development during the 1930s.[35] To Stalin, the traditional peasant commune *(mir)* represented one of the largest obstacles to full-scale socialization, intrinsically opposed to the structures of the new regime. The peasant was a dark, primitive, and untamed force in opposition to Soviet power (an extension of the metaphor of light and darkness discussed in the context of "electrifying the village").[36] The *mir* was opaque in structure, a system based on tradition and unspoken hierarchy. It had no place in the cult of visibility and publicness that underpinned Stalinist development. There was an urgent need to expose and subject the "irrational" peasant to the new rational order, to transform the peasantry into a rural proletariat. Collectivization would provide clear points *(lampochki Il'icha)* on the map of the Soviet territory.

In practice, of course, the collectivization process was not the rationally ordered transformation anticipated and publicized by propaganda but a vivid demonstration of the centrifugal spin of development during the early period of modernization, showing how state-initiated and -directed projects during the First Plan were in reality often decentralized and, more importantly, *decentralizing*. There were no exact instructions as to how to carry out *sploshnaia* (total) collectivization that was demanded, and central government had little control over its transmission belts. As a result, the assault on the countryside was at best disorganized, and often violent and coercive. Three forces were at work: directives from the centre initiated and ostensibly oversaw the process; local communist officials, specifically in rural soviets at *raion* (region) and *okrug* (district) levels, modified and implemented it; and, at the same time, rural Soviet officials met vast "mobilizations" of urban communists, Komsomols, students and workers, sent for long- and short-term service in the countryside. These activists performed a kind of shock therapy and coercion, descending on the countryside to unearth and destroy these capitalist "saboteurs" of the Bolshevik dream.[37] In the propaganda of the period, this was represented as a form of *smychka,* and documentary films showed brigades of workers arriving in the village, bringing technical "education" to the peasantry.[38] Just as films of industrialization showed peasants leaving the village and travelling to the *stroiki* (construction sites), so during collectivization workers travelled from village to village.

Like industrialization, therefore, collectivization created a fluid and decentred space. It was perhaps politically pragmatic for the centre to incite and unleash an attack on the territory for which it was later able to disclaim responsibility.[39] Whatever the political reasoning, however, it was certainly a practically impossible task in the Soviet Union of the late 1920s to retain full command over, and knowledge of, activities on the periphery. As a result, the years between 1929 and the end of the First Five-Year Plan constituted a period of chaotic flux in the Russian countryside that radically transformed the nature of settlement and called into question the very notion of peasant identity. Nothing, and nobody, was fixed in space, and the divide between peasant and worker was blurred. Chaos created a particular kind of mobility—in the words of Sergo Ordzhonikidze (head of the State Commission for Heavy Industry), a "*chemodannoe nastroenie* [suitcase mentality]."[40]

This mobility transformed the imagined geography of the nation, effecting dramatic shifts in the spatial limits of the peasant imagination, traditionally village-centred, and in which travel was difficult and unusual.[41] "Overcoming the isolation of the peasant village," so central to Bolshevik ideology in this period, placed the local space in a new relationship with the greater whole of the national space. During collectivization, the village became a place into which people from *elsewhere* would frequently intrude. Throughout the First Plan, categories of identity were fluid, as state-generated notions of Sovietness met with community-bound, traditionally created and sustained identities.[42] The mass influx of "outsiders" into peasant communities dislodged previous categories of local and national; in effect, it necessitated peasant self-identification as a prerequisite for resistance. The transformed structure of the land forced a reevaluation and in many cases a solidifying of regional allegiances as awareness was suddenly focused on the map of Soviet socialist identity: one documentary film newspaper of 1929, for example, pictures peasants gathered at an exhibition organized by the Peoples' Commissariat for Land and scrutinizing a map of collectivization.[43] These maps marked the position of the local space within a larger national space, emphasizing interconnection. In parallel, documentary film "journal" series such as *Za sotsialisticheskuiu derevniu (For a Socialist Vil-*

lage), Sotsialisticheskaia derevnia (The Socialist Village), and *Kolkhoznyi byt (Everyday Life on the Collective Farm)* encouraged villages to collectivize by offering positive examples from elsewhere in the territory. The successful policy of *sotssorevnovanie* (local "socialist competition"), where neighbouring communities were encouraged to compete to overfulfil the Plan's targets, was a common theme in documentary films and the press and emphasized the necessity of local allegiance. The metaphor of the network *(set')*—the equalized territory—rendered the local space a key point of identification.

FILMING LOCALNESS: THE FILM TRAIN
OF ALEKSANDR MEDVEDKIN

The significance of the relationship between local and national spaces in propaganda about collectivization and other key "modernizing" projects is particularly evident in the work of Alexander Medvedkin's *kino-poezd* (Film Train), a complete travelling film studio, which was formed in August 1931 by order of the Central Committee and travelled the Soviet territory between 1931 and 1935, documenting the construction of socialism.[44] The Film Train had the explicit mission of propaganda, teaching—or more importantly, *showing*—correct Soviet socialist construction and contrasting it with the reality of bad practice. It would travel, generally from Moscow, to key sites across the territory: "Wherever there was something amiss, like the Plan not being fulfilled, wherever there was bad management, there our train went," Medvedkin recalled; "it was a kind of public prosecutor's cinema."[45] On arrival, the team would film the local community, collective farm, or provincial factory in its everyday activities, "like a newsreel." The film would then be edited and processed on the train and shown immediately to the community in question.[46]

The Film Train filmed the effects of the Plan at the level of the particular, in local communities, establishing new spatial connections between centre and periphery. It developed the concept of "competition" *(sovrevnovanie)* on a larger scale. One of the expeditions, undertaken during harvest time in 1932, focused on collectivization, travelling from farms in the south (in Crimea) northward into Ukraine. The route was carefully planned so that films shot early in the trip could be used during the later period, creating examples of good and bad practice. Two films produced during this trip demonstrate how this dynamic was to work. The first, *Veitlus: ili opyt luchshego vsem kolkhozam (Veitlus: or, the Experience of the Best to All Collective Farms)* showed "socialist competition in action." In this film, the Veitlus collective farm was held up as an example of good production discipline: everybody works together, and plans are drawn up daily to encourage a rapid and good-quality harvest. The success of this farm was represented through a combination of shots of labouring workers and painfully "realistic" (lengthy, and filmed in real time) discussions of targets, together with idealized landscape shots that emphasized the pastoral harmony achieved by Soviet agricultural methods. In contrast to the positive example of *Veitlus*, the second film, *Da, Zveno (Yes, A Chain)*, showed poor harvest methods and lack of incentive. It emphasized the necessity for teamwork (the "chain") and problems caused by poor work discipline, proposing the remedy of socialist competition in order to engage the community directly: "they have no stake in it," a title proclaimed, "and quality suffers." *Yes, A Chain* offered no scenes of rural harmony, emphasizing rather the disharmonious relationship of peasants and land and the failure of the harvest brought about by the failure of collective action. Shown together, these two films set good example against bad, seeking to encourage shame and self-criticism in those communities that were, implicitly, failing to fulfil the Plan's targets. They were part of a multilevelled process of agitation undertaken by the Film Train team, organizing socialist competition and a series of local "rallies" *(slety)* between neighbouring communities. After this expedition, Medvedkin boasted of having encouraged twenty-one collective farms to join the "All-Union Competition" for grain yield.[47]

Encouraging the community to identify itself as a competitor in a regional race was a means of linking local and national identities—and this was the self-proclaimed task of the Film Train. Using a similar structure, a third film of the Collective Farm Expedition *(kolkhoznyi reis)*, *Pis'mo kolkhoznikam (A Letter to the Collective Farm Workers)*, made explicit links between local and national achievements. "The plan for grain procurement has so far not been fulfilled in your farm," it announced gravely. This small failure was contrasted with the mighty achievements of the nation as a whole: "Together with the workers," a title portentously proclaimed, "we are building the fortresses of socialism." Within the context of the national plan, the local failure gains in significance; the film showed the dilapidated state of the collective farm: a single, forlorn tree in the yard, broken equipment, rundown barns and houses. "Whose fault is this?" an intertitle demanded, and the camera cut to the faces of the guilty. Thus the film acted directly as prosecutor, rooting out culprits: Medvedkin recounts how members of his team would stalk culprits in order to catch them in the act of anti-Soviet action. The train did not have the right to punish, however: it sought instead to encourage change. Like *Yes, A Chain, A Letter to the Collective Farm Workers* was used in combination with *Veitlus* to encourage improvement. Public humiliation—seeing one's guilty face on-screen—and the shame of comparison were to be sufficient.

The *kolkhoznyi reis* was only one of six major expeditions that the Film Train undertook in its first year of operation (1931–32).[48] The scope of these first expeditions—focusing on transport, industrialization, and collectivization in diverse areas of the territory—echoed the national imperative to build socialism "at all levels" of society and to balance large-scale events with the local and small-scale. In Medvedkin's words, the task of the train was to "raise the great issue of construction on the screen."[49] Film was to be a direct participant in the construction of the new regime: "Cinema can be not only a weapon 'in general,'" Medvedkin proclaimed, "but a very real weapon of the party cell, in concrete sectors of socialist construction."[50] The practice of the train differed significantly from that of other propaganda trains, however: it did not bring films from centre to periphery. The films made by the train were made *in place* and aimed primarily at local use: "The main difference between the Film Train and any other film factory," Medvedkin claimed, "is that the making of the film is intrinsically and inseparably linked with its screening in the place of production."[51] In the 1932 film *Kak zhivesh', tovarishch gorniak (How's Life, Comrade Miner?),* for example, the camera lingered on a forlorn tree outside a shared residential block, emphasizing the reality of hardship within which local inhabitants were living (Figure 11).

In this sense, the Film Train was an answer to the pressing questions raised during the 1920s: how to communicate with the masses?[52] Show them what they know best, the train proposed: "To see on-screen one's own friends, one's factory floor, one's own street—that's interesting for anyone."[53] Medvedkin's accounts of reactions to the films emphasized the shock of self-identification on-screen.[54] This he identified as the key effect of the Film Train: showing the community how they themselves live. On-screen, the peasants or workers saw themselves as Soviet citizens: their everyday lives were represented "as a newsreel." In this way, the train films seemed to make the localized everyday *newsworthy,* recognizing it as a crucial part of the national space. The familiar environment of communities was transformed into a cinematic category. During the first trip, for example, Medvedkin developed an animated camel, which could be superimposed onto films to symbolize shame.[55] The effectiveness of the device, it was believed, was the combination of such film "technology," generally new and startling to the viewer, with the familiar locations of the films: "the caricature moved in a place familiar to the spectator."[56]

Although little evidence remains of concrete reactions to screenings, and it is

Figure 11. The Film Train: filming localness. Film still from *Kak zhivesh', tovarishch gorniak?* (Karmazinskii, 1932).

not clear how communities used the films after the train left, it is certainly the case that copies of each film made in a given community were left in the hands of local administration. Medvedkin recounts how the Mine Committee of the Kribass region purchased three films "for future work."[57] Although Medvedkin bemoaned what he perceived to be insufficiently serious use of the films as educational propaganda after the departure of the train, the films did enter the entertainment repertoire of small, local communities.[58] The local space was marked on the imaginary map. In addition to local self-identification, however, the structure of the train's activity also demanded recognition of the situation of the local space within a network of other spaces. On arrival in the Donbass, for example, the train encouraged workers to come and see the films that it had brought, shot in the Kribass mining region.[59] Screening films in one community, produced during previous trips or in other mines or collective farms visited earlier in the same expedition, created a reciprocal network.

Through this representational process, the regions were envisaged as a functioning cog in the larger machinery of the Soviet state. Just as the "little people" (in Medvedkin's words, the "invisible heroes") had a role to play in the creation

of socialism, so the local community was summoned to fulfil goals for the national good.[60] This summons—the iconic finger pointing at "You!"—played
an important part in the creation of the "Soviet citizen"; and the model may
also apply to the "naming" of local communities and regions, creating the unified Soviet space. Everybody, in every space, was called to work. To suggest,
however, that this constituted a radial dynamic that subjected the periphery to
a strong centre is to underestimate the consequences of *interpellation,* according to Louis Althusser's definition. Althusser suggests that the success of any
ruling system depends on the *interpellation* of the individual citizen as subject.[61] His model is inflected by the psychoanalytic theories of Jacques Lacan:
Lacan's "mirror stage" suggests that the entrance of a child into the "symbolic"
realm, the first stage of which was the recognition of the self as "other" in the
mirror, is the beginning of subjectivity.[62] Similarly, interpellation depends on
the citizen recognizing him- or herself as a subject (in the national sense). This
is a useful structure through which to understand the exploration of the periphery undertaken by the Film Train, offering a more nuanced reading of the
integrational process during the First Five-Year Plan. It might be argued that
the process of representing local communities *to themselves* constituted a fundamental stage in the construction of local identities within the Soviet space.
The local was a more valuable category than the national in the Film Train
films. Although organized from the centre, the train in practice symbolically
elided that centre, envisaging regional networks and encouraging local self-
identification, embedding localness within the "symbolic realm" of Sovietness.
The Film Train represented the local to the localized and gave the periphery a
voice, as the community recognized itself on-screen.

SHAPING SOVIETNESS: ARCHITECTS PLAN
THE TERRITORY

The films made by the Film Train pictured a space in transition, providing
snapshots of the dynamic chaos engendered by the Great Leap Forward. This
chaos had a profound effect on the actual organization of the territory. The
rapid and massive industrialization of the First Plan necessitated enormous
population movement, with millions of people travelling around the country
to supply urgently needed labour. Travelling recruiters, often with crude mar-
keting devices such as pictures and pamphlets, travelled rural Russia to mobi-
lize workforces for large construction projects, disseminating images of the territory.[63] The traditional *otkhod,* the peasant's seasonal departure to urban

centres for work, was transformed into mass movements to and from cities and construction sites. According to Moshe Lewin, about seven million *otkhodniki* moved around the country in 1931 alone.[64] The *smychka,* in its broadest sense, found a peculiar realization: the distinction between peasant and urban worker was blurred, as the nation became a land of mobile labour. Lewin describes peasant Russia during this period as *Rus' brodiazhnaia* (roaming Rus'), a country of vagrants or nomads, and indeed, this describes the urban population as well and goes some way toward describing the extraordinary mobility that characterized the new Soviet space during the First Five-Year Plan.[65]

"Modernization" transformed the nature and perception of the Soviet space, seeking to eliminate the distinction between peasant and worker, town and village. In symbolic terms, the drive for *smychka* threw the very categories of urban and rural into profound flux, actively seeking to redefine them (Figure 12). And this flux was not only symbolic, or rhetorical. Collectivization sought to transform the organization of the territory, replacing the isolated rural "village" with a semi-industrial "collective farm," connected—symbolically and practically—to the new communicative network. Rapid industrialization launched the nation into flux, with dispersed, temporary housing springing up around industrial sites, altering the characteristic organization of Russian space. The *poselok* (workers' settlement)—neither urban nor rural—was a symbol of industrialization and the *otkrytie* of space, a significant and signifying image throughout the First Plan.[66]

During the First Five-Year Plan, the shape of the new socialist city (of the many new socialist cities), and indeed of the new Soviet nation, became an urgent practical task for architects and planners. In 1928, Gosplan published a document entitled "The Problem of Space in the First Five-Year Plan," which spoke of producing "spatial descriptions" of plan proposals.[67] "Are architects ready for the plan?" asked a headline in an architectural journal in 1929 (Figure 13).[68] Debates that had begun during the 1920s in response to electrification intensified: the problem of *sotsialisticheskoe rasselenie* (socialist patterns of settlement) was at the forefront. How should the new socialist space be physically organized?

The projects of key groups of urban planners during this period represented a radical attempt to create an alternative political and social space, to redraw the national map along socialist lines—to create, that is, a decentralized space.[69] The very term *rasselenie (ras-selenie),* used throughout the Soviet period to describe "settlement" and planning, describes the spreading of population across the nation and suggests extension and dispersal. Between 1929 and 1931, two

Figure 12. "The total liberation of humanity from the chains of the past can take place only through the destruction of the opposition between town and village" (Engels). "The predominance of the town over the village, in economic, political, intellectual, and all other relations, is the general and unavoidable feature of all countries with commodity production and capitalism" (Lenin). Cover of *Sovremennaia arkhitektura*, 1930, no. 3.

groups dominated urban planning debates: Urbanists and Disurbanists.[70] The Urbanist group was led by a Gosplan economist, Leonid Sabsovich, who presented important papers to Stroikom (the Building Commission) in 1929. The Disurbanists were largely members of the OSA (Association of Contemporary Architects), a Constructivist group of architects working under Moisei Ginzburg in the planning section of Stroikom and linked with the Trotskyist theoretician and sociologist Mikhail Okhitovich.[71] For all their differences, the two

Figure 13. "Architect. Is your team ready for the Plan?" Cover
of *Sovremennaia arkhitektura,* 1930, no. 4.

groups were in fact united in an antiurban drive, their difference primarily one
of extent. All were agreed, it seemed, on the impossibility of continued urban
expansion: the *razgruzka* (unloading) of the city, an ideological catchphrase
that appeared as early as 1920, was an urgent task—an attempt to control the
burgeoning urban population.

Despite their name, the Urbanists were not in fact in favour of large-scale urban agglomeration. In place of the traditional divide between town and country, Sabsovich proposed a new intermediate form of settlement: the "agro-
industrial" town.[72] The ideal socialist town, he suggested, would contain a
maximum of forty thousand to fifty thousand inhabitants housed in a number
of large communal residences (the *dom-kommuna* [house-commune]). These
communal houses were to be constructed on an enormous scale, providing
each individual with a minimum unit of five to six square metres of living space

and with all services rendered collective. The town itself would consist of a number of these residences, constructed near the industry for which their inhabitants would provide the labour force. As such, it would have neither centre nor periphery. In parallel, the Soviet Union itself would have no centre. Spatial hierarchies would be abolished: "The whole territory of the Union will be more or less evenly covered with industro-agricultural and agro-industrial towns, closely tied to their production base," Sabsovich announced.[73] Distance was conquered *(osvoen)* through the development of a national and local communications infrastructure, and full-scale decentralization was possible.[74] The national centre would become irrelevant in economic and cultural terms, and local spaces would become new social and economic centres of gravity.

The Disurbanist group offered a reimagining of *sotsialisticheskoe rasselenie* even more radical than that offered by the Urbanists, calling for the complete abolition of the city—indeed, of any kind of urban conurbation—in the new socialist utopia. The city, Okhitovich maintained, was the product of particular historical conditions (those of capitalism) and was rendered both unnecessary and untenable by the new socialist society. In its place, the development of infrastructure, and in particular of transportation, would permit the dispersion of population evenly across the territory.[75] "There will be no town and no village," Okhitovich wrote; "there will be no divide between them."[76] In practical terms, this total decentralization was made possible by electrification: "Fuel!" Okhitovich enthused: "The transportation of fuel! It is the revolution in the transmission of energy which is the condition that allows us to hope for the abolition, on the one hand, of the unbelievable isolation [of the peasant village] and the hypertrophied overcrowding [of the big city], on the other."[77] Symbolically too, the electrical grid was a metaphor for equalized territory: "there are no centres of energy," Okhitovich wrote, echoing earlier discussions of electrification: "There is a single *network* of energy. There is no central source, only local, large, small, and very small, sources of energy everywhere. Every centre is a periphery and every point on the periphery is a centre [emphasis in original]."[78]

Centreless, the Disurbanist Soviet Union would become a network of interconnecting arteries along which human habitation would be evenly distributed: "The network will be victorious and the centre die away."[79] Even housing was to be rendered mobile—a flexible, dynamic form, able to adapt to the changing needs of the individual. Moveable housing units for single people were proposed, offering individuals the freedom to travel around the country, providing a mobile workforce. In 1930, the Stroikom committee offered de-

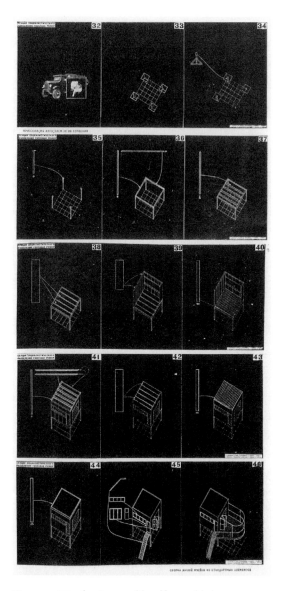

Figure 14. Disurbanist portable self-assembly houses (showing the house arriving in a car and the stages of assembly). From *Sovremennaia arkhitektura,* 1930, no. 6: 13.

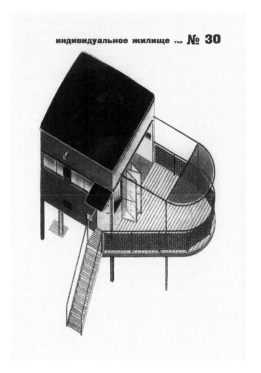

индивидуальное жилище тип **№ 30**

Figure 15. The end result: A Disurbanist model
housing unit. From *Sovremennaia arkhitektura*, 1930,
no. 6: 14.

signs for several types of housing unit or "box" *(iashchik),* all of which were
compact, prefabricated, and individual (Figures 14 and 15).[80]

These housing cells echoed the futuristic prophesies of the Futurist poet
Velemir Khlebnikov almost ten years earlier, who had pictured human habitation as "a box made from moulded glass or a mobile housing cell," which could
be put "on the train or the boat" so that "the inhabitant, not leaving [the cell],
travels."[81] Like Khlebnikov's utopia, the Disurbanist vision was premised on
an ideal of movement. It was, in symbolic terms, the attempt to design a pattern for spatial organization that would capture the "blood circulation" of the
new world, embodying revolutionary energy. "This new complex will not be
called a point, a place, or a city," Okhitovich proclaimed, "but a process, and
this process will be called disurbanization."[82] In this sense, Disurbanism
echoed a broader preoccupation with dynamism and mobility that can be
traced through several campaigns and projects of the period in which the
utopian and the practical intersect. In 1930, for example, one N. Osinskii pub-

lished the first edition of a journal called *Avtomobilizatsiia SSSR (The Automobilization of the USSR)*, in which he pictured a Soviet Union where all citizens had a motor vehicle and the nation became, effectively, mobile: "we must make our Soviet Union traversable *[proezzhim]*."[83] Osinskii's society, Avtodor, promoting automobile mania, functioned between 1927 and 1935 and had a membership of some forty thousand in 1930.[84]

The drive toward universal mobility was central to the reformulation of the imaginary geography of the Soviet Union during this period. The unknowable, *neob"iatnyi prostor* became a territory crossed by roads and rail tracks, a space ripe for exploration and, crucially, accessible to all. The Disurbanists located their projects within this imaginary map: in the words of Anatole Kopp, their projects were "an attempt to make the inhabitants of the space into participants and not observers."[85] The space was to be *lived* and experienced: it was the new adventure space for the *malen'kii chelovek* (little man). This echoed the broader movement of incorporation: everybody was part of the construction of the new world. The imperative of incorporation, however, raised important questions about the status of local and national identities in the new Soviet imaginary. In one respect, the Disurbanist grid suggested an ambivalent attitude toward localness, launching what might in many ways be seen as a challenge to any notion of fixed identity. In particular, the grid might be seen as a means of suppressing localness; the linear, mobile space of the Disurbanists would disrupt settlement and remove the basis of local self-identification. In this sense, like the electrical network or grid, the Disurbanist grid was a vision of homogeneity. The integration of the periphery would suppress local difference and establish a single, unified Soviet space. As we have seen in the context of electrification, however, in practice the rhetorical emphasis of the grid presented a more ambiguous dialectic of sameness and particularity. Although the Disurbanists sought to create a "single network" of population dispersion, abolishing spatial hierarchy, Okhitovich's vision nonetheless depended on a clear conception of localness."[86] Industrial processing was to be linked with localized resources; residence was to be linked with place of work, and the provision of amenities abolished the need for travel to a distant centre. The local space would thus function independently as part of a network of independent and equal regions.

Disurbanism might be understood, therefore, as a radical reformulation of the coordinates of identity, in which "Sovietness" was to function as an umbrella identity that overlaid local identification. According to this vision, identity was not mediated through a symbolic national centre, but directly between the local space and a "Soviet," supranational identity: the *International.* Moscow was symbolically elided and attention focused on the periphery. This denial, or destruction, of the centre was expressed in concrete terms in a plan for the reconstruction of the Moscow region that members of the Disurbanist group produced in 1930. The Green City Plan proposed the systematic evacuation of Moscow and the dispersion of its industry, scientific institutes, and administration across the Soviet Union (Figure 16).[87] Inhabitants were to be relocated along major axes linking the city with surrounding towns. The same would be done with the agricultural and rural populations around the city, thus effecting a crucial intermingling of the town and village, with all using the same collective services. New construction in Moscow would cease, and the space liberated in the city by the transferral of industry and administration would be used to create green spaces for recreation, ultimately becoming a vast cultural park toward which the new ribbons of dispersed habitation would converge: a museum city. Thus the gradual disintegration of Moscow as a capital would be initiated; the centre of the Soviet territory would be emptied.

This desire to decentre the capital had its roots in much earlier debates about the reorganization of the territory. Moscow had long been considered an impossibly overcrowded and anachronistic blight on the socialist landscape. Between 1918 and 1922, for example, the architect and land surveyor Boris Sakulin, a member of the first state planning commission (Komgosoor), had produced a plan for the redevelopment of the Moscow region which prefigured that of the Disurbanists. This plan retained the notional structure of the major city but proposed a process of emptying out the core or centre *(razgruzka)*. All significant development and amenities would be shifted to the periphery, with a rail network providing a system of communication between peripheral areas that would bypass the centre. The traditional centre would thus become a purely cultural node, surrounded by a green belt, permitting the conurbation to expand without fear of overcrowding. The city would be what might be described as an "open system," without boundaries, part of a larger network that would extend across the territory.

The Disurbanists' Green City Plan for Moscow was rooted in a conviction of the ultimate imperfectability of the city. Furthermore, it was premised upon what was described as the "maximum proximity of man to nature"[88] Illustrative photographs by Aleksandr Rodchenko accompanied the published plans, carrying the headings "For every house, light and sun; for every house, open space" (Figure 17).[89] Habitation would be distributed along axes that would extend organically through nature, protected from pollution by green belts, and each individual cell or housing unit would be positioned in such a way as to

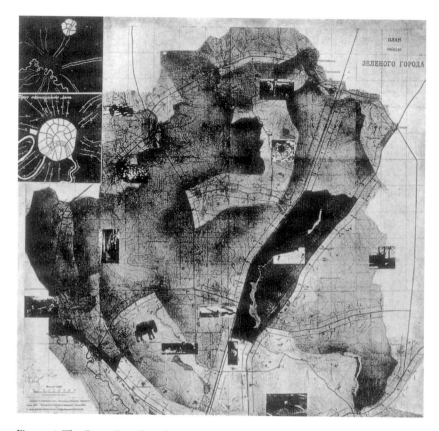

Figure 16. The Green City Plan of Moisei Ginzburg and Mikhail Barshch. Private collection.

allow it maximum space and freedom. There was nothing particularly new here: echoes of a "return to nature" philosophy can be traced through urban planning in many of its manifestations—from the ostensibly practical to the overtly fantastic—during the first years after the revolution. In 1918, one Mark Elizarov (then government commissar in charge of fire protection) commissioned plans for a suburb to be built west of Moscow. Naming that suburb Privol'e, Elizarov drew on a term—*volia* (will)—often used in Russian to refer to the vast expanses of the Russian steppe and expressing both space and liberty (see the Introduction).[90] The entire Moscow population would be resettled in such suburbs, such that the city would be an uncrowded cultural centre, and suburban communities would offer rural (pastoral) harmony.[91] The influence of the Garden City movement of Ebenezer Howard and his followers in England had been felt in Russia even before 1917 and seemed to many to offer a so-

Figure 17. The Green City: Socialist reconstruction of Moscow.
"For every house, open space." From "Zelenyi gorod:
sotsialisticheskaia rekonstruktsiia Moskvy," *SA,* 1930, nos. 1–2: 17.

lution to the hierarchical division of urban and rural space. Howard's theories, realized in English towns such as Letchworth, proposed a harmonious blend of urban and rural features in small "garden cities" of some thirty-two thousand inhabitants, linked by roads, and separated by agricultural land. In 1921, Ivan Zholtovskii, later to become a key figure in architectural design under Stalin, produced a "scheme for a small settlement," which was clearly indebted to the Garden City model of decentralization, and a number of Soviet planners visited Letchworth in 1924. Similarly, El-Lissitskii's *gorod-kommuna* envisaged the whole world as a single spatial form in which the town-commune was the key unit of settlement, and population dispersion would permit proximity to nature.[92]

A similar pastoral urge was expressed in Aleksandr Chaianov's utopian tale of a peasant utopia, *Puteshestvie moego brata Alekseia v stranu krest'ianskoi utopii (The Journey of My Brother Aleksei to the Land of the Peasant Utopia)*, published under a pseudonym in 1920.[93] The story tells of Aleksei, who falls asleep and awakens into an "ideal" world of the future (in 1984) in which the difference between town and country has been dissolved: towns have been destroyed by the "great decree on the destruction of towns," and Russia has been remapped. "Now, if you like," an inhabitant informs the bemused hero, "there aren't really any towns at all, there are only nodal points of social connection. Each of our towns is simply a point of assembly, a central square for a district—a point, but not a social phenomenon." The success of this utopia is, we learn, premised on axes of communication; a "law of obligatory movement" has been established for young people, on the basis that it provides for wider horizons and creates more fully rounded citizens. No towns can exceed a population of twenty thousand; the old, overcrowded Moscow has become a "a new Moscow, transformed and brightened up," surrounded by green space. Through these transformations, it is claimed, "the circle of individuals who drink from the original source of culture and life is widened."[94]

The creation of a closer relationship between the human body and the physical world was the motivating ambition of this return to nature. This permits a reevaluation of the ideological significance of the "pastoral" in early visions of the Soviet utopia. Through the metaphor of the grid, or network, the Disurbanists offered a vision of the Soviet space that mirrored the ideal socialist society composed of a collective of individual, independent citizens: "Individuality must not be opposed to the collective, or vice versa. The stronger the collective links, the stronger the individuality."[95] The Green City Plan was grounded in this principle of individual self-realization as the fundamental precondition for true collectivity: "we believe that a task of fundamental importance for the socialist organization of society is the fulfilment of every individual."[96] And this "individual fulfilment" was premised upon a productive and creative relationship between the individual and his or her environment: an *appropriation* of the physical world. This newly productive relationship was enabled by a kind of sensual rapprochement, which echoed Marx's call for an "emancipation of the senses."

Ultimately, moreover, the Disurbanist vision was not pastoral but *dynamic;* it was not premised on a romantic or individualist connection between man and nature, but rather responded to an ideologically sponsored imperative to discover a new way of looking at space—a new and mobile perspective.[97] The symbolic weight of *energetika* (the catchall term, used both literally and metaphorically, for power and energy) is revealing here. Energy was an enabler, distributing development, but it was also a metaphor for a new vision of movement as mobile and experiential. The dual emphasis of *energetika,* which evokes a more organic sense of energy in addition to its primary meaning, points to a complexity that can be traced in many representations of technology, and in particular, electricity, during this period. Energy provided a new, dynamic axis along which the Soviet space was to be organized. It also transformed the relationship between the new Soviet man or woman and the "electrified" Soviet space (the physical world). The cult of energy created around electrification responded to the vision of progress and dynamism that was propagated by Soviet culture but also echoed the Marxist thesis of "the appropriation of human reality."

The connection between Okhitovich and Moisei Ginzburg's Constructivist architectural group (the OSA) was premised on this reenvisaging of the experience of space. Ginzburg and the OSA developed what they called a "functional" *(funktsional'nyi)* theory of architectural and spatial design, underpinned by the belief that architectural form must be active, that is, dynamically linked to movement through space. For them, Disurbanism was the logical extension of this founding principle. The task of architecture was the organization of movement, to construct a built environment that would be suited to the needs of the new proletariat.[98] The creation of a *novyi byt* (new everyday life) was a key task for Soviet planners during the 1920s; it was a process of *zhiznestroenie* (lifebuilding).[99] Architecture was to create social condensers (or, using an electrical metaphor, "transformers")—habitats that would create the conditions for the realization of a new type of society: "The building of socialism is the building of a new material and cultural basis for humanity . . . it is the reorganization of our economic life and the construction of new forms of everyday life."[100] Like many of the avant-garde movements of the period, these architects were influenced by the "flow diagrams" of production offered by Henry Ford and Frederick Winslow Taylor in the United States. The Soviet Taylorist movement for the Nauchnaia organizatsiia truda (Scientific Organization of Work), led by the poet and Proletkul't (Proletarskaia Kultura, the Proletarian Culture Movement) member Aleksei Gastev, was part of a broader interest in understanding (and rationalizing) the processes of everyday life: forms of time and motion studies.[101] In parallel, the Constructivist Disurbanists proposed a kind of urban flow diagram, structured according to local transport systems, public routes, and squares. The built environment must become a functional part of the new society, constantly created and *appropriated* by daily activity.

This "functionalism" was grounded in a rethinking of the nature and experience of space and time. "The exceptional growth in the strength, quality, quantity and speed of the means of mechanical transport now permits separation from centres," Okhitovich wrote; "Space is here measured by time. And time is itself beginning to be shortened."[102] The implications of this statement bear further consideration. Space is now measured by time; that is, space exists *as it is traversed.* The perception of space becomes a physical, experiential process of *practice,* in which it is the action of the body in moving around and across that space that constructs it. Furthermore, "time is itself beginning to be shortened"; that is, the very nature of space, measured by time—by the experience of travelling through it—is altered by a revolution in transport that creates new conceptions of "real time."[103] In parallel with the remapping of the territory, then, the early Soviet planning project was an attempt to discover an architecture, and an urban system, that would be created by the body (individual and collective) in an ongoing, dynamic process. "Thanks to movement," Ginzburg wrote, "we define the most important and the secondary aspect of man—the organic meaning of the development of the human body."[104]

Chapter 2 Feeling

To discover life, in what there is that's true, in what it contains that's so prodigiously intense, varied, multiple.
—*Le Corbusier*

Placing the human body at the centre of their theories, the "function-alist" architects sought to reorganize perception, to create a new way of looking at the world. Citing Lenin's statement that "in order really to know an object, it is necessary to comprehend, to study all sides of it, all its 'connections and means of mediation [*sviazi i oposredstvo-vaniia*],' external and internal," Moisei Ginzburg argued that art (in the broadest sense of the word) must seek to convey the three-dimensional, sensory fullness of experience.[1] It had a key part to play in the "emancipation of the senses" that, as discussed in the Introduction, was the ideological foundation of the new order.

Film, naturally, was conscripted into this broader project. And it seemed uniquely equipped for it. For Dziga Vertov, the primary goal of film was to offer a "a cinematic feeling [*oshchushchenie*—the term incorporates both "sensation" and "experience"] of the world."[2] This emphasis on physical sensation—the *oshchushchenie*—underpinned Soviet revolutionary culture. Vertov was part of a much larger movement in the cinematography of the 1920s that viewed film as a means of exploring, even reconstructing, space and of establishing a new relationship between the human body and the physical world. The task of film was to project a space belonging to the young revolutionary culture—in Vertov's words, "the creation of a fresh perception of the world," through "fragments of real energy."[3] The camera would liberate the eye from the constraints capitalist society imposed on it, enabling fresh (and implicitly *socialist*) perception, and experience.

This new experience was, above all, mobile. In 1923, Vertov's *kinoki* (Cine-eye) manifesto called for film to render unmediated the immediacy and dynamism of the revolutionary period, the destabilized and decentred space and time of the 1920s: "I emancipate myself from this day and forever from human immobility. I am in constant motion."[4] This ideological emphasis on mobility corresponded to social realities. In the words of the Constructivist theorist Aleksei Gan, the task of art was to "actually formulate fluidity *[tekuchest']* and its concrete content."[5] This term *tekuchest'* carried concrete social resonance during the 1920s and into the Great Leap Forward, describing the extraordinary social and physical mobility caused by rapid industrialization and huge-scale transformation. The poet Vladimir Maiakovskii, using an electrical metaphor that demonstrates the symbolic power of electrification, described cinema as a "conductor of movement": "For me," he proclaimed, "cinema is almost a way of looking at the world."[6] Film was both creator and reflector of a new *mirosozertsanie* (way of looking at the world), in which mobility was the primary referent.

Through movement, Vertov's Cine-eye group sought to remake the relationship between the individual and space (the physical world) and to do so through the body. Film, they believed, was uniquely placed to express a physical apprehension *(oshchushchenie)* of the world. It stood in a unique relationship with reality. There was nothing obviously new here: the inherently mimetic quality of cinema's "moving pictures" had preoccupied filmmakers and theorists since the Lumière brothers' first films in 1895. Film theorists of the first half of the twentieth century divided broadly along Realist and Formalist lines. How was film to be at once an art and a photographic (mimetic) reproduction of the "real"? While Formalist theorists such as Rudolf Arnheim sought ways for film to escape from its inherent mimetic qualities and to become truly "artistic," other critics such as Siegfried Kracauer and Walter Benjamin (and later André Bazin) claimed that it was precisely film's unique ability to record the "real" that was its artistic quality.[7]

FILM: THE REDEMPTION OF REALITY

The attention of early film theorists to film as a representation of the physical world has been largely lost in the increasing attention given to structures of identification ("the gaze") and to narrative as film theory has developed. The "what is represented" of film has become, apparently, a subject less worthy of analysis than structures of how and why. Cinema has been viewed principally as bearer of ideology, implicated in dominant and dominating structures of gender, power, etc.[8] The introduction of the gaze as the key category of cinematic analysis has, in effect, sidestepped the problem of film's relationship to reality. In so doing, it has separated cinema from that which had been initially identified as its key point of difference from other media: the suggestion of a limitless representation of reality. Returning to this early "difference" may enable a better understanding of film's particular role in the remapping of Soviet experience. Writing in 1934, the film theorist and art historian Erwin Panofsky claimed that the cinematic image would never be reducible to narrative: it would always be immutably "physical."[9] In this sense, he suggested, "It is the movies, and only the movies, that do justice to that materialistic interpretation of the universe which, whether we like it or not, pervades contemporary civilization."[10] In the first decades of the twentieth century, film seemed to offer a new representation of the world—and one that corresponded to the material experience of the modern world.

Early attempts to understand the nature of cinema were often preoccupied by the strangeness of the medium and the curious revelation of reality that it seemed to provide. In his pioneering study of early cinema in Russia, Yuri Tsivian recounts how, for the first film spectators, certain stylistic techniques (such as the camera tracking "into" and "out of" the filmic space) created a special type of sensory involvement, disturbing their established sense of "spatial identity."[11] In Russia and the West alike, the shock of cinema was, he points out, often expressed as the shock of the experience of viewing "a world without me"— of viewing the object world from unexpected, otherwise impossible perspectives.[12] This "world without me" was something of a revelation: in the words of the Hungarian Béla Balázs (who lived in Moscow from 1931 to 1945), film "revealed the mainsprings of a life" and "widened our vision of the world."[13] By focusing on small details, the camera seemed to uncover the physical "truth" of the world.

In terms similar to those of Balázs, Siegfried Kracauer claimed that truly "cinematic" films "incorporate aspects of physical reality with a view to making us experience them."[14] The term *experience* is important here. Miriam Hansen has argued that cinema was "the single most inclusive, cultural horizon in which the traumatic effects of modernity were reflected, rejected or disavowed, transmuted or negotiated."[15] Following Kracauer and Benjamin, she argues that film from its very beginnings "engaged the contradictions of modernity *at the level of the senses,* the level at which the impact of modern technology on human experience was most palpable and irreversible [emphasis added]."[16] It seemed to re-create the visual and tactile experience of modern life—not through its narratives, but through its techniques.

The impact of cinema, Hansen suggests, was in part due to its creation of "a new sensory culture"—what Benjamin called the "unconscious optics" of cinema.[17] These unconscious optics were not merely optical, however. The experience of cinema was tactile as well as visual, and it was this multilevelled sensorium that, for Benjamin, gave cinema its peculiarly redemptive quality. "The tasks which face the human apparatus of perception at the turning points of history cannot be solved by optical means, that is, by contemplation, alone," he wrote; "they are mastered gradually by habit, under the guidance of *tactile appropriation* [emphasis added]."[18] For Benjamin, cinema had a crucial role to play in the *appropriation* of reality that was the human project, and which would, in Marx's terms, bring about the "end of alienation." It would bring people into a closer sensory relationship with the object world. As the subtitle of Kracauer's later book proclaimed, film promised a "redemption of physical reality."

It is clear, then, that an emphasis on the sensory experience of space was at the centre of early cinema and film theory in Europe. This found exciting and politically charged expression in the cinematic exploration of space in Soviet film in the first decade after the revolution. Film was a means of *appropriation* and, as such, had a key political role to play. In the words of one L. Shipulinskii, writing in a collection of articles published in 1919, and dedicated to the *"kinematograf,"* film "sees everything, knows everything, and shows everything to everyone."[19] Shipulinskii's enthusiastic inclusiveness here demonstrates both cinema's mass, democratic character (it shows everything, to everyone) and its revelatory capacity (it *shows*). The coincidence of these two categories guaranteed the importance of film to the revolutionary project—it was at once democratic and transformative, offering the mass dissemination of a sensory revolution.

MONTAGE, PHOTOGÉNIE:
THE TRANSFORMATION OF REALITY

Examining the spatial structures of films in the first decades after the revolution, therefore, provides us with a revealing index of shifting aesthetic and ideological preoccupations. Prerevolutionary cinema, as Tsivian has shown, had drawn substantially on theatrical models of mise-en-scène. The innovations of the prolific and talented director Evgenii Bauer, for example, lay in the reshaping of the mise-en-scène, creating vast and dramatic film sets that offered new cinematic possibilities of depth and shadow. They relied, however, on sequences of long shots that were carefully staged and not significantly edited. Bauer's *Deti bol'shogo goroda* (*Children of the Big City,* 1914), for example, represented the space of the city through slow-paced street shots that showed his protagonists gazing through ornamental ironwork gates and glass shop fronts. Behind the grand façades of his cinematic city lay high-ceilinged interiors, in which the glamorous paraphernalia of the high bourgeois interior played a starring role.[20]

For the young filmmakers such as Vertov who aligned themselves with the revolutionary experiment, however, cinema had an entirely new message to convey and a new world to represent: a new visual language was required. It was out of this quest for a new means of expression that the art of montage was born. Although the history of Soviet montage is well-known as a foundation of modern film history, it may nevertheless bear reexamination here. Much has been written about the complex distinctions between the diverse practitioners and theorists who make up the canonical history of Soviet montage: Lev Kuleshov, Sergei Eisenstein, Vsevolod Pudovkin, and Dziga Vertov. All, however, were united by their conviction that the power of cinema lay in its specificity—in its distinctly "cinematic" nature. Praising the achievements of American filmmakers such as D. W. Griffith, Kuleshov said that they alone had recognized that the true value of cinema lay in its potential to create energy and impact from the combination of shots: from editing. The value of a film lay not in the aesthetic weight of individual shots, and not in the mise-en-scène, but in the creative possibilities offered by editing. Setting up a workshop with several associates (including Pudovkin), Kuleshov set out to experiment with the effects achieved through the combination of shots as "building blocks" in the film sequence.

Acknowledging the hegemony of editing (montage) over mise-en-scène in film meant acknowledging the potential of cinema to reconstruct temporal and spatial categories. Montage changed the relation of film to its material referent, and it was, from its very beginnings, tied to a reshaping of space. For the montage director, space was not just setting, but a structural component of the film. In his experimental laboratory, Kuleshov discovered the possibility of creating what he called "created geography" *(tvorimaia geografiia):* the splicing together of film shots taken in diverse places to create an entirely new geography, a purely cinematic space. His first experiment in this respect linked diverse places in Moscow with the White House in Washington.[21] Vertov celebrated the revolutionary possibilities of this spatial collage in his 1923 article "The Film Eyes: A Revolution," in which he spoke of combining Chicago and Petrograd, Astrakhan and Moscow as a single filmic space: "I juxtapose any points in the universe, regardless of where I fixed them."[22]

Montage, then, appeared to separate film from its problematically mimetic relationship with the "real." Things were not so clear-cut, however. The shaping of cinematic space was linked, crucially, to the shaping of "real" space—and it was there that film's truly revolutionary potential lay. In 1922, Kuleshov called for art to have "precision in time" and "precision in space," in order that it establish an "organic connection" with contemporary (implicitly revolutionary) life.[23] This temporal and spatial precision must, he wrote, be tied to what he described as "the reality of raw material *[deistvitel'nost' materiala]*." This prescription bears further consideration, for it demonstrates how the early principles of Soviet montage were tied to a belief in increased proximity with the experiential reality of everyday life. The task of film was to fix "human and natural raw material." The dynamic editing of montage was not just a means of telling a story better, but the only true way to tell that story (the story of contemporary life) at all. It was a stylistics of the present.

Here, then, we confront a key paradox of early Soviet film theory and aesthetics. The editing principle would appear to have suggested that the "raw material" of film was less important than the transformation of that material through film. Kuleshov's emphasis on the "reality of raw material," and on an "organic" connection with life as it is lived, however, seems to contradict this. It suggests that montage was a means of capturing a sense of the raw material of life that, in his view, could not be conveyed through traditional art forms. This call for "natural" or "real" material was common to Kuleshov, Vertov, Eisenstein, and Pudovkin. Films must be set in "real" space: the created geography of cinematic space was created through the montage of fragments of real space, and not through the fantasy of set design.

Two key ideas are blurred here. On the one hand, the possibilities of "imaginary geography" seemed to render space less than real—to transform the materiality of the physical world into visual simulacra that could be manipulated and reshaped by editing. On the other hand, film enabled a closer encounter with natural raw material. The delimitation of the cinematic frame seemed to isolate fragments of raw material from the chaos of the totality and to permit a visual and sensory reevaluation of those fragments—a form of "redemption."[24] It liberated the material world from human (capitalist) intervention, picturing a new "world without me." In the words of Susan Buck-Morss: "What is perceived in the cinema image is not a psychological fact, but a phenomenological one."[25]

This apparent contradiction—between the "transformation" of the material world and its discovery or "redemption" through film—was central to discussions of montage. It is particularly evident in the response of Soviet critics and practitioners to the theory of *la photogénie,* formulated by two French theorists and practitioners, Jean Epstein and Louis Delluc, in the 1920s. Photogénie was premised on the idea that film provided an apprehension of a reality that was "more than real." Delluc, an "impressionist" filmmaker, saw cinema as a means of creating a "lived experience" in which nature (the natural world) was "alive."[26] For Epstein, who studied with Delluc, film was unique and "superior to man," in that it captured the universe in four dimensions—that is, in space and time. It "discovers movement where our eye sees nothing but stasis" and reveals the fullness of the natural world, in which "everything is alive."[27] Film, according to photogénie, was capable of "developing the range of our senses," and in so doing, of renewing the human apprehension of the world.

For Epstein, film was a means of exposing the pure material surface of the physical world, and this pure materiality would provide "a specific form of knowledge" of the world, at once physical (corporeal) and emotional.[28] Film heightened the effect of the object world on the perceiving subject. In Epstein's words, cinematography was a "means of thinking"; it shaped the relationship of mind to matter. The "psychology" of photogénie was premised on the physical, however; it was a *phenomenological* conception of experience. Above all, Epstein and Delluc saw in cinema a new relationship between the perceiving subject (the body) and the material world.[29] Cinema was to function as a redemption of the experience of reality that had been lost by industrialization and the excessive visualization of culture. It would represent a heightened ("photogenic") reality, *created* by cinema. This heightened reality was "embalmed in motion": that is, it depended upon the specific characteristic of cinema, uniquely able to represent a mobile physical world.[30]

In the Soviet film press, photogénie had been generally discredited by 1927. Delluc's 1920 book *La photogénie* had been published in translation in both Moscow and St. Petersburg in 1924, and the work of Epstein as both filmmaker and theorist was known, at least to those who read the cinema press.[31] Epstein's films *La belle Nivernaise* (1923) and *La goutte de sang* (1924) were released in Russia in 1925 and received a poor critical response (leading one critic to exclaim of *La belle Nivernaise* that "it really is a meaningless film; like many French films, it offers a combination of pornography and sentimentality").[32] The publication of Delluc's book provoked an immediate storm of controversy among Soviet filmmakers and theorists, with Pudovkin publishing a virulent repudiation of the theory of photogénie in April 1925.[33]

Pudovkin's critique of photogénie was based on the belief that the theory neglected the most important element of the film art: the "selection" *(vybor)* and combination of material. He admitted that the "photogenic" quality of the filmed material was the most important element of any film but insisted that the task of the filmmaker in selecting and combining (editing) the material of the film was vital. Montage provides the "net" that structures and the "rhythm" that defines the effect of the material. Pudovkin took issue with the "lyrical" and "individualist" underpinnings of Delluc's theory and argued for the importance of the "organization" and "order" of potential chaos that editing can create.[34] Other Soviet critics criticized Delluc on similar ideological grounds: Viktor Pertsov stated that photogénie paid insufficient attention to the "transformation" of material.[35] The mere revelation of the material world was inadequate: what was needed was to alter radically the *relationship* between that material world and the individual. For Pertsov, Delluc and Epstein represented a bourgeois conception of experience. They did not transform this experience, but rather exaggerated it through film. Indeed, Epstein's euphoric celebration of the world as it is, revealed by cinema, displays a (somewhat unfocused) sensual delight in the plenitude of the physical world: "Life recruits atoms, molecular movement is as sensual as the hips of a woman or young man."[36]

This tension between the apprehension of reality and its transformation, evident in the photogénie debate, was central to the representation of space in film during the 1920s and early 1930s, posing fundamental questions about the relationship between man and woman and the physical world. The key need was for film to offer a new, *appropriative,* experience of space. Even in Marx's original use of "appropriation," however, we have identified a fundamental ambiguity. On the one hand, man must seek a renewed sensory relationship with the object world (the material). On the other, the means of achieving this was through the transformation of the object into a "social object."[37]

Eisenstein's 1925 article "Toward a Materialist Approach to Film Form" (published side by side with Pudovkin's repudiation of photogénie) approached these questions directly, distinguishing his own cinematic method from that of Vertov according to a different attitude toward the filmic "material." Vertov, he suggested, "rushes after objects *as they are* without rebelliously interrupting the inevitability of the statics of the causal connection between them, without overcoming this connection through a powerful social-organizational motive, but yielding to its 'cosmic' pressure [emphasis added]."[38] In contrast to this "pantheistic" enslavement to the material world, Eisenstein called for film that "recarves reality and real phenomena," that would "interrupt" and "overcome" reality *as it was* and, implicitly, recast it *as it should be.* Thus while he, like Vertov, viewed film as the means of "a concretization of a new attitude and approach to objects and phenomena," for him this approach was one of control, not of discovery.[39]

Three years later, in 1928, Eisenstein articulated his conception of the status of "raw material" in film more explicitly. Writing about the making of his 1928 film *October* (made in celebration of the tenth anniversary of the revolution), he reflected on stages in the development of Soviet cinematography, claiming that *October* represented a new kind of cinema, which moved beyond the kind of films produced during the earlier part of the 1920s.[40] He articulated this new stage as a changed relationship with raw material. The "nonplayed" film of the 1920s (a clear reference to the work of Vertov's Cine-eyes) had, he suggested, fallen victim to a "fetish for raw material" that was not "materialist." In Eisenstein's words, "When the question of the hegemony of 'raw material' merged into general usage, a hysterical scream, the 'cult' of raw material, it meant the end of raw material."[41] The end, that is, of raw material as the stuff of *production.*

Eisenstein decried the emphasis on increased proximity with the material world that we have identified as central to the montage aesthetic in its early stages. He suggested that material "in itself" was no longer enough and called for a transformative, constructive relationship with that material: "Slaves of raw material are becoming masters of raw material."[42] The distinction made here is an important one and strikes at the heart of the complex status of "material" and "raw material" in Soviet Russia during this period. Eisenstein was at pains to claim that his use of the term "raw material" was meant "in the formal cinematic sense and not as something historical or factual." This distinction is itself revealing, seeking to distinguish the material out of which a film is constructed from the "material" reality of the physical world. In practice, however, the distinction does not hold. The fetish for material to which Eisenstein referred was certainly fundamental to the reconceptualization of space that can be traced in film during the first half of the 1920s. But it was not limited to aesthetics. In the climate of rapid modernization of Soviet Russia during the 1920s and into the First Five-Year Plan, "raw material" *(syr'e)* carried a particular symbolic weight. Russia was the raw material out of which socialism was to be constructed; the Soviet territory (the earth itself) was the rich raw material out of which a powerful state was to be moulded—provider of riches and potential.

In practical terms, then, the material world was at once something to be discovered and something to be transformed. In artistic terms, this led to an ambiguity that can be traced through many avant-garde writings on sensory perception and art, and particularly in the work of Formalists Viktor Shklovskii and Boris Eikhenbaum.[43] For Shklovskii, the aim of art (through *ostranenie* [defamiliarization]) was to "bring back the feeling *[oshchushchenie]* of life, to feel things, to make the stone stony."[44] Shklovskii's use of the term *oshchushchenie* echoed Vertov's *kinooshchushchenie:* through film, the "feeling of things" could be rediscovered and made available to all. The filmic image could create a heightened sensory awareness of the material world. For the Formalists, this emphasis on "feeling"—physical sensation—was set against the mental, conscious representational model offered by language: Shklovskii's fellow Formalist Eikhenbaum saw cinema as part of a larger rejection of language (and by extension, narrative) as the primary means of creating meaning. "The film spectator wants a rest from the word," he wrote; "he wants only to see and to guess."[45] Meaning, in cinema, is constructed outside language—*materially,* in space: "The film spectator thinks in [through] space *[myslit prostranstvom],*" Eikhenbaum declared; "it exists for him beyond the characters."[46] We are able to sense space because of our knowledge of our own bodies, and the process of cinematic perception is situated between cognitive and physical experience.

In prioritizing "the thing," Eikhenbaum and Shklovskii placed the material world at the centre of their theories. In this respect, they echoed the Constructivist "culture of materials" elaborated by Aleksei Gan. Gan agreed with Moisei Ginzburg in seeing art as a means of reformulating the relationship between man and the material world (see Chapter 1): it would "create a system for the presentation *[oformlenie]* of things in general." For Gan, three principles underpinned Constructivism: *tektonika, faktura,* and *konstruktsiia. Tektonika* described the synthesis of aesthetics and ideology (form and content) that was essential to the new culture, in which "art," in a traditional sense, was rendered irrelevant. *Faktura,* he claimed, was the "texture" of a thing—the "how-it-is-made." Constructivists must approach the material world "as if for the first time," Gan asserted, "not putting prior meaning into our conception of the *faktura*." This was, in a sense, an attempt to arrive at a preconscious apprehension of the world, to "emancipate" the senses. Emancipation was only the first stage, however: a "real" understanding of the material was achieved only through a synthesis of the raw material and its "processing" *(obrabotka).* Through processing, the "natural" object would become a "social" object: *Faktura,* Gan explained, "is the organic state of the *processed* material." The final principle, *konstruktsiia* (construction), describes the process by which the material is assembled into a system, a whole.[47]

This tripartite process of "(re)construction" sought to follow Marx's dictum of transforming the "thing," or object, into a *social* object, articulating a complex relationship with the material world. The quest for a fresh feeling/sensation *(oshchushchenie)* of the physical "texture" of the world was a guiding imperative. Once this was achieved, however, the essential task of the artist was to transform that texture through *obrabotka).* This emphasis on *obrabotka* demonstrates the ideological weight of "work" or labour in Constructivist theory: "work" was a creative and sensory process, a means of forging a relationship between the body and the material world. The object was *appropriated* through its processing (and in art, implicitly, the very act of representation was a form of processing). The paradox is evident here: it is through the processing of the object world that it is *restored* to a fully sensory relationship with humanity.

This paradox underpinned debates about film. The Constructivist emphasis on the "processing" of raw material anticipated Shklovskii's attack on Vertov's Cine-eye movement in 1925. Shklovskii's initial definition of the task of cinema as the representation of the "feeling of things" appeared to correspond to Vertov's own manifesto of 1923. In the same year as publishing this "definition," however, he argued that Vertov's aesthetics denied the very essence of cinema, which lay in articulating a particular "relationship to the material." In the Cine-eye films, he wrote, "objects are impoverished, because there is no bias, in the artistic sense of the word, in the *relationship* to objects [emphasis in original]."[48] The primary material of film, Shklovskii suggested, was not the object that was filmed, but the method of its filming; the task of film was to transform the material.

DYNAMISM: THE CINEMATIC MOVEMENT IMAGE

Shklovskii's criticisms prefigured Eisenstein's accusations of Vertov's enslavement to "raw material." But they also presented a problem. Shklovskii sought to explain how the "physical" could be transformed by film into the "signifying" and to avoid the supposedly bourgeois mysticism of photogénie. In its emphasis on the "material" level of cinematic signification, however, Formalist film theory had itself raised several obstacles to this: the "material," in film, Eikhenbaum had suggested, offered *prelinguistic* meaning. It was constructed through sensation (feeling). As such, it resisted classification as a signifying code. The resolution of this apparent contradiction lies, perhaps, in the dual meaning of the Constructivist *faktura.* "Processing" *(obrabotka),* for the Constructivists, was both redemption and "transformation"—the successive emancipation of the senses and *appropriation* of the object. For Vertov, the moving pictures of film offered the same double function. Movement itself assumed almost the status of ideology: it was both redemptive and transformative, creating a new, and implicitly revolutionary, relationship with the world. The cinema of the Cine-eye group, for example, placed *movement* at its centre and substituted the logic of movement for the logic of signification.

For Vertov and the Formalists alike, film's mobility underpinned its unique relationship with the material world. In Eikhenbaum's words, it "dynamized the photographic shot, turning it from an enclosed, static singularity into a frame—into the infinitely small part of a moving stream."[49] Here we encounter a key ideological opposition between closure and openness, stillness and movement. The film liberates the enclosed, motionless "fragment" of reality and re-creates it as part of a "stream" of mobile energy. This representational stream was perceived to respond to the experience of "real" space.

The influence of Henri Bergson (whose philosophies of time and movement as predicated upon subjective experience were well-known in Russia at this time) can be sensed here.[50] For Bergson, perception depended on movement, and movement was heterogeneous and indivisible: "A moving continuity is given to us, in which everything changes and yet remains."[51] Bergson's reconceptualization of the nature of perception is richly suggestive for film theory, and in particular for consideration of the representation of movement and space in Soviet film. In 1919, the film critic Shipulinskii's words seemed to echo Bergson directly: "We experience movement, and any living process, taking place in time, as something single and undivided, as a process, and not as a collection of images or pictures spread out (even if only in our minds) in space."[52]

Through its "moving pictures" film seemed uniquely placed to do justice to the "moving continuity" that, for Bergson, was "modern" experience. Bergson himself, however, had criticized cinema for "abstract movement," claiming that the succession of frames (twenty-four per second) upon which cinematic representation depends necessitated a "synthetic" creation of movement by the eyes and brain of the spectator. The film shot, he believed, was merely a single instant *(coupe)* to which an abstract, mechanized succession was added in order to simulate movement. Real movement, by contrast, has a "concrete duration"— that is, it takes place in the present and is heterogeneous. It cannot be broken down into instants. Thus cinema, for Bergson, was "false movement," in direct opposition to the experience of real movement, experienced as a continuous process, *through the body.*[53]

Shklovskii agreed with Bergson, arguing that it was precisely cinema's "synthetic mobility" that transformed the real material of the world photographed by the camera into "movement as sign."[54] Where "real" vision is continuous and indivisible, he asserted, the cinema emerges out of a stylized "broken-up *[preryvnaia]* world."[55] Further consideration of the nature of cinematic movement, however, offers an alternative view. Gilles Deleuze has suggested that Bergson's dismissal of cinema as abstract, or false, movement was "overly hasty" and failed to grasp the true essence of cinema. The cinematic image, he suggested, is in fact an "intermediate image *[image moyenne]*": it cannot be reduced to the still frame *(photogramme)* but is in reality always in the process of transition to another image. The film image is never static.[56] In this sense, cinema is intrinsically part of what Deleuze calls "a modern conception of movement." It is a means of representing (even embodying) the nature of flux and contingency that Bergson defined as the "modern" experience of time. Film places the physical experience of the body (in motion) at the centre of perception.

Deleuze's interpretation of Bergson provides a useful interpretive angle on Soviet cinema of the 1920s. He links the "modern conception of movement" to the development of mechanized transportation, suggesting that the rapid movement made possible by train (and later airplane) travel transforms the human experience of time and space (see Chapter 5). In this respect, for Deleuze, the camera, and montage, captures the "mechanical succession of instants" that, he suggests, has become the predominant scientific and philosophical understanding of the nature of time and movement in the modern age.[57] Where the photograph abstracts the image from time, the cinematic "movement-image" (to use Deleuze's phrase) produces a spatial representation of time as mobile experience.[58] Cinema thus becomes a representation of experience as dynamic and corporeal: movement through space.

For the Soviet avant-garde, similarly, film was to transform "real" movement into a representation of the symbolic dynamism of the revolutionary experience. Cinema was able to represent a kind of embodied perception—vision as a mobile, physical experience. It could encapsulate the new synthesis of body and technology, apprehension and transformation, that defined the Soviet aesthetic project. It was in this sense that film had such a crucial role to play in the creation of the Soviet imaginary map.

DZIGA VERTOV: THE "FEELING"
OF THE TRAVELLING EYE

The ideological weight of "mobility" is made clear in Vertov's early films. His *Chelovek s kinoapparatom (Man with a Movie Camera)* of 1929 is the most fully developed demonstration of his Cine-eye theories and one of the purest demonstrations of the cult of dynamic space that is the subject of the present book. The "man with a movie camera" was the natural counterpart of the "man with a suitcase," who was a central figure of Soviet culture throughout the 1920s and who found a practical incarnation in the travelling workforce and exploratory dynamic (the *chemodannoe nastroenie* [suitcase mentality]) of the late 1920s. The film ostensibly tracks the adventures of a cameraman as he roams the contemporary Soviet everyday, apparently unlimited by constraints of time or space. In practice, however, the cameraman provides only the most tenuous narrative thread, and the film subverts the conventions of plot and signification in favour of an exploration and interrogation of the potentiality of the cinematic "eye." In this film, Vertov's aesthetic represented the experience of space as a process of exploration and discovery—as *embodied perception*.

Filming an unnamed Soviet city, and the activities of a man with a camera in that city, Vertov produces an image of space that is without a centre. It is both decentred and, perhaps more significantly, centreless. In the first place, the city is unmapped—that is, it is not named or geographically located. Its authenticity as a "real" space is irrelevant to the dynamic of the film. Vertov's city exists outside a controlled or known structure of the Soviet space: the cityscape is fragmented into a series of isolated and partial shots, and montage reconstructs a vision of a city that cannot be mapped. Parts—fragments—of monumental architecture, landmarks that identify different cities, occur but are never articulated relationally or geographically such that the city becomes an abstract composite of physical experiences. Arteries predominate, as urban scenes are presented crossed by trams, roads, pedestrians. Furthermore, the arteries themselves are always crossed, as the intersection of vertical and horizontal shapes constructs the frame. All coherent axes are refused and replaced by a dynamic of flux in which space can be remade according to alternative principles: a logic of the body.

Vlada Petric has undertaken a sustained analysis of Vertov's montage in the film as a formal representation of the machine aesthetic of Constructivism.[59] Vertical and horizontal movements are juxtaposed, both within single frames and between shots. Petric describes this cinematic method as based on "kinesthesia": creating an emotional and *sensory* effect (the *oshchushchenie*) on the viewer through the juxtaposition of stasis and movement: the opposition of static shots of buildings (factories, etc.), for example, with highly mobile tracking shots of movement, located principally in images of the human body and of mechanized transport. Vertov's montage theory depended on what he called a "theory of intervals." Cinematic perception, he suggested, was primarily dependent on the points of transition between individual shots. Each frame is in itself dynamic (contains movement), and the juxtaposition of different movements (frames) creates the kinesthetic effect. As Deleuze suggested, no filmic frame may stand alone: there can be no such thing as a filmic "still." Editing, therefore, becomes the "organization of movement"—a "dynamic geometry."[60] This aesthetic may be differentiated from the Eisensteinian conception of montage as signification, in which the juxtaposition of shots constructs "intellectual" meaning.[61] Where for Eisenstein montage was a kind of language, "transforming" the material, Vertovian montage was premised on a logic of sensation. The dynamic and destabilizing energy of the film represented a new kind of perception, liberated from common (and by implication, capitalist) constraints. It reproduced the perceptual experience of a new kind of physical movement through space.

This, then, offered a new vision of the body in space. Vertov's position on the role of the human body in perception was ambiguous. Discussing the superiority of the camera eye over the human eye in 1923, he wrote: "The position of our body during observation, the quantity of moments of this or that visual phenomenon perceived by us in a second of time, are not at all obligatory for the movie camera, the powers of perception of which are as much greater and better [than a human's] as it is more perfect [than a human]."[62] Petric describes Vertov's camera as an "omnipotent eye," ready to capture life unawares (Vertov's expression was *zhizn' vrasplokh*).[63] Rather than validating the camera (the eye) at the expense of the body, however, a closer examination of Vertov's writing, and his films, suggests that the Cine-eye was premised on a complete *re-thinking* of the nature of the body in space, on a newly active relationship between the individual and the physical world. While I accept that the camera eye, for Vertov, is an all-powerful means of penetrating beyond the external surface of reality, I would add an important caveat. Vertov's camera eye may appear omnipotent, but it is never *omnipresent*. Instead, the spatial limits of vision are consistently made explicit. In *Man with a Movie Camera,* vision is fragmented and mobilized as the cameraman travels around the city. The camera adopts different viewing positions, some of which are channelled through human figures who appear, however briefly, in the film, and others of which have no point of origin, but rather are that of the camera. This camera moves around and within space, but the limits of its movement are anthropomorphized. That is to say, it achieves a form of omnipresence, but only by physically *moving* from one position to the next. Throughout *Man with a Movie Camera,* Vertov emphasizes the sheer energy and ingenuity involved in creating this cinematic vision: the cameraman travels on a crane across a dam, climbs buildings, even lies on rail tracks, etc. Although the movements of the cameraman are not always seen, they are a constant subtext of the film. The animated camera scene in the film makes this theory explicit. In it, the camera rises from its case, constructs itself (with tripod, etc.), and moves offscreen. It exhibits human characteristics, as it shows off its various parts and seems to bow for a cinema audience.

Thus the film eye does not provide a vision of totality: the perceptual experience of space is rendered material and corporeal. It is rooted in the body, and as such challenges the controlling, perspectival notion of vision. In this sense, Vertov's aesthetic echoed the phenomenological emphasis of early Marxism.[64] All knowledge (all meaning) depends on experience of the physical world. It cannot be formulated outside that experience. It is the ability of film to represent this experience that differentiates it from the photograph. Where the photograph abstracts the image from time, the cinematic movement-image represents vision as a mobile, physical experience. Again, *Man with a Movie Camera* made this distinction between film and still photograph explicit. In one sequence Vertov shows Elizaveta Svilova (his wife and editorial colleague) examining still photographs of faces. The stills become single frames. Then they are shown *in action,* as part of a filmic sequence. This serves two functions. It is part of the broader project of the film, which creates a *mise-en-abîme* of the process of filmmaking: Svilova is constructing a mobile picture from a series of still fragments. It is clear, however, that for Vertov film is valuable precisely because it is able to capture the experience of "real" movement, as Bergson defined it: an indivisible, heterogeneous *durée.* The cinematic system is an "open system," and the frame appears permeable.

Man with a Movie Camera, then, pictured what Gan described as a "concrete interrelation" between people and objects (space): "people are always in concrete interrelation with the objects of their daily life."[65] Vertov's cinematography represented the experience of the world as premised on practice, conditioned by the material facts of that world. This was not necessarily a disempowerment of the individual, however. Rather, it was envisaged as *liberation:* the new Soviet man and woman would be free to experience the world in all its fullness. His/her "eye" would be transformed—and transformed by revolution. The Cine-eye aesthetic sought to reformulate the relation between space and time to respond to the revolutionary model of experience. Vertov claimed that "the film eye is a concentration and deconstruction of time."[66] His montage, I suggest, replaced the temporal axis with a spatial axis. It "spatialized" time through a series of cinematic techniques. Movement, in *Man with a Movie Camera,* has no defined goal but is a thing in itself. The dynamic composition of the frame is a visual "fact." In this sense it is a formulation of *tekuchest'* (fluidity), according to Gan's prescription. In Vertov, time was removed from a historical narrative of past—present—future and placed in the present. The present moment, the dynamic moment of change, was all-important. The *put'* was reconfigured, not as progression to an elusive but significant goal, but as the dynamic *process* of transformation itself, and the nation was mobilized.[67] In 1919, Roman Jakobson wrote: "The overcoming of *statics,* the discarding of the absolute, is the main thrust of modern times."[68] The camera was an appropriative mechanism, enabling a new relationship with the physical world. Its task was to represent—and to encourage—a new kind of sensate relationship between the body and space.

Chapter 3 Decentring

Вообще центр сдвигается с места.

(The centre is getting moving.)
—*Viktor Shklovskii*

This new relationship between the human body and space was frequently expressed through a focus on the periphery, both real and metaphorical—and in the transformation of traditional centres (ideological and spatial) into new peripheries. In *Man with a Movie Camera,* the decentred space of Vertov's unnamed and composite metropolis transformed urban space into a kind of periphery, denying the possibility of any kind of centre, geographical or spectatorial. In parallel, across a broad spectrum of cultural texts in the 1920s, pictures of decentred space emerged. In 1921, for example, a group of young artists who collected around Grigorii Kozintsev and Leonid Trauberg in St. Petersburg named themselves the Factory of the Eccentric Actor (FEKS). Between 1924 and 1929, FEKS produced five films under the banner of *Ekstsentrizm,* defined by their manifesto in 1922 as a multi-levelled rejection of all that was "central"—that is, of dominant social and cultural forms—in favour of the marginal or peripheral, understood both ideologically and spatially.[1]

Eccentrism was a negation of the past, of traditional, "high" culture and authority. In this, FEKS had much in common with the Futurist rejection of the past, famously expressed in their manifesto *A Slap in the Face of Public Taste*.[2] They used "vulgar" and "low" forms of entertainment as the weapons through which to launch an assault on the "centre." Above all, FEKS rejected *immobility:* "To the machines!" they cried, "Driving belts, chains, wheels, hands, legs, electricity. The rhythm of production."[3] The machine aesthetic merged with what Eisenstein called the "attractions" of the fairground and circus, with movements that were "acrobatic, gymnastic, balletic, [and] constructive-mechanical."[4]

The very term *eccentrism* (*ex-centrism*—out of the centre) expressed the dual thrust of FEKS's decentring and destabilizing impetus. Naum Kleiman has suggested that, for the "ex-centrics," "the shift of axis from the former centre guarantees the self-propelled movement not only of art, but also of reality."[5] The conscious process of destabilization that the Eccentrics undertook sought to create a kind of *perpetuum mobile,* in which the system was forced into continual movement. It would break down traditional axes and create alternative patterns of movement. The dynamism of the perpetuum mobile depended, above all, on the dissolution of the established centre: the "shift *[sdvig]* from the centre."

URBAN HERITAGE: THE TRANSGRESSIVE CITY

This did not mean, however, that the city had no part to play in film. Rather, it was itself configured as a decentred space. FEKS's third film *Chertovo koleso* (*The Devil's Wheel,* 1926) is set "on the outskirts of Leningrad," in run-down apartment buildings that, the titles suggest, may appear "dead" but are in fact "teeming with life." An upright young sailor, Vania (recently arrived "from the village"), descends into the urban underworld, drawn into a frenetic, unstable milieu of fairgrounds and bars. The excitement causes him to lose track of time (visually, the spin of the "devil's wheel," a popular fairground attraction, echoes the uncontrolled spin of time) and to miss his required return on-board ship. Throughout the film, the city is represented as dangerously dynamic: one scene provides fragmented cityscapes from the perspective of characters on a roller coaster. In another, as characters dance in a bar, drinking, the background quite literally moves around them, such that the relationship between setting and protagonist is disrupted: everything moves. The metropolis is pictured as a living organism, an unstable space.

The energy of the cityscape is central to the impact of the film. In his memoirs, Kozintsev describes *The Devil's Wheel* as based on the belief that in film, "everything must be active *[deistvovat']*": the opposition between background and action was irrelevant and outdated. In his words: "on the screen are not 'places for action' but 'acting places' [*deistvuiushchie mesta,* playing with the term for dramatis personae—*deistvuiushchie litsa*]."[6] Props, too, were "acting things." This dynamic aesthetic sought to transform the relationship between actor and set, and, implicitly, between man and the material world. The physical environment—the set—was a character in the film. In parallel, in life itself, man was brought into closer contact with the textures and surfaces of things—with the *material.*

The "living" city that we encounter in *The Devil's Wheel* was common to many early twentieth-century images of the metropolis in film, poetry, and visual art. It can be identified in images of Moscow and St. Petersburg alike, and indeed in Western representations of the city. A similarly mobile, fragmented picture of the new capital was echoed, for example, in Il'ia Kopalin and Mikhail Kaufman's documentary film *Moskva* (1927),[7] and indeed in Walter Ruttman's *Berlin: Symphony of a Great City* (1927), as well as *Man with a Movie Camera.*[8] FEKS, like Vertov, used montage to create a vision of the city as fragmented and dynamic. Revolution is movement: the tempo of the age rendered space dynamic. The "acting," living city existed in a transformed relationship with the human body.

Much has been written about the effects of the modern city on Western European culture. The Soviet city can be viewed both within and against the framework of such analysis. In the words of Georg Simmel writing in 1903 the modern metropolis was characterized by "the rapid crowding of changing images, the sharp discontinuity in the grasp of a single glance, and the unexpectedness of onrushing impressions."[9] The sensory experience of the city was one of competing sensations and, ultimately, of the fleeting and the ephemeral. Walter Benjamin, who was much influenced by Simmel, has memorably described the experience of the urban male *flâneur* in terms of contingency and fluidity. A walk through the city offers the freedom of anonymity, the possibility of chance encounter. For Benjamin, the clearest expression of this sense of the city was Charles Baudelaire's poem "A une passante," where, in the midst of a "rue assourdissante," the poet has a moment of epiphany, "un éclair," as an unknown woman passes by, catches his eye, and then disappears, lost in the crowd forever.[10] The city is a liminal space, offering the possibility of transgression. Within the crowd, the individual is profoundly alone—and strangely free. A similar link between urban experience and bodily freedom has been explored by Richard Sennet, who suggests that the experience of the modern city can be dated from the late eighteenth century and tied to the emergence of modern individualism. For Sennet, the urban phenomenon was an epidemic of "circulation," as bodies were thrust into motion, finding themselves in the city both "restless and alone." The mobile experience of the city, he says, changed the sensory relationship between the human body and space: the relentless energy of the city alienates the human body, and the "modern problem," for Sennet, is "how to find a sensate home for responsive bodies in society."[11]

Such ideas of the city as an individual, not collective, space inflect modernist ideas of the liminal city familiar in prerevolutionary Russian culture of the first decades of the twentieth century. Many of Aleksandr Blok's poems of the first two decades of the century, for example, pictured the city as a solitary dreamscape for an increasingly disaffected poetic soul. Andrei Belyi's novel *Petersburg* (1914) offered a vision of that city as a shifting, hallucinatory space that seemed to rush precipitously toward impending apocalypse.[12] In prerevolutionary cinema, too, the city played an important part: in Evgenii Bauer's *Grezy (Daydreams)* of 1915, for example, the urban space is the site of precisely the kind of chance amorous encounter of which Baudelaire had written, as its central *flâneur* finds himself compelled to pursue an alluring stranger. Eleven years later, the influence of the modernist idea of the city as inherently transgressive could still be felt in *The Devil's Wheel,* in which FEKS blended urban "reality" with the urban folklore of popular culture. The city was transformed into a series of peripheries, both spatial and social, in which norms are suspended. The cultural heritage of this vision of St. Petersburg in particular needs little introduction: from Aleksandr Pushkin's *The Bronze Horseman* through Belyi's *Petersburg,* that city has a long history as the archetypal "liminal" site of Russian culture.[13] During the 1920s, Moscow and St. Petersburg alike were frequently represented in cinema within these essentially modernist frames of reference, as a space in which transgression was possible and lowlife could flourish. The creation of Moscow as the new capital, and as an alternative urban experience, was gradual.

Yet alongside this transgressive energy, the emergent metropolis also represented modernity, and technology. As such, for young Futurist poets such as Maiakovskii and Alexei Kruchenykh in the years leading up to the revolution, it represented a positive force for change. It was, moreover, the natural habitat of the nascent revolutionary force: the proletariat. After the revolution, crucially, the city needed to offer a new kind of experience, to correspond with new ideological and social imperatives. The solitary experience of the individual *flâneur* must be remade as the collective experience of the mass; transgression must become conformity. It was imperative to reconfigure the city as, using Sennet's term, a "sensate home" for the *malen"kii chelovek* (the little man). Discussing the space of revolutionary Paris, Sennet describes how the "visceral experience of freedom" and independence offered by urban space was manipulated and legitimated by the political project of revolution and transformed into an ideal of "mass" freedom and revolutionary energy.[14] In the Soviet context, similarly, we can trace a complex set of cultural practices that both exploited and transformed the "freedom" and "transgression" of the urban space. The dynamism of the city was appropriated as the dynamism of revolution; the liminal qualities of the city were mediated and blurred, as the urban space was gradually transformed into the lived space of the ordinary citizen.

Kuleshov's *Neobychainye prikliucheniia Mistera Vesta v strane bolshevikov (The Extraordinary Adventures of Mr. West in the Land of the Bolsheviks),* made in 1924, set two Moscows against one another at the level of plot. The first is the liminal Moscow of the urban underworld into which the naive American businessman Mr. West, visiting Soviet Russia for the first time and full of trepidation, unfortunately falls. It is located in peripheral, run-down apartment buildings similar to those of *The Devil's Wheel* in which the transgressive elements of society flourish. Here, Mr. West is deceived by a band of mercenary lowlife into believing that Soviet Russia is rife with danger and that this peripheral space represents his only safe haven. Within it, it seems, he will be protected from the terrors of Moscow that he has anticipated from the safe distance of the United States (reading magazines in which Bolsheviks are pictured as Viking-like primitive figures—a myth that his "saviours" are keen to encourage him to believe). In the course of the film, this Moscow underworld is set against the public space of the "real" capital, in which flourish true Soviet citizens. It is into this pure moral space that Mr. West's faithful companion, Jeddy, is drawn. And at the end of the film, when Mr. West has been mercifully rescued from the darker forces of society—the "remnants" of a petty-bourgeois society of petty criminals—he, too, is taken into this space. The final sequences of the film show Mr. West taken on an official tour of the "real" Moscow, through the public spaces of the city, to factories and a radio-telegraph centre, beacons of Soviet achievement.

These visions of the city during the 1920s as breeding ground of corruption were ideologically ambiguous. Although the narratives of *The Devil's Wheel* and *Mr. West* set the pure forces of a "true" Soviet hero or heroine against the protagonists of urban lowlife, there is no clear moral position from which to view the transgressive behaviour of the protagonists. In *Mr. West,* the triumphant, positive vision of the city lacks the authenticity of the other Moscow that has formed the narrative locus of the film. It appears, rather, as a city of images and postcard views, a tourist's itinerary. In *The Devil's Wheel,* there is no pure moral space within the city that can be set against the implicit immorality of the peripheral, tumbledown apartment houses. Although these buildings will, a title assures us at the end of the film, "collapse" in the near future, still these marginal spaces provide the most coherent locus in the film.

CORNERS AND CHAOS: THE CITY LIVED

A similarly ambiguous city starred in the *bytovaia* film comedies (comedies of everyday life) that proliferated during the mid-1920s, picturing the curious hybrid of life under Lenin's New Economic Policy (NEP). Like *Mr. West* and *The Devil's Wheel,* these films refused to construct the city as a coherent public space. An early example of the genre, produced in the same year as Kuleshov's *Mr. West,* is Iurii Zheliabuzhskii's *Papirosnitsa ot Mosselproma (The Cigarette Girl from Mosselprom)* of 1924. This film followed a clerk, a typist, a cigarette salesgirl, a fat American entrepreneur, and a cameraman in a complex series of romantic intrigues and farcical adventures. It was set in Moscow and thematically centred around the phenomenon of the "new" city, as the cameraman, Latugin, is commissioned (by the fat American) to make a film of the "everyday life of the new Moscow."[15] Yet the "new Moscow" that Latugin films, like the city the protagonists inhabit, is no clearly articulated public space, no monumental centre for the new regime. It is, rather, an urban space characterized by chaos and energy, a vision of a city in transition. On the street, old meets new as cars and trams cross traditional horse-drawn carts. Zina sells cigarettes for a state industry but is seduced into working as a film star, and then as a model for the fat American entrepreneur himself. The city is shaped, above all, by the experience of its inhabitants: the film-within-the-film that is Latugin's, "Everyday Life in the New Moscow," turns out to be a paean to his new love, the "photogenic" cigarette girl, Zina. And in the film itself, the grand public spaces of the city appear only in passing, as the backdrop for adventure: we spot the Bol'shoi theatre, we see monumental arches and the central Moscow River, but our attention is drawn not to them, but to the action that surrounds them. The grand urban space is reduced to the chaos of narrative.

The chaotic city played a similarly vital role in Iakov Protazanov's *Aelita*, also produced in 1924 but set three years earlier in December 1921, during the difficult period of "War Communism" enforced during the civil war. This film told the story of an engineer and intellectual, Loss, who constructs a machine that enables him to travel to the planet Mars, where he has fallen in love with the exotically beautiful Princess Aelita. Despite the striking futuristic images of the Mars sequences of this film, its key message lies in the representation of the earthly chaos of Moscow and the difficulties of the War Communism years.[16] This chaos centres principally around the experiences of Loss's wife, Natasha, whose work for the revolution brings her into close contact with the realities of postrevolutionary life. Through her, we encounter the sites and experiences of the everyday: crowed railway carriages and stations, the bureaucracy of documentation, housing committees, and the underground drinking clubs of the bourgeois remnants of prerevolutionary capitalism.

In the Moscow scenes of *Aelita*, the spectator confronted some of the practical truths of the utopian age, and these everyday truths were contrasted with the other-worldly excesses of Mars. Ultimately, Loss's journey to outer space reveals the ostensibly futuristic world of Mars as a feudal and despotic regime, and he is responsible for inciting the oppressed workers of the planet to revolution before returning to Moscow, to the "real" utopia of Communism in construction. The sci-fi utopia of Mars to which he aspired is revealed as illusion, and the "real" Moscow is pictured as an authentic utopia in the making. The stylized movements of the Martians are contrasted with the implicitly more authentic bodies, lives, and experiences of Moscow's inhabitants. Thus, we infer, chaos was to be excused; it was even to be valued, for it represented the dynamic process of transformation. Rejecting the Martian princess and returning to his Natasha, Loss discovered "truth," back in the gritty disorder of the city, and in the task of building the socialist world.

The lived reality of the 1920s was indeed one of gritty disorder, and social comedies such as these continued to be made into the final years of the decade. The heroine of Boris Barnet's 1927 film *Devushka s korobkoi (The Girl with a Hatbox)*, Natasha, lives with her grandfather on the outskirts of Moscow and travels daily to the city, carrying hats to the millinery shop of the bourgeoise Madame Irene. For her, Moscow is a familiar space, and her experience of the city renders it merely functional. For Igor Snegirev, however, whom Natasha meets on the train, it is an alien and unknown space. In his increasingly forlorn wanderings in search of habitation, and his nights spent in railway stations, the city appears not as the impressive centre of the national imagination, but rather as disorientating and unwelcoming. His experience is initially one of disillusion. For both characters in this film, the principal spaces of the city are the railway station and the millinery shop and rooms above it. Landmarks do not appear. Within the capital city—the implied centre of the new state—there is no centre. Ultimately, in this film, as in so many others, Moscow is configured not as a capital city, but as an urban space of action. The village, moreover, is not distanced from the city, as several of the characters seem to travel freely between the two spaces. This normalization of travel serves to dedramatize the capital and allows Barnet to forge an imagined *smychka* of more pragmatic than ideological justification.

The end of *The Girl with a Hatbox* is one of romantic resolution rather than revolutionary consolidation, as Igor and Natasha fall in love and marry. The city is merely the backdrop against which personal dramas take place. Barnet's next film, *Dom na Trubnoi (The House on Trubnaia Square)* of 1928, scripted by Viktor Shklovskii, seemed to offer a more ideologically driven narrative of its heroine's path to consciousness. Like Igor in *The Girl with a Hatbox,* its heroine, Parasha, arrives in Moscow from the countryside. She finds work as a domestic servant in the home of the reprehensibly petty-bourgeois hairdresser Golikov and his indolent wife. The film charts Parasha's path to political consciousness as she is brought into the Workers' Union and assimilated into the collective. This move is echoed in her rejection of the bourgeois domesticity of her employers and her move into social space—the space of the workers' club, and of the city.

Despite this ostensibly clear ideological thrust in the narrative, however, the visual level of the film offered a more complex picture. Where *The Girl with a Hatbox* was structured around the train line connecting village and city, along which its characters travel, *The House on Trubnaia Square* is a fundamentally urban film. Seen from many differing points of view, the city evolves and mutates through the film, seeming to echo the shifting attitudes of its protagonists and their changing relationships with it. The opening sequence is a long shot of a single apartment building by night, in which lighted windows, darkening one by one, symbolize private space. Shortly afterward, we see a broader picture of the city, viewing Moscow empty of people as it "awakes" and cleans up, ready for the day. Yet this "awakening" is shown in details, and not in grand establishing shots; the city is not mapped through its landmarks. As such, the eponymous house on Trubnaia Square remains the only real spatial anchor, the structural centre of the film.

Parasha's arrival in Moscow (with a duck under her arm) pictures the city as a disorientating and chaotic space. Armed with the address of her Uncle Fedia, the heroine embarks on a marathon trip around the city, which takes her the many miles from the central station square, past the Kremlin and other landmarks of the centre, toward the apartment buildings of the outskirts. Yet even here the city is not articulated as a monumental space. Landmarks, such as the Historical Museum and Red Square, appear only as background, often strangely fragmented, viewed from unexpected angles, as the bewildered Parasha asks ever more people for directions. Instead of serving as points of orientation for the visitor from the countryside, the landmarks of the capital serve as symbols of *dis*-orientation. Moscow is thus denied its ostensible status as urban centre, and denied monumental stature. It becomes, instead, a space of lived experience.

This "lived" city was characterized by new types of physical experience. People walk, are driven, and travel in carts and on trams. Urban transport systems, the tram in particular, offered a mobilized perspective on the dynamic city space. Vertov used the shapes and energy of intersecting trams and tramlines in his *Man with a Movie Camera* to convey the "dynamic geometry" of the revolutionary age, and his trams were by no means unique: in *The House on Trubnaia Square,* the tram spelled terror for the disorientated Parasha, as it nearly ran over her wayward duck. In *The Cigarette Girl from Mosselprom,* it was through the window of a tram that Latugin was able to spot his beloved Gina, the eponymous *papirosnitsa,* and to leap out in order to embrace her on the spot. In Barnet's *The Girl with a Hatbox,* a brief montage of shots through moving tram windows was used to create the energy and adventure of Natasha's chase after Igor through the city, and in Friedrikh Ermler's 1929 film *Oblomok imperii (Fragment of an Empire),* the interior of the tram itself was pictured as an unfamiliar social space, offering the film's protagonist new encounters (including the unheard-of sighting of female legs). In all its manifestations, the tram was at once a collective and an individual experience, enabling a new kind of mobile experience of the city, and shaping the cityscape itself.

THE BENIGN CROWD: THE CITY SHARED

As the heroine of *The House on Trubnaia Square* progresses through the city, she begins to inhabit the urban space and to make it her own. Through affiliation to the collective, she moves into the social space of the city and is liberated from the stifling domesticity of the petty-bourgeois Golikov household. This shift in Parasha's relationship with the city is most clearly marked in the changing representation of the urban crowd. In early sequences, the film offers a vision of the urban crowd as alienating and disconcerting. As Parasha moves through the unknown city, she is jostled and harassed by the threatening proximity of the crowd, intimidated by urban chaos. Later in the film, she is pictured in a quite different relationship with the crowd—first at a theatre performance in the Workers' Club and later during a city council election parade. In these later scenes, the crowd is transformed into the collective; it is, in both cases, the instrument of Parasha's awakening. In the theatre, she is carried away by the spontaneous joy of shared experience, stamping and applauding the play. In the parade, she moves further on her path to political consciousness, as her spontaneous joy is slowly modified into conscious participation in the collective.

The changing status of the crowd in films of the 1920s and 1930s echoed the changing shape of the city. Crowds, of course, were part of urban reality—and in particular part of the overcrowded cities of the early Soviet period (Figure 18). In *The Cigarette Girl from Mosselprom,* made three years earlier than *The House on Trubnaia Square,* the urban crowd functioned as an apparently accidental participant in the film. Large numbers of strangers gather to watch the somewhat hapless clerk Miliutin (played by the consummate comic actor Igor Il'inskii) jump to the mistaken rescue of what he believes to be the drowning object of his affection, the film's heroine, Zina. (In fact, of course, as the crowd knows full well, Miliutin mistakes the shooting of a film for reality and jumps into the river after a dummy, as Zina, now a film actress, merely pretends to jump.) Later, another crowd follows Zina, and her true love Latugin, when he is arrested for jumping out of the tram in order to kiss her, and then continues to follow them as they register their spontaneous marriage. In this film, the crowd is benign and shapeless; the "mass" is present, but unformed. The individual experiences of the protagonists are shared with a larger community, but this crowd is not a collective; in contrast to the symbolic evolution of the relationship between Parasha and the crowd in *The House on Trubnaia Square,* in *The Cigarette Girl from Mosselprom* the crowd carries no ideological weight.

The representation of the mass, of course, was an important ideological imperative, and a task that Sergei Eisenstein had taken on in his revolutionary films *Stachka* (*The Strike,* 1924) and *Bronenosets Potemkin* (*Battleship Potemkin,* 1925). There was no place for film stars in revolutionary cinema. Eisenstein sought to make films without heroes—to use film to capture the unique phe-

Figure 18. Urban chaos: Moscow in the 1920s (the Sukharevskii Market). From Alexys A. Siderov, *Moskau: Das Gesicht der Städte* (Berlin: Albertus, 1928), 78.

nomenon of the revolutionary *massy* (the masses) and of collective action. For him, and indeed for many left-wing artists, writers, and theorists, the crowd represented spontaneous revolutionary energy. The task of the new culture, and of the new order, was to harness that spontaneous energy and to render it conscious, organized, and creative. The "freedom" of the urban experience is transformed by revolution into a force of liberation. The power of film, it seemed, was to enact a parallel transformation. Eisenstein's 1928 film *October,* for example, celebrated the artificially organized power of the masses in a vast restaging of the October revolution. The crowd that peopled the streets of Moscow, and starred in the *bytovye* comedies of the 1920s, however, was quite different from this revolutionary mass. In contrast to the striking visual geometry of the "mass" body, the ordinary crowd was composed of disparate individual bodies struggling to find their ways in the new world.

DOMESTIC SPACE: THE CITY AS HOME

Through Parasha's evolving relationship with the city, and the crowd, *The House on Trubnaia Square* explores the relationship between public and private life. This theme was of pressing importance, central to the revolutionary project to transform the social structure and central, too, to the remaking of the Soviet space. In his essay on Moscow, published in 1927, Benjamin suggested that the Bolsheviks had "abolished private life."[17] Certainly, for the revolutionary generation, the private domestic space of the prerevolutionary bourgeoisie, immortalized in Anton Chekhov's four most famous plays, was a symbol of the old order and brutally satirized in the 1921 introduction to the second version of Maiakovskii's play *Misteriia-buff (Mystery-Bouffe)*, first written in celebration of the anniversary of the revolution, in which the prologue asks: "What do we go to the theatre for?"—not, it assures us, to watch the lives of Aunt Mania or Uncle Vania. "Aunts and Uncles you can find at home," the play asserts: the task of art is to move life beyond the "home," out of the domestic sphere.[18]

The task of the new order was to create a *novyi byt*—a new kind of everyday life, and a new domestic environment—but this ideological imperative was beset by practical obstacles. In the first decade after the revolution, the problem of living space was urgent in the principal Soviet cities, as rural workers flocked to urban centres to find work. The mass influx of the peasantry into the cities effected a "ruralization of the cities *[okrest'ianivanie]*," breaking down established social relations and making for new kinds of adventure. In films from *The Girl with a Hatbox* and *The House on Trubnaia Square* to Abram Room's 1927 *Tret'ia Meshchanskaia* (*Third Meshchnanskaia Street,* commonly translated as *Bed and Sofa*), to name only a few, the influx of workers to the city, and the shortage of living space, provided narrative momentum and structure. There was an urgent need to provide living space for the new ruling class: the proletariat. Moreover, ideological imperatives demanded not just any kind of home, but a new kind of habitat for a new kind of social life, and for the new kind of Soviet man and woman.

As early as 1918, recognizing the power of cinema as a propaganda weapon, Anatolii Lunacharskii, head of Narkompros, himself scripted a short agitational film entitled *Uplotnenie (Overcrowding)* dedicated to the housing question. One of the very first Soviet films, it recounted the story of the encounter between the prerevolutionary elite and the working class, when a worker and his family are moved into a spare room in the apartment of a professor at St. Petersburg University. It begins by establishing the separateness of the domestic lives of the two classes, showing the eminent professor lecturing to students and then returning to his spacious apartment and private study. In contrast, the worker is shown with aching limbs, in a cold cellar. We then follow a process of adaptation and assimilation, as the worker and his daughter move into the professor's apartment, and his worker friends begin to visit them there. Ultimately, domestic space is transformed into social space, as the professor begins to engage in apparently healthy debate with the visiting workers. Eventually, he gives lectures at the Workers' Club, and full happiness and class entente are guaranteed when the professor's youngest son and the worker's daughter announce their engagement. In this joyful final scene, public and private space are fused as street celebrations and parades, viewed through the window of the apartment, seem to echo the private contentment of the protagonists.

This comparatively simplistic early film, shot in long tableaux, is interesting for its tentative treatment of a subject that became increasingly common in films of the 1920s: the transformation of private space. During the mid-1920s, with the flourishing of petty industry under NEP, private space was increasingly configured as an indicator of revolutionary credentials.[19] While the Communist utopia envisaged collective living space, with furniture reduced to the functional and decoration to a minimum, the relaxing of strictures on small-scale profit seemed to lead to a rehabilitation of private ownership, and thence to the lure of petty-bourgeois domesticity. The corrupting dangers of interior design were encapsulated in one term: *meshchanstvo*. For a committed revolutionary such as Maiakovskii, the lure of *meshchanstvo* threatened the core of the revolution: his poem "On Trash" warns of Communism "killed by canaries" and destroyed by "cozy cabinets."[20] Yet the protection of a secure, personalized domestic space retained its value in this rapidly changing world.

The positive values of private space within the city are evident in *Kat'ka-bumazhnyi ranet* (*Kat'ka's Reinette Apples*, 1926), directed by Friedrikh Ermler, former Chekist officer turned director.[21] This, Ermler's first film, is the story of a peasant girl, Kat'ka, who has come to Leningrad to make money to support her family in the village. She falls in with a gang of petty black marketeers, illegally selling apples on the street, and has a child by the irresponsible and morally suspect Semka. In the early sequences of the film, the city appears to Kat'ka as a space of transgression and uncertainty. Eventually, however, she finds happiness in a relationship with a simple, good-hearted man—Vad'ka, a former *intelligent*. Together they create a sustainable and fulfilling private life, protecting themselves from the urban chaos that is the public space of the city, and in which they both feel threatened. Thus the film constructs a disjunctive relationship between the protagonists and the public sphere. It locates "real" experience in private corners of the space and in the informal structures of community that people establish in order to *appropriate* a part of the urban world. Although at the end of the film, Kat'ka and Vad'ka decide to cease their illegal trade and take up work in a factory, the abiding sense of the public space of the city is one of fracture and disunity, within which the microsphere is the only refuge.

Ermler's representation of private space in this film was ambiguous and failed to engage with the imperative of social and personal transformation. One year later, and ten years after *Overcrowding,* Barnet's *The House on Trubnaia Square* explored more directly the complex transformation between "old" and "new" forms of private life during the 1920s. Life in the house on Trubnaia Square is a curious hybrid of the collective and the private. The central staircase of the building provides the space where the two worlds collide: a remarkable early sequence in the film charts the "awakening" of the inhabitants of the building through a single long shot that moves slowly up through this staircase, encountering a whole series of individuals and activities (Figure 19).

Figure 19. The shared staircase. Film still from *Dom na Trubnoi* (Barnet, 1928). Courtesy of B. F. I. Stills, Posters and Designs.

The staircase sequence is structured around domestic chores, as households prepare for the day. Chaos reigns: ornamental tigers are pushed onto the landing for cleaning, and firewood is chopped on an already structurally weak staircase. Domestic necessity is given a starring role in *The House on Trubnaia Square*. The functional realities of everyday life—dusting, cooking, laundry—provide much of the narrative momentum of the film. Parasha's virtue is revealed through her dedication to her duties in the Golikov household. The contrast between her simplicity and the disordered faux-sumptuousness of her household is telling: the Golikov apartment is crammed with house plants and heavy furniture in a deliberate parody of *meshchanstvo*. Surrounded by the accoutrements of petty-bourgeois decadence, Parasha's honest labour acquires a particular poignancy and moral weight.

A similar focus on the value and dangers of domesticity can be found in Room's *Bed and Sofa*. Like *The House on Trubnaia Square* (and produced in the same year), this film charts the move toward revolutionary consciousness of a female protagonist.[22] Unlike Parasha, however, Liudmila is not innocent. She is, by contrast, when the film begins, in thrall to the morally suspect comforts of private life. Opening shots show a sleeping couple, buried deep beneath feather eiderdowns and surrounded by the paraphernalia of *meshchanstvo* (the word even finds its way into the title of the film, as the name of the Moscow street where the Batalovs live) (Figures 20 and 21). In the course of the film, which tracks Liudmila's shifting relationships with her husband and her husband's old friend in a bizarre ménage à trois, we follow her dilemma between private and public lives. Finally, she abandons both lovers and leaves for what we understand to be a socially responsible, ideologically correct independence. She seizes control of her own life.

This final "escape" from the confines of petty domesticity into an implicitly Soviet freedom, however, is rendered more complex than similar narratives of the path to consciousness in later films of the 1930s by the cinematic refusal to offer a stable public space within the city. The end of the film shows Liudmila *leaving* Moscow, implicitly for a more authentic life elsewhere. The status of the capital city in this film is complex. As in so many other films of the period, it is represented as a series of partial views, fragmented cityscapes, in which the dynamism of urban life predominates over any monumental, ideological stability. Liudmila's husband, Batalov, works as a construction worker on the renovation of the Bol'shoi theatre, and his bird's-eye view motivates many of the dynamic montage sequences of the city. As he lounges on the top of the landmark during his lunch break, leaning on a sculpted horse with his legs dangling over the busy

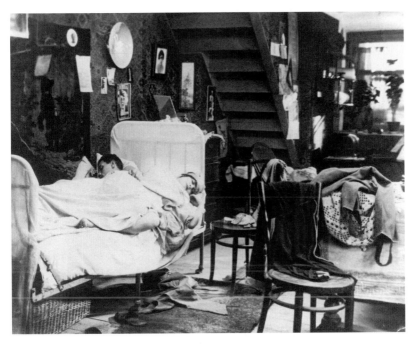

Figure 20. The bourgeois dangers of pillows. Film still from *Tret'ia Meshchanskaia* (Room, 1927). Courtesy of B. F. I. Stills, Posters and Designs.

squares of Moscow, the city appears as a kind of giant playground. The traditional landscapes of the capital appear, but from unexpected angles and distances that transform their grandeur into energy. The camera seems to revel in "Moscow in full swing *[v razgare]*," emphasizing the unceasing movement of the city streets through horizontal level shots that approach passing tram windows and peer through moving bicycle wheels. Ultimately, the city offers no obvious collective space. We read it, instead, as a space that is at once private and public, lived by individuals within the crowds and chaos of public life, but not yet organized as the shared collective space of the capital city.

The focus on private space in these films thus operates at several interrelated levels. On the one hand, we find a clear polemic with bourgeois domesticity, and an assertion of the value of everyday life pared down and lived through the collective. On the other, we discover an urban space that is never articulated as a monumental, public space, but which is lived and experienced in the microenvironments of shared apartment buildings and work spaces. Despite their refusal to map the city, Barnet and Room incorporate concrete Moscow addresses into the very titles of these films, identifying Trubnaia Square and Third

Figure 21. Liudmila in thrall to materialism. Film still from
Tret'ia Meshchanskaia (Room, 1927). Courtesy of B. F. I. Stills,
Posters and Designs.

Meshchanskaia Street. This apparent paradox serves, in fact, to reinforce the rejection of public space, emphasizing the particularity of the streets and corners
of the city in which these narratives unfold. The immediate locality of the protagonists is a more defining space than that of the city as a whole, or by extension, of the nation as a whole.

The status of Leningrad in films of the period was perhaps even more complex than that of Moscow. As the original revolutionary city, in the early years
after the revolution St. Petersburg had impeccable credentials and status. Yet
for the new regime, it was also the prerevolutionary capital, representative of
the old order, and a cityscape inseparable from a long literary heritage of Gogo-
lian chaos and decadence. A new capital was needed, and Moscow seemed, ar-
chitecturally and historically, to offer a promising blend of the new and the
old—less tainted by Russia's immediate Imperial past and yet displaying the
weight of ancient Rus' in its architecture. Such a dramatic shift in the imagi-

nary geography of the nation was by no means simple, however. Representations of Leningrad during this period display much in common with images of Moscow, picturing the city as a similarly dynamic and unstable space, but they are inflected with further emphasis, clearly displaying Leningrad as Soviet Russia's "other" city. Ermler's last silent film, *Oblomok imperii* (*Fragment of an Empire*, 1929), used the status of St. Petersburg/Leningrad as a city caught between past, present, and future in order to explore the conflict between public and private spaces in the city. It charted the story of former worker and noncommissioned officer Filimonov, wounded in battle during the civil war and falling into a coma. Reviving, he discovers that he has lost his memory and is thus unable to recapture his former life. The film follows his attempts to construct a narrative of his past through which to approach the present. In so doing, it explores the relationship of the Soviet present to its Imperial past, and does so through the cityscape.

The film offers Filimonov two locations through which to reestablish his life. The first is a village, in which he finds shelter after awaking from his coma. There he finds a kind of peace, which is disrupted when he sees a woman's face at a train window in the station, prompting flashes of memory to return.[23] These fragments of memory lead the hero inexorably to Leningrad—"to his native place *[na rodinu]*, to St. Petersburg, to the place where his wife is, his home is." The move to the urban "centre" from the village is linked to an attempt to recapture the past. It is part of an attempt to reestablish the narrative of his life, to link past, present, and future. The city, therefore, is supposed to fulfil the function of an organizing centre, in which the diverse threads of Filimonov's life will be linked.

Filimonov's vision of St. Petersburg evokes a city of the past and does not correspond to the Leningrad of the present. His *rodina* is transformed. The cityscape is dramatically altered: new, unfamiliar statues dominate the skyline, disorientating the protagonist. The city is *uncanny:* both familiar and unfamiliar and profoundly disorienting.[24] Filimonov searches for an organizing centre and heads, logically, for the historic centre of the city: Palace Square. New, Constructivist-style buildings loom behind the buildings he knows and loves, prompting the despairing remarks: "So where is Petersburg? Where am I? I don't understand." The centre—narrative and geographical—for which Filimonov is searching does not exist. Indeed, the whole quest for a centre, the film implies, is itself misplaced. The new Soviet space has no need for the old centres. And especially no need, of course, for prerevolutionary "Petersburg," with its associations of Imperialist decadence and oppression.

In place of the stable, centred space he desires, Filimonov's new city is represented through rapid montage, emphasizing the dynamic fluidity of the urban
landscape. For him, as for so many cinematic heroes and heroines of the period,
the movement of the city is disorientating. Shots of the new Soviet Leningrad
create a disparate and partial picture of urban utopia. On arrival at the station,
Filimonov finds hens and ducks on the platform (brought there, perhaps, by
Parasha of Barnet's *The House on Trubnaia Square*). The rural penetrates the urban—the village dwells within the city. New buildings obstruct and disorient,
jutting into the harmonious cityscapes of old Petersburg. Filimonov's confusion is expressed stylistically through the alternation of speed and stillness:
rapid montage and tracking shots as he runs through the streets of Petersburg
searching for his past, and single still shots that emphasize incomprehension
and paralysis in the face of the new society (Figure 22). The movement of the
city acts to disorient Filimonov, "fragment of the empire."

Filimonov eventually locates the pieces of his past—his former employer
and his wife—only to find that they do not offer him a continuation of his former narrative. His former wife, Natasha, is now married to an unsympatheti-
cally portrayed *kul'trabotnik* (a "culture worker," responsible for improving be-
havioural standards among the population), who lectures on the new *byt* while
treating Natasha as his slave. She will not leave him, however, and thus Filimonov's past is effectively nullified; a new story will begin. He takes on a new
life in the factory, as a comrade. The narrative of the film suggests, therefore,
that Filimonov will *appropriate* this new dynamic space. He will inhabit the
modern urban space and make it his own. The urban space of prerevolutionary
St. Petersburg becomes, initially, the disorienting space of Leningrad but will
become, ultimately, a lived and appropriated space.

Here, then, we see how the modernist trope of the liminal urban space was
reconfigured as the merely *disorienting* urban space of the city films of the
1920s. For Filimonov, as for Parasha, and for Igor in *The Girl with a Hatbox*, arrival in the city is accompanied by disorientation. In addition to its roots in the
reality of the chaotic Soviet urban experience of the period, this disorientation
served an important aesthetic and ideological purpose. It allowed the urban
space to retain its energy, but to lose its transgressive force. The city was a
chaotic and fragmentary space, yet that chaos held, ultimately, a positive value,
for it represented the dynamic energy of the new world. The cinematic city offered a kind of freedom to its diverse inhabitants—the freedom to craft a new
way of life, to *appropriate* the urban space. In the end, as these narratives
showed, the city could be navigated; it could be lived. It was lived, however,

Figure 22. Filimonov confronts the New City. Film still from
Oblomok Imperii (Ermler, 1929). Private collection.

largely in the interstices of public space. Representations of the city during the
1920s shared a focus on the *bytovoe* (the everyday) at a micro-level and explored
the relationship between the individual and the new environment.

Thus the city was decentred. For all its urban credentials, Barnet's *The House
on Trubnaia Square* seems to transform the city into a peripheral, even rural,
space. The courtyard of the eponymous house operates almost as a village, blur-
ring traditional values of community with the new values of the urban proletariat. The reality of the Soviet urban experience during the 1920s is important
here: Moscow as a public space was not a clearly mapped space during this period. The words of Walter Benjamin, describing the city he experienced during

1926–27, seem an apt description of the cinematic Moscow of the 1920s: "Nowhere does Moscow look like the city itself; at the most it resembles its outskirts. . . . In the streets of Moscow there is a curious state of affairs: the Russian village is playing hide and seek in them."[25]

Like the architectural projects that proposed to "empty" the capital, films of the 1920s pictured Moscow as a centre that was at once chaotically overcrowded and symbolically "empty." The capital was transformed, in effect, into local space—it was another "space of experience" in the dynamic, changing world of Soviet Russia, open to *appropriation* by the ordinary man or woman. As such, the national map lacked a clearly defined centre. As we shall see in Chapter 6, by the mid-1930s the ideological space of the centre would be clearly established; in the meantime, the collective gaze of the nation was focused on the vast territory—on a space for exploration.

Chapter 4 Exploring

Нам нужно знать свою страну

(We need to know our country.)
—Title of an article in the journal *Sovetskoe kino (Soviet Cinema)*

The *neob"iatnyi prostor* inherited by the new regime was, both practically and symbolically, "ungraspable." It was a *chuzhaia rodina*—an alien native land.[1] This ostentatiously paradoxical phrase is revealing. The territory was both native and unknown. It belonged to the new state—and hence "to the people"—but it needed to be discovered, *appropriated*. The paradox of the *chuzhaia rodina* was also, pragmatically, its strength: the very strangeness and mystery of the territory meant that it could be shaped—mapped—according to new criteria. Through "discovery," it could be transformed from Tsarist empire into Socialist union. It was a space in transition, dramatically mobilized by the project of modernization. The mobile, malleable territory became a new adventure space; the key task, for everyone, was to explore it—to rush to the periphery.

The dynamic of exploration was presented not just in film, but in the popular press. One journal, *Vokrug sveta (Around the World)* described itself in 1928 as "a journal of travel, discovery, inventions and adventures." Descended from a journal first founded in 1861, the Soviet version of *Around the World* differentiated itself from its Imperial predecessor by a somewhat tendentious claim: "the bourgeoisie sought to know the earth in order to enslave it," an editorial proclaimed. "In our magazines," by contrast, "we tell how the victorious proletariat is changing the earth so that it blooms with the joyful beacons of socialist towns."[2] The Soviet adventure, the journal proclaimed, was one of discovery, not conquest—of exploration, not exploitation. The new Soviet space would consist of equal territories, liberated from the yoke of Imperial control, in which, supposedly, no hierarchy of centre or periphery would exist.

The project of exploration was tied to that of modernization, focusing the national gaze on the discovery and transformation of the periphery. Between 1928 and 1931, *Around the World* popularized a vision of industrialization underpinned by the ideals of decentralization. The rhetoric of industrialization was accompanied by a vocabulary of *equalization:* the primary task was the extension of development (of influence) *across* the territory: "Build socialism, build powerful factories. Dneprostroi, railways and bridges, electrify and build new towns only on this side of the Urals? No, that cannot be. *We must build socialism in the whole country.* In Turkestan, in the Caucasus, in Ukraine and in Siberia. We have to remake the whole of the Soviet land [emphasis added]."[3]

Modernization, the rhetoric proclaimed, was a project that must be carried out at a *national* level—it implicated the entire Soviet space. Although Dneprostroi and other large projects were important cornerstones of industrialization, they were to be understood as merely paradigmatic examples of a process carried out continually at a smaller scale across all strata of the community. The entire Soviet space was to be "remade" and transformed.

TRANSFORMATION: "DISCOVERING" THE PERIPHERY

The *otkrytie* of the territory was the theme of many stories and articles in the popular press: "This used to be the steppe. Limitless *[bezkrainaia]*, vast steppe. Pampas grass. Now there is no steppe."[4] *Otkrytie*, during the First Plan, was pictured as a form of *appropriation:* "Come, settle, work, bring the region alive!" It was a task for everyone. Vast population shifts would transform the steppe from the wild and exotic (the mystery of the territory is emphasized here by the somewhat eccentric use of "pampas grass"—hardly a familiar feature of the Russian landscape) into the known and inhabited. Exploration and travel were pictured as the prerogative of the mass: the explorer was the ordinary man or woman, not unusually heroic, incited to set off and discover the nation. The Soviet version of exploration, presented in journals like *Around the World,* was located in the everyday, in the exploits of the ordinary hero: "we do not have to dream up adventures and heroes: they are all around us."[5] The travel and mobility offered by the new vision of Soviet space were accessible to all.

Aiming at a mass audience, *Around the World* presented a curious blend of high fantasy with the "reality" of Soviet industrial transformation.[6] This conflation of exploration and construction marked many cultural representations of the First Five-Year Plan. Adventure yarns with titles such as "At a Far-Flung Station" and "In the Taiga, On the Threshold" showed how habitation transformed the mysterious territory into a mappable and familiar space.[7] In one story, for example, one Petr Nikolaevich Osipov, an ordinary bureaucrat working for Gostorg (the State Trade Commission) is sent to a distant valley in the Amu Daria region on official business. There he has a series of adventures that link Sovietization with more traditional tropes of exotic difference, as he wonders at the strangeness of those he encounters.[8] Another tale charts the adventures of a group sent to explore Siberia and recounts how they learn the language of local tribes, discover resources, etc.[9] Ultimately, all these outsiders establish, according to the tales, productive and reciprocal relations with local inhabitants. They explore but—we infer—they do not conquer.

These "official adventures" developed into a major genre in Soviet cinema during the 1930s, but the early Soviet adventure was one of learning and discovery above all. In *Around the World,* scientific description was consistently integrated with the heroics of development, emphasizing the need to "find out" (*uznat'*) and to disseminate information about the Soviet space—to get to know the *chuzhaia rodina.* In the rallying words of a school primer: "They say that as yet our country has not even been discovered."[10] In practical terms, of course, knowledge of the territory was a prerequisite of development: scientists—geologists in particular—were enlisted in the service of the Plan, and in 1929, the discipline of geology was placed under state jurisdiction. *Pochvennye* (topographical) maps of the territory were vital aids to industrialization, uncovering the "riches" of the *rodnaia zemlia* (native land, or earth): in 1930, the first full topographical map of the "European part" of the Soviet Union was produced; in 1932, it was matched by one of the "Asian" *(aziatskaia)* territory. Geologists and cartographers mapped the terrain to be transformed; they were the "scouts of the Five-Year Plan *[razvedchiki piatiletki],*" setting out to uncover the riches of the territory, "opening up hitherto unknown deposits of natural wealth."[11] The myth of the rich *rodnaia zemlia* was thus appropriated to an apparently rational discourse of discovery and exploitation. *Razvedchik* (scout)— a military reconnaissance term—was frequently used during this period: the same school primer of 1931 claimed that "throughout our entire country our scouts *[razvedchiki]* are at work." And not all of them were specialists: the *razvedchik* could be either a scientific expert (the geologist) or, crucially, an ordinary citizen. Everyone was called upon to explore the territory and to discover the rich "raw material" *(syr'e)* that would be used to build the new world.

This urge to explore the territory had gained in popularity during the 1920s. Vertov's seventh *Kinopravda (Film-Truth)* featured geologists studying the rock layers along the banks of Lake Baikal. Between 1925 and 1926 alone, 633 "scientific" expeditions were organized with the aim of gathering "historical and ethnographic" material about the various component regions of the new state. Il'in's primer claimed that between 1919 and 1929, the Academy of Science alone had organized 371 expeditions of *razvedchiki* across the territory.[12] In addition, the explosion of local museums in the first decade of Soviet power is testament to the state's ideological investment in ethnographic and geographic information about the national space. Between 1918 and 1923, 270 new museums were created by the young Soviet state, of which a startling 193 were local, *kraevedcheskie* (local knowledge/study) museums.[13]

This growth continued through the 1920s. "Local study" *(kraevedenie)* itself (which had begun in the eighteenth century and developed through the 1800s in connection with the Geograficheskoe obshchestvo [Geographical Society]) expanded to become a significant political and social movement, involving leading party members such as Nadezhda Krupskaia, Anatoli Lunacharskii, Gleb Krzhizhanovskii, and Mikhail Kalinin, together with academics and historians. As early as the Eighth Party Congress in January 1918, *kraevedenie* had been identified as a national imperative. The TSBK (Central Bureau of Local Study), set up in 1921, sent "experts" to the provinces to train local *kraevedy;* the number of *kraevedcheskie* organizations, dedicated to local research in geology, ethnography, and history, increased tenfold between 1917 and 1927, from 155 to 1,688.[14]

The provision and dissemination of information about the nation was a key task for the Soviet propaganda machine: it was represented as a process of illumination, demystifying "adventure" and making it available for all. In 1929, a substantial "manual" of "the whole Soviet Union" was produced, with the proclaimed intention of providing all the information necessary to the ordinary traveller.[15] In addition to guides such as this, of course, the new explorer also needed certain key skills, and many articles in *Around the World* focused on "popular science." Articles explained oil processing, the function of a hydro-electric power station and a turbine, different types of fuel, and other vital technological miracles.[16] A similar genre developed in documentary cinema: *nauchno-populiarnyi* (popular-scientific) documentaries explored themes such as electrification or geological rock formation in simple terms aimed at a mass audience.[17] The ideal of knowledge provision as an enabler for the ordinary citizen is demonstrated by the example of an animated film produced in 1928 entitled *Chto dolzhen znat' rabochii i krest'ianin o SSSR (What the Worker and Peasant Should Know About the USSR).*[18]

As part of this dream of a knowledge economy, real maps, too, had an important part to play (Figure 23). In 1919, the task of mapmaking was given special importance by a state decree, calling "for the study of the territory of the RSFSR with respect to topography, for the purposes of advancing and developing the productive forces of the country."[19] From 1920, a special commission worked on the production of a new, complete atlas of the Soviet state, which, for Lenin, was to serve a vital educational function.[20] The all-important role of mapmaking is demonstrated though the article in *Around the World,* cited in the Introduction to this book, that boasted of a vast increase in mapmaking capacity. The globe and the map were essential tools in the creation of the new, liberated Soviet space; knowledge of the space was a prerequisite for the consolidation of citizenship. Vertov's fifteenth *Kinopravda* newsreel opened, for example, with a map of the nascent USSR, locating its viewer squarely on the national map. The map was a means of incorporation, involving everybody in the space: "this globe is not an object of luxury, not an amusement or a game," the journalist in *Around the World* declared, "but a visual aid for the peoples of the USSR, who strive for knowledge."[21] As a result, it must be provided for *everyone:* "now globes are produced in twenty-nine languages of the peoples of the Soviet Union."

Symbolically (if not actually) armed with these new maps, then, everybody had the right to travel during the late 1920s. And everyone was a hero. The balance between the large-scale and the small was carefully maintained. In 1929, for example, a documentary newsreel of the *Soiuzkinozhurnal (Union Film Journal)* linked the glorious exploits of the pilot Mikhail Gromov, who had flown from Moscow to Berlin, with the exploratory adventures of pioneers in Orel whose "expedition" had a more low-key, yet equally crucial ambition: "having rigged out their boat, the young tourists set off to study their re-

Figure 23. Topographical map of the USSR. From: *Karmannyi atlas SSSR* (Leningrad, 1939), 3.

gion."[22] Vertov's twentieth *Kinopravda* (1924) followed the excursion of young pioneers into the countryside to explore the new Soviet reality *(deistvitel'-nost')*.

The task of these ordinary *razvedchiki* was to discover the local. Il'in's primer of 1931 ended its description of national exploration with a general exhortation: "Do you know the locality in which you live? Can you tell whether it contains peat swamps, forests, lime, phosphate, brick and pottery clay, building sand? You of course do not know such things. And the first journey that you should undertake is a journey through the region surrounding your city or village. Organize expeditions, prepare detailed maps. On these maps indicate everything that could be used in the Five-Year Plan."[23] The local space was pictured as a crucial part of the "whole" of the national space, and it had to be mapped. All forms of exploration were to be valued: in 1929, the eminent academician Nikolai Antsiferov published a short book with the title *Kak izuchat' svoi gorod (How to Study Your Town),* aimed at use in schools.[24] Knowledge of one's environment was a prerequisite for the exemplary citizenship; the local was metonymically symbolic of the national. Discovering the "raw material" and everyday life of one's own space was a means of appropriating that space, of entering a closer physical and mental relationship with the material world.

In film, too, local space began to emerge as an autonomous mark on the bigger national map. The status of the local space as setting for adventure, for example, is evident in the 1927 film comedy *Dva druga, model' i podruga (Two Friends, Their Girlfriend, and a Model),* directed by Alexei Popov. This film provides a lighthearted interpretation of the theme of modernization. It tells the story of two young factory workers, Makhov and Akhov, who live on the "farthest outskirts" of the territory and who have invented a machine that makes wooden crates, with the possibility of radically improving productivity at their local factory. As they try to bring their invention (the "model") to the attention of local authorities, struggling against the ferocious opposition of a local troublemaker, Akhov and Makhov undertake a long and exciting journey through their local space (their *uezd*)—to the local capital—accompanied by their female friend Dasha.[25]

In this film, the periphery is the principal signifying space. The tale begins with an affirmation: that Soviet modernization "has reached to the distant outskirts of the Soviet country." This links the "distant outskirts" with an imagined ideological centre. The spatial axis thus established, however, the film proceeds to ignore the centre altogether and to locate its narrative and its implied message firmly within the local space. Discussing their invention, for example,

Makhov and Akhov pronounce that it will "destroy *local* capitalism [emphasis added]." Our heroes travel to their regional centre, and not to Moscow. The local space lacks specificity—it is not named or mapped—but retains, nevertheless, an important structural autonomy.

In addition to its focus on the autonomy of peripheral space, *Two Friends* made an important link between *razvedka* (exploration) and *izobretenie* (invention). As the subtitle of *Around the World*—"a journal of travel, discovery, inventions and adventures"—made clear, the two were intimately connected, both newly available to the Soviet citizen. Through the dissemination of popular science, everyone had the chance to aid the shared cause. Makhov and Akhov are distinctively ordinary; their invention is the result of commitment and energy; and their often clumsy adventures mark them not as heroic, but as familiar and loveable. *Razvedka* and *izobretenie*, we understand, are accessible to all. This link between exploration and invention is not accidental. Both are rooted in the ideal of information provision that we have discussed. The *nauchno-populiarnyi* genre, of which *Around the World* is a revealing example, celebrated scientific achievement. During the First Plan, travel was rarely undertaken for its own sake; the heroism of the inventor was celebrated alongside the heroism of the traveller.

INFRASTRUCTURE: CONNECTING
THE PERIPHERY

The construction of transportation networks—the *puti soobshcheniia* (routes of communication) that were the new skeleton of the nation—was vital to the creation of the new territory, enabling the mobility and interconnection crucial to efficient Sovietization. Key projects of the First Plan sought to link constitutive parts of the Soviet space, establishing alternative lines of influence: they were not centred on Moscow. One of the most important of these, the Turksib railway project, was initiated in 1927. Its purpose was to link Turkestan's cotton fields with Siberia's grain and timber regions. The opening of the railway in 1930 provoked a storm of documentary films, press eulogies, and literature in celebration. The most famous and successful of these films was Viktor Turin's 1930 film *Turksib,* part scripted by Viktor Shklovskii.[26]

Turksib presents the construction of the railway as an adventure of exploration and discovery. It shows how prospectors *(izyskateli)* travel into the steppe with measuring equipment and binoculars, "make friends" with the natives, and produce piles of documents that "map" the *neob"iatnyi prostor*. An animated map charts the progress of construction. Difficulties are overcome, the steppe is gradually cultivated, and the railway is built. In this, as in all films about Turksib, the steppe represents extremes of isolation: Kazakh herdsmen live without the benefits of Soviet civilization, until: "across the limitless space of Kazakhstan ... over mountains and rock faces ... steel paths ... are forged." A similar emphasis on physical difficulty is evident in the section dedicated to Turksib in *Giganty raportuiut (The Giants Report),* a documentary film series of the First Five-Year Plan created for the Sixteenth Party Congress in 1930. The first section of this film is entitled simply "Sand" and links the desert terrain of the steppe with the cold intransigence of Siberia. The railway will "transform Kazakhstan from a neglected region into an agroindustrial region." The rhetoric of transformation *(preobrazhenie)* here, however, is subtly different from that of *osvoenie.* Although intransigent *(upriamaia),* the steppe is not hostile. It is not "conquered" or dominated by heroism. Instead, the new railway is harmoniously integrated into the "natural" world: the end of Turin's *Turksib* shows a train metaphorically "galloping" across the landscape, accompanied by cheering children, Kazakhs on horseback, and camels. Its final frame sees a lone camel investigating the tracks and then calmly settling to graze around them. The railway has become part of a new vision of nature. This process of transformation *appropriates* space, creating a harmonious relationship between the natural world and those that inhabit it. This relationship is expressed cinematically in the prominence of striking organic imagery, which endows industry and agriculture alike with a natural energy and significance that take them beyond the mechanical. Modernization, we infer, is tied to a heightened sensual relationship with the natural resources of the territory.

This nuanced idea of transformation also inflects the representation of the Kazakh peoples who inhabit the "intransigent" steppe. The herdsmen are romanticized, pictured as living in harmonious connection with nature. Their "backwardness" is rendered decorative. In this film, and in other representations of Turksib, there is little emphasis on the need to homogenize and assimilate the Kazakhs to a model of Sovietness that extends from a dominant centre. Instead, these films demonstrated the rhetorical emphasis on connection and integration that was central to infrastructural projects of the period. The railway does not—and need not—pass through Moscow. It links the peripheries in a structure that is independent of the centre.

The "first Soviet railway" was both industrial enabler and social integrator. In propaganda, the opening of Turksib was frequently declared to be "in celebration of the *smychka*," and this image provided a consistent axis for imagery.[27] The Soviet train was symbolically differentiated from the "coloniza-tion" of Imperial and capitalist rail expansion and celebrated as part of a broader project of integration: "All hail the brotherly union of the nationali-ties!"[28] For the Soviets, the railway was to be an enabler and not a subjugator: it was "a project that has quite different aims [from those of the Tsarist railway], and arose on a new basis."[29] The message here is clear: the train, so crucial to Imperial industrialization during the late nineteenth century, was appropriated as a fully Soviet myth. It was a new kind of railway, premised on equalization rather than subjugation, and it forged a new path *(put')* through the unknown Soviet territory.

A similarly urgent focus on the need for interconnection—the *put'*—is evi-dent in another film of 1930, *Sol Svanetii (Salt for Svanetiia),* produced by the young director Mikhail Kalatozov (later to gain international fame with the 1957 *Letiat zhuravli [The Cranes are Flying]*).[30] Like *Turksib,* this film focused on the values of interconnection and on the need to integrate the isolated areas of the territory into a single Soviet space. It concentrated on the life of a single community in the isolated region of Svanetia, in the Caucasus Mountains, and showed how the lives of the inhabitants were rendered difficult through a lack of connection with the wider world. Like the Kazakhs in the steppe, they are "cut off from the world" and "waiting for a wide path *[doroga]*," which will link them with that world. Life in this community is "immobile" and at the mercy of the elements. Above all, the community suffers, as the film's title makes clear, from a potentially fatal lack of salt. As the film progresses, the urgency of the call for a *doroga* increases, as the imagery becomes increasingly dramatic: we watch dogs licking newborn babies to taste the salt in blood, see children dying, and are told that "pregnancy is cursed." What begins as a romantic evocation of a natural life, lived in proximity to nature, becomes a horrifying vision of a life lived in desperate isolation. Finally, as things rise to fever pitch, the tension is broken: "Thousands of Svanetians are forging a path into Soviet Svanetiia." Svanetiia becomes Soviet Svanetiia—it becomes connected, part of the net-work that constitutes the new territory.

Salt for Svanetiia offers a revealingly ambiguous view of the project of inte-gration. Its images of the isolated "natural" life of this rural community appear initially somewhat fetishistic: the film is remarkable for its stylized close-ups of thirsty faces, of desperately probing animal tongues, seeking salt in human urine or in their own sweat. The slow-paced, highly stylized cinematography creates an impression of Svanetiia as a kind of mythic archetype. It is at once majestic and tragic in its archaism. The camera eye that views this world makes no secret of its lack of objectivity; the message is clear: Bolshevik power is needed here. The film begins with a map and a quotation from Lenin, making overt its propagandistic intent: the purpose of infrastructure is to eliminate the remnants *(ostatki)* of backwardness in all corners of the territory. Yet it avoids condescension. Its emphasis is on hardship, not on backwardness, on the extraordinary exigencies of a climate that sends deep snow in mid-June, not on the failures of the community. And when the road finally arrives, it is built by Svanetians themselves. They are not "saved" by the Bolsheviks; they save themselves. Thus the structure of interconnection comes not from Moscow, not from an implied centre, but from a more generalized symbol of Sovietness.

The structures of interconnection provided by infrastructural projects such as the railway and the road to Svanetiia were crucial to the emergent imaginary geography of Soviet Russia. The space was to be reconfigured as a single whole, within which links between individual members were crucial. The destruction of social and spatial boundaries meant the creation of alternative connections, between peasant and worker, and between proletariats across the world. The molecular model of ideal society valued each atom in the total structure, and its linear connections with other atoms (other individuals, other spaces), but offered no controlling centre. For Vertov, for example, the *Kinopravda* film newspaper "links city with country, south with north, winter with summer, peasant women with working women."[31] Documentary film newspapers such as *Kinopravda* sought to offer a vision of the USSR as an interconnected territory. The seventh edition, for example, incorporated features from Siberia (Lake Baikal), Sochi, Tuapse, Moscow, and the Caucasus. All, implicitly, were part of the (unbounded) socialist space.

Vertov's comments on the seventeenth *Kinopravda* of 1923, devoted to the first All-Russian Agricultural Exhibition in Moscow (vsкhv), echoed this vocabulary of integration: the film showed, he claimed, "not so much the exhibition itself, as the 'blood circulation' *[krovoobrashchenie]* brought about by the idea of the agricultural exhibition."[32] Large sections of the film were devoted to showing workers and peasants on trains, travelling to the exhibition: they are the "blood circulation" of the new revolutionary body. So although ostensibly a film about the centre, in practice this *Kinopravda* focused on the periphery. Thus it suggested that the Agricultural Exhibition was a collaborative, incorporating event, constructed by the wider Soviet nation and not by the centre.

The exploration of the periphery was an integrative movement designed, ostensibly, to eliminate difference in the creation of a unified Soviet "body," and the exploratory imperative was expressed in films of and about the Soviet na-

Figure 24. A film expedition: Dziga Vertov and Mikhail Kaufman on location filming
A Sixth of the World (1926). Private collection.

tional space. This became particularly important in the second half of the
1920s. In 1926, Vertov produced two films, *Forward March, Soviet!* and *Shestaia
chast' mira (A Sixth of the World)*. Between these two films, a complex picture of
Soviet imaginary geography emerges. *Forward March, Soviet!* was a eulogy to
the achievements of the Soviet state, defined by a clearly articulated image of
Moscow. *A Sixth of the World*, by contrast, is an almost internationalist, decentred vision of the Soviet space. It was made on commission for Gostorg to encourage internal trade and as an international advertisement of the achievements of the new social order of equality and interdependence between the
republics. For it, Vertov and the Cine-eye group organized a series of expeditions across the Soviet territory, collecting an enormous amount of documentary, ethnographic material (Figure 24). *A Sixth of the World* explicitly seeks to
create a map of the Soviet Union, and the image of the globe is a leitmotif
throughout the film. Representing all the republics and areas of the *neob"iatnyi
prostor* in sequence, it presents ethnographic images of everyday life in the far-
flung regions of the Soviet space—from the Siberian taiga to Dagestan. The final scene shows a globe, presented to a group of men, women, and children,
with the title: "One-sixth of the world is in your hands" (Figure 25).

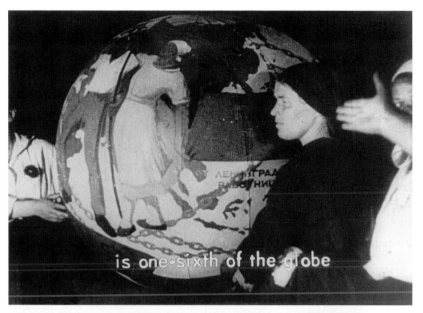

Figure 25. Film stills from *A Sixth of the World* (Vertov, 1926). Courtesy of B. F. I. Stills, Posters and Designs.

The principal intent of this film is to offer a decentralized vision of the consolidation of empire. Vertov's description of the film's aims is suggestive here: "We were supposed to present a marathon race along the chain of the Gostorg apparatus."[33] The Gostorg "chain," as represented in *A Sixth of the World*, links the republics of the Soviet Union as contributing areas of the national production. It has ideological implications: the use of the word *chain* to describe the Gostorg apparatus is explicitly contrasted, by Vertov, with the *okruzhenie* (encirclement) of capitalism, thus opposing a linear structure of interconnection with a circular, enclosing one. The Soviet model is linear: all parts of the system are equal in the chain. The space is envisaged as a grid, or network, in which there is no centre.

This vision of national particularity emphasized scientific interest and ethnographic learning over "local colour." Vertov's images focused on the *specificity* and difference of all the cultures represented as part of the Soviet Union. The region was represented as an independently functioning part of the greater totality that is the state. Unlike many later films, in which the centre was seen reaching out to educate and integrate the periphery, to create *sameness,* the spatial organization of *A Sixth of the World* was not centripetal: nothing either ends or begins in Moscow. Vertov's national spaces were not connected by road and rail to a symbolic centre: they belonged instead to a supranational Communist International, the "sixth part of the world."

This vision of the Soviet territory reflected the realpolitik of the period in relation to the non-Russian nationalities. As Yuri Slezkine has argued, the "Great Transformation" of the First Five-Year Plan was an "extravagant celebration of ethnic diversity," a genuine attempt to foster diversity *(raznoobrazie)* and particularity *(svoeobrazie)* within the new Soviet state.[34] Between 1924 and 1930 approximately, the process of state formation for the Union of Soviet Socialist Republics involved the identification and designation of the non-Russian national republics, and in some cases their creation as clearly defined national groups.[35] The first All-Union census in 1926 sought to identify the key determinants of "nationality" in the Soviet Union, claiming, as Francine Hirsch states, "that this formal registration of nationality would guarantee each people *[narod]* the right to 'establish its life in its own way' *[ustraivat' svoiu zhizn' po svoemu].*"[36] Ethnography was a natural companion to the state-sponsored exploration of the territory that was an urgent task for the new regime: mapping and identifying the constituent parts of the space. In 1925, the opening of the central Muzei narodovedenii (Museum of the Study of the Peoples), dedicated to the study of the "everyday life and art *[byt i iskusstvo]* of the peoples of the USSR," was celebrated.[37]

A Sixth of the World is thus indicative of a key moment in Soviet spatial imaginings: a rush to the periphery and exploration of the specificity and difference that constituted the Soviet national space. In this respect, Vertov's image of the capital in his other film of that year, *Forward March, Soviet!*, bears examination. Despite being set principally in Moscow, this film also emphasizes the networks of communication that integrate centre and periphery, creating the single Soviet space that is defined by its transformative energy which moves from city, to town, to village, to individual home. The power of film, in both cases, was to enable such radical visions of interconnection. Vertov's "sixth of the world" was an imaginary Soviet space in which hierarchy was abolished. In his words: "The Cine-eye means the conquest of space, the visual linkage of people throughout the entire world based on the continuous exchange of visible facts."[38] The "creative geography" of film offered a reenvisaging of real space as ideal Soviet space—the space of the immediate future.

THE FILM EXPEDITION: SCREENING
THE PERIPHERY

A Sixth of the World was among the first of a large number of cinematic "explorations" of the periphery between 1926 and 1929. Cinema was a vital tool in the exploration of the Soviet territory. In April 1927, the journal *Soviet Cinema* produced an edition with the heading "We Need to Know Our Country," an impassioned call for film to engage with the problem of "the study *[izuchenie]* of the ethnography of the USSR."[39] This was not, the editorial suggested, to be a romantic vision of exotic otherness, but rather a "precise documentation of the everyday life, labour, and folklore of the peoples of the USSR." Cinema, it continued, had a role that was to study, and not merely to "show," to inform, and not merely to entertain.

In another article in the same edition of *Soviet Cinema,* the head of the Moscow Muzei narodovedeniia, Professor F. Sokolov, called for cinema to discover "real" ethnographic material and not to filter its ethnographic images through the material available in his museum.[40] Cinema, he claimed, had a unique ability "to imprint the genuine dynamic of life," in contrast to the museum, which was "unavoidably static." Film seemed able to escape from a fetishized, implicitly colonial vision of ethnic particularity into a more genuine understanding of the real life of the national republics. And significantly, this genuine under-standing would be, according to Sokolov, dynamic and mobile, not static. Cin-ema was ideally and uniquely placed to provide a newly dynamic vision.

The significance of cinema to "scientific" study had been recognized long be-fore the revolution. In 1909, *Around the World* had published a pamphlet dedi-cated to the new *kinematograf*—"The Living Photograph"—in which film was proclaimed an invaluable aid in geographical, ethnographic, and scientific study.[41] In the new, equalized space of the Soviet Union after the revolution, however, cinema had a unique task: "In no other country can there be such a vi-tal need for cinema to work at acquainting us with the authentic everyday life of those nationalities which populate our Socialist Union, the only place in the world where the many nationalities are in the unique position of total equal-ity."[42] The revolutionary quest for information, explicitly linking cinema with exploration and ethnographic research and education, led to an explosion of ethnographic films during the second half of the 1920s. A state-sponsored proj-ect of 1926–27 organized film expeditions in the Urals, Siberia, and Far East, with various articulated aims, both geographical and ethnographic.[43] Statistics from the Moscow department of Sovkino published in *Soviet Cinema* in 1927 showed that of fifty-eight *kul'turfil'my* (cultural/educational documentary films) produced by Sovkino in 1926, seventeen had an explicitly "ethnogeo-graphic theme."[44] The geographical scope of these films encompassed Kazakh-stan, Crimea, Kamchatka, Siberia, Dagestan, the Volga, and other areas. The "ethnogeographic" was the single largest category, and the call went out to in-crease it.

In 1925, one director, Vladimir Shneiderov, produced two of the first exam-ples of the emergent genre of the travel film: *Po Uzbekistanu (Around Uzbek-istan)* and *Velikii perelet (The Great Flight)*. *Around Uzbekistan* is, as its title somewhat unimaginatively suggests, an account of travel around a Soviet re-public. The equally literally named *The Great Flight* tells the story of a major air expedition between Moscow and China, which Shneiderov and a small team, including the cameraman Georgii Blium, were able to accompany.[45] This film, providing an "ethnographic" account of China, provoked particular critical in-terest. In the words of one review, the response to the film demonstrated not the film's qualities (which were, he suggested, questionable), but "our interest in the real construction of human life," which film was uniquely placed to sat-isfy.[46] This, he went on to suggest, was the most important task of Soviet cin-ema.

Although focused abroad, and not on the internal "unknown," Shneiderov's

The Great Flight demonstrates how, in this period, the adventure space was implicitly *unbounded:* under the banner of world revolution, the Soviet Union was to extend beyond its frontiers into a unified global space, the workers' International. The national border represented not a protective divide, but rather a point of transition or contact, Russia's immanent link with the international proletariat. China, of course, was of particular interest: a near neighbour, to be transformed—ideally—from potential enemy into member of the Socialist brotherhood. The periphery was configured as a point of positive potential, a site of transition. In similar terms, one documentary film of 1931, *Po sovetskim granitsam (Along the Soviet Borders),* demonstrated this idea of the border: border guards peered across into the West with "Greetings to Workers," and emphasis was placed on the gate *through* the divide. Communism, the film proclaimed, dissolves boundaries. The border represented a site of transition into the wider socialist world.

The rhetorical emphasis of the debate around cinema and ethnography between 1927 and 1929 focused on the need to discover a mode of objective representation that would liberate ethnography from the complex heritage of Tsarist colonialism. Predominantly, the film expedition had as its aim the production of a film that was scientific and not "artistic." The "objective" eye of cinema would permit a decentred knowledge and understanding of the particularity of the regions.[47] This was to be aided by the establishment of locally based filmmaking organizations, such as the East Siberian Studio of the Film-Chronicle (Vostochno-sibirskaia studiia kinokhroniki), established in the early 1920s with the explicit mission of producing documentaries founded on local (principally ethnographic) material.

The stated aim of the film expedition, and indeed of all the ethnographic projects of the period—to acquaint centre with periphery, with the "real, working life of the peoples of our Union"—raises complex ideological questions. These questions are central to anthropology more generally and have been explored in recent debate among Western theorists and practitioners such as James Clifford and George Marcus.[48] Although their studies focus on areas other than the Soviet Union, they provide an interesting perspective through which to consider the rhetoric of difference that characterized representations of the noncolonial Soviet "empire" during this period. Knowledge, after all, is not neutral; it is itself implicated in the colonizing process. Knowledge is an assertion of power, part of the drawing of boundaries, the constitution of self and other that sustains and objectifies the Imperial structure. In Russia, the heritage of this reached far back beyond the revolution: the earliest expansion into

Siberia during the reign of Peter the Great was accompanied by intense carto-graphic and geological research, which sought to "map" the region at a number of levels.[49] It is clear, certainly, that the Soviet state recognized the need for in-formation as a prerequisite for solid state building: "In the tenth year of revolu-tion we must have an authentic scientific picture."[50]

The Soviet ideological apparatus during the 1920s, however, was at pains to differentiate itself from the construction of empire as a form of *osvoenie*. Knowledge was consistently articulated as the means of liberating the nation from repressive Imperial structures and building an equal society. An article in *Around the World* claimed, for example, that "the equality of the nationalities, achieved by the October Revolution, by definition excludes the possibility of even the slightest inattention or carelessness in relations with those nationali-ties."[51] However spurious this distinction between knowledge and control may appear, the significance of the debate in the early Soviet context should not be underestimated. "Authentic" ethnographic detail was presented as a prerequi-site for the genuine equality of the peoples. As Francine Hirsch has shown in the context of the census, "ethnographic" nationality was to be the basis of a new kind of social life, which would take account of difference. An awareness of the objective thrust of this exploratory urge offers a more nuanced under-standing of the process of *osvoenie*. The quest for "authenticity," however illu-sory, was a rhetorical cornerstone of the ethnographic project.

The film expedition had two stated, and apparently contradictory, aims: sci-entific study and intervention (to encourage the building of socialism).[52] Early articulations of ethnographic and travel cinema demonstrated a greater focus on the former category, in which travel was valued *for its own sake* as part of the cult of exploration. In 1928, for example, a film called *Lesnye liudi (The Forest People)* was extensively advertised as a new kind of travel film.[53] The film was an ethnographic introduction to the peoples of the Far Eastern mountain re-gion of Kharbin (a Soviet territory within China). It shows the daily life, habits, and habitat of these peoples, demonstrating how they fish, build yurts as homes, and generally survive. A series of maps demonstrates the location of this community within a global space, identifying it within the Soviet territory, be-fore narrowing to a more local map that focuses on the area around Vladivos-tok. Any suggestion of transformation or homogenization is avoided in this film, which focuses on the ostensibly objective dissemination of information.

A similar emphasis on learning about and "understanding" the non-Russian nationalities can be traced in stories in *Around the World* that have an ethno-graphic slant. "In the Taiga—on the Threshold," for example, recounts how a young explorer encounters an older native and from him, learns about the traditions and habits of those who live in the Taiga. The language of incorporation and *otkrytie* is inflected by a reciprocal dynamic in which the centre has things to learn from the periphery. Similarly, "A Year Among the Forest People" took on a task similar to that of the film *The Forest People*: spending a year living among the people of Kharbin, a young Soviet man undertakes a form of rite of passage toward understanding the beauty of diversity.[54]

The difficulties and ambiguities of this quest for an ostensibly objective ethnographic eye are made overt in a feature film such as Pudovkin's *Potomok Chingis-khana (Storm over Asia),* made in 1928 and offering a very different vision of ethnic otherness. *Storm over Asia* exploits the exotic drama of the Mongol tribes of Asia, creating an epic tale of revolutionary insurgence. The implicit message is that *all* the Soviet peoples fought for revolution. In practice, however, the film offers an unobjective, fetishized vision of otherness in which the camera seems to function as voyeur, framing and aestheticizing the wild Mongol. The apparent opposition between these visions of exotica and the rhetoric of objectivity and exploration in documentary film can be partly explained through an understanding of the status of the camera. The ethnographic documentary films of the late 1920s often focused on the *experience* of travel and exploration, positioning the camera explicitly as part of an adventure. The experience of the participants in film expeditions was often recounted in accounts in *Soviet Cinema* during 1927, describing in detail the daily trials and adventures the travellers encounter, and in particular the reactions produced in local populations by the arrival of the expedition.[55] The camera was part of a drama of representation in which the emphasis was on the interaction of the local population (those who were being represented) and the outsider (the expedition itself). In Pudovkin's feature film, by contrast, the camera is invisible, and the film provides no space for self-reflexive distance.

VLADIMIR EROFEEV: FROM REPRESENTATION
TO ASSIMILATION

The complexities of the filmed—filming relationship, elided by Pudovkin, are made particularly evident in the work of the director and critic Vladimir Erofeev. In particular, Erofeev's 1927 film *Krysha mira: ekspeditsiia v Pamir (The Roof of the World: An Expedition to Pamir)* reflects and problematizes the ethnographic urge of the early period. Erofeev was much interested in the connections between cinematography and scientific ethnography and was a key player in discussions of the role of the cinematic expedition in 1927.[56] As director, he made twenty-five documentary films in thirteen years, of which at least eight were explicitly of the national ethnographic/travel genre.[57] *The Roof of the World,* his first *kino-ekspeditsiia,* was the product of an expedition jointly organized by Sovkino and the Geological Committee.

Extracts from Erofeev's travel journal were published in *Soviet Cinema* in association with the ethnographic push of 1927–28.[58] In 1929, he published his account of the journey as a book, *Po "kryshe mira" s kino-apparatom (puteshstvie na Pamir) (Over the "Roof of the World" with a Movie Camera: A Journey to Pamir).* The book was published as part of a series by the Molodaia gvardiia (Young Guard) publishing house entitled "A Contemporary Library of Travel, Local Lore, Adventure and Science Fiction," which included accounts of the construction of the Turksib railway as well as the encouragement of "national tourism." The brief of the series was to offer "a focus on the more distant and lesser known corners of our country," part of the broad *nauchno-popularnyi* genre in which exploration and adventure were reformulated as scientific expedition.[59]

In the foreword to the book, Erofeev emphasized that the diary would be "only facts," filling in those details that the camera cannot show. The camera is neither omniscient nor neutral. Indeed, throughout his written accounts of this first expedition, Erofeev directed attention to the problem of representation and the role of the camera as intrusive observer. In a curious reversal of roles, they—the expedition—are more strange, more "other" than those whom they have come to film: women, for example, refuse to be filmed, and a scandal ensues in which the local community demonizes the filmmakers.[60] Further, Erofeev consistently emphasized the materiality of transportation—from the train at the beginning of the film that carries the expedition from Moscow to Pamir, through the trucks and donkeys that take them on the more difficult parts of the journey. Obstacles to travel, such as wheels of a truck stuck in mud, serve similarly to emphasize the role of the expedition as interloper. The expedition itself becomes the key protagonist of the film, a self-reflexive document of exploration that explicitly problematizes the role of the viewing, camera eye. By stressing the contingency of representation, Erofeev pictured a reciprocal dynamic between centre and periphery in which the camera eye was clearly represented as subjective. Ethnography, in this vision, was not a neutral exercise.

Erofeev was one of the earliest Soviet directors to use panoramic shots consistently, initiating a cinematography of long takes and mobile panoramas. Erofeev's camera eye was a mobile eye, but it was explicitly the eye of a traveller and explorer. *The Roof of the World* features long tracking shots that emphasize the scale of the territory to be traversed. Erofeev stresses the limits of representation, suggesting as much what the camera cannot show as that which it does. He reveals an acute awareness of his own role and that of his team as observer-participants in the world that they film. Although at first glance it would appear that his panoramas and slow editing are sharply contrasted with Vertov's dynamic montage, in fact there are marked similarities between the two filmmakers. As Vertov's aesthetic foregrounds the experiential limitations and possibilities of vision, so Erofeev takes this awareness into his early travel films. Erofeev's geologists-with-a-camera (the presence of the camera is made explicit throughout the film) recall Vertov's man-with-a-camera, exploring the extent to which the camera reveals new aspects of the world. They reject monumental, static images in favour of a contingent vision.

In this, his first travel film, Erofeev emphasized nonideological exploration as motivation: "Both film and book," he wrote, "can convey only weakly the feeling of the traveller, placed face to face with nature, sensing directly a surprising, diverse life, full of as yet unknown pleasures."[61] The traveller, here, is explicitly not colonizing. He confronts "nature" directly, and this confrontation, enabled by the cinematic eye, permits a clearer apprehension of a world that is crucially *mnogoobraznyi* (diverse). Feeling and sensation *(oshchushchenie)*, accessible through experience, are here prioritized over message. *Oshchushchenie* is the prime channel for "knowledge." Travel is valued for its own sake: the key imperative is to explore the territory, to be part of the "suitcase mentality" of the time, and to access new experiences.

In their work during the 1920s, both Vertov and Erofeev refused the reification of the "exotic" associated with colonial vision. Like *A Sixth of the World*, for example, *The Roof of the World* featured little in the way of folk dances and national costume. Although in sections of the film the enlightening influence of Soviet power was shown to be transforming and modernizing ("they already know Lenin here," one title points out), this integration did not provide the dominant dynamic of the film. In its place was a representation of exploration that sought to be nonassimilative.

Yet the exploratory initiative was, at the same time, part of a broader project of mapping. In the *Roof of the World*, this emphasis on the experience of travel coexists with a need to mark routes through the territory—to *map* the space. The route of the expedition is clearly mapped from Moscow, and an animated map recurs throughout the film to confirm and reconfirm the position of the Pamir Mountains on the Soviet map. A larger scale map of the region itself also charts the progress of the expedition through the area. Further, the scientific objectivity of the expedition is emphasized through the figures of two geologists who accompany them. In an interesting scene, the geologists are pictured with measuring equipment, plotting the territory; a title boasts that "our geologists have seriously taken on the task of exploring the territory of the Union"[62] The discovery of the territory is a means of grasping the "ungraspable" (the *neob"iatnyi*).

The Roof of the World can be revealingly compared with Erofeev's later film *Daleko v Azii (Far Away in Asia)*, made in 1931. Taken together, the two films provide an index of the development of Soviet attitudes to the periphery during the Cultural Revolution. *Far Away in Asia*, made in collaboration with the documentarist Roman Karmen as cinematographer, was another *kino-ekspeditsiia*, in which Erofeev and his crew travelled to Uzbekistan. In comparison to *The Roof of the World*, this film made explicit in its very title a view that originates in Moscow: "far from Moscow" positions the centre and constructs Asia as a periphery. The map from Moscow that was nascent in *The Roof of the World* became the dominant axis for *Far Away in Asia*, echoing a new phase of Soviet *osvoenie*. Although it continued the technique of *The Roof of the World* in problematizing its own status as representation and the role of the filmmakers as intruder and voyeuristic eye, this later film nonetheless presented a clear vision of a backward Asiatic world transformed by the arrival of Soviet enlightenment. Homogenization and integration are the key aims of the expedition. Soviet machinery accelerates the harvest, otherwise held back by the primitive laziness and even foolish superstition of the local people. The cinematic eye was implicitly linked with the modernizing vision of the Soviet centre. In this respect, *Far Away in Asia* is indicative of a broader trend: ethnographic films from the early 1930s on tended to emphasize integration and transformation. "Grant culture to the distant Pechora region," one indicative film proclaimed: "Let us transform the distant Pechora into a factory of meat, dairy products, and fish." The entire territory was to be reconfigured as provider to the centre, the red star of Moscow.

The shift of emphasis between *The Roof of the World* and *Far Away in Asia* echoes a broader transformation in attitudes to the periphery. The exploration of difference that I have identified in ethnographic film of the late 1920s should be differentiated from the reification of "local colour," which began to emerge in later Stalinist representations of the peoples and nations of the Soviet periphery. In parallel with the drive toward assimilation, a growing "Orientialism" emerged in images of the non-Russian nationalities.[63] Ethnic particularity was reduced to ethnic decoration, "local colour" was superimposed onto a vision of homogeneity, and real difference was suppressed. The changing status of localness and particularity was also reflected in a change in attitude towards kraevedenie. In 1937, many *kraevedcheskie* organizations were officially liquidated, and a decree in 1938 declared that its practitioners were enemies of the people. Henceforward, the work of the *kraevedy* was to be carried out by central organs of *prosveshchenie.* The fates of *kraevedenie,* and of ethnography, are rooted in transformations in the Soviet ideological map in the mid-1930s and mirror a more general shift in Soviet attitudes to the territory: from exploration to assimilation. In its original formulation, *kraevedenie* was explicitly local in origin and orientation: it focused on the dissemination of local knowledge to a local population. Its liquidation marked a stage in a progressive shift in the ideological emphasis of territorial exploration and information gathering. *Osvoenie,* the extension of power radially, was not an exploratory practice. Its primary need was enlightenment over exploration.

Chapter 5 Travelling

The twentieth century is a century which sees the earth as no one has ever seen it.
—*Gertrude Stein*

Cinema's role in shaping the imaginary geography of the Soviet Union was twofold: it represented the territory, of course, and, perhaps even more importantly, it also offered ways of looking at it. Shifts in attitudes to the territory—the movement between exploration and *osvoenie*—may be explored through an examination of two models of vision presented in Soviet cinema of the period: the train and the plane. Both represent different ways of looking: they offered different relationships with the space.

TRAINS OR PLANES: VIEWING THE TERRITORY

From the first years of Soviet power, a cinematic obsession with the train and with rail travel was testament to the quest for mobilized perception. Trains, train wheels, and tracks abound in early Soviet film.

The mobilized gaze of cinematic perception found its natural counterpart in the train.[1] Although the Lumière brothers' film *L'arrivée d'un train en gare de la Ciotat* (1895), first shown in Russia in 1896, is the origin myth of Russian cinema, just as it is in the West, Russian cinematography as a whole came to the train later, and it was really in the 1920s that the train entered Soviet film in its full force as cultural myth and practical necessity.[2] The Soviet railway served important symbolic and practical functions in the drive to abolish spatial hierarchy, overcoming the divide between town and country, centre and periphery. In the new world of equalized spaces, the symbolism of the train suggested more than just the ideological message of integration. Vertov's "train of revolution," so named in the *Leninskaia kinopravda (The "Lenin" Film-Truth),* together with the rail imagery of much of his documentary film, was at the centre of an emerging cinematic myth of the railway. The train was an expression of a liberated and mobilized experience of seeing and a new way of living in the world; it functioned at thematic and stylistic levels in the creation of new visions of the Soviet space.

Train travel seemed to offer a type of experience uniquely appropriate to the spirit of the age (Figure 26). In Vertov's films, from the first *Film Week* to *Man with a Movie Camera* of 1929, the view through the train window—the moving landscape—functioned as a metaphor for *dynamic* vision and a means of representing the flux of experience associated with the revolutionary transformation of everyday life. It was essential to the representation of movement that was, as we have seen (Chapter 2), central to Vertov's cinematic aesthetic. Several of the early Cine-eye documentaries pictured the cameraman leaning out of the train window, shooting the landscape as it flashed past. In the seventh *Film-Truth,* for example, processing plants on the banks of Lake Baikal were shot from a train window. In the nineteenth, the camera goes on a "journey" by train from Moscow to the Arctic Ocean, and the journey is shot at length through the window of the train. In one of the best-known sequences of *Man with a Movie Camera,* the cameraman positions himself on the train tracks at ground level in an attempt to capture the energy of the approaching train.

More generally, much Soviet film during the 1920s pictured the landscape through the train window as a dynamic space. People craned heads (and cameras) out of windows to capture the fleeting landscape. Dynamism was the central characteristic of representations of space. The experience of train travel offered a new vision of the Soviet space—one that was accessible to all. The train was the means through which the territory was to be explored: railway lines facilitated the new "blood circulation" of the nation, allowing journeys to and

Figure 26. The suitcase mentality. From *SSSR na stroike,* 1930, nos. 5–6: 13.

from the capital (in Abram Room's *Bed and Sofa,* for example [see Chapter 3], the train brings Fogel to the city at the beginning of the film and carries Liudmila away from it at the end) and across the vast *prostor.*

The predominance of the train in film of the 1920s and early 1930s contrasts with the cinematic adulation of the airplane that can be discerned in Soviet film from the mid-1930s onward. The use of aerial shots in Soviet cinema of the 1930s paralleled the emerging ideology of *osvoenie.* In real terms, the plane overcame distance, transforming the vast spaces of the Soviet Union into a controllable territory. In parallel, the aerial shot expresses control over the landscape, rendering it tame. It offers an alternative model of cinematic perception. Where the train window creates a linear, contiguous, experiential vision of space *as it is traversed,* the airplane (the aerial shot) offers a controlling gaze that maps and orders. It is a gaze that is not subject to movement but is abstracted and framed.

The differences between these two perceptual experiences stimulated much reflection during the 1920s. In 1925, discussing Shneiderov's *The Great Flight,* Viktor Shklovskii described the aerial perspective in the following terms: "the land, seen from above, is single faceted and geometrical *[odnoobrazna i geometrichna]*."[3] The view from above, he suggested, erased the "individual fate"—the marks of human experience—from the landscape. Sergei Tret'iakov expressed a similar sense of shock at this transformed space, viewed from the air: "the landscape is nature seen through the eyes of a consumer."[4] For Tret'iakov,

the relationship of consumer to landscape was explicitly non-Soviet: it was a relationship of possession—a capitalist relationship. Furthermore, he added,
when looking from above, "you start to long for knowledge": the aerial view removed the spectator from the experiential "knowledge" of the space, which was
the crucial characteristic of the Soviet vision of exploration.[5]

Tret'iakov's comments here are highly revealing. Echoing him, some fifty
years later, the French theorist Michel de Certeau points to a distinction between views from above (the aerial shot) and horizontal/experiential views
when he writes of viewing New York City from the top of the World Trade
Centre. The spectator at the summit, he says, is as an "Icarus flying above the
waters," who can "ignore the devices of Daedalus in mobile and endless
labyrinths far below. His elevation transforms him into a voyeur. It puts him at
a distance. It transforms the bewitching world by which one was 'possessed'
into a text that lies before one's eyes. It allows one to read it, to be a Solar eye,
looking down like a god."[6] In opposition to this scopic totalization, de Certeau
situates "practice": the *appropriation* of the city by the act of walking through it.
This is a horizontal experience of the urban landscape, which "manipulates
spatial organizations, no matter how panoptic they may be."[7] The horizontal
model of space, constructed by human *appropriation,* breaks down the hierarchical, radial organization of the space associated with Panopticism. The
"knowledge" that Tret'iakov sought corresponds to this experiential knowledge
of space—produced by practice, by movement through the space. For him, the
aerial view ran counter to the exploratory initiative that was central to the revolutionary remapping of space.

During the Soviet 1920s, a new—implicitly *Soviet* and revolutionary—vision of the world was offered. In this context, I would suggest, the aerial shot
drew a *map* of place, where the train represented an *experience.* In cinema of the
1920s, the use of the train as a metaphor for transformed vision incorporated it
within a broader aesthetic of spatial "practice." The train functioned, during
the 1920s, as an expression of a horizontal, physical experience of space, which
was sharply contrasted with the controlling, panoptic vision of the aerial shot,
a purely specular experience. The train was a vehicle for exploration—and implicitly for *appropriation.*

LOOKING OUT: THE TRAIN EXPLORES

This view of the train is largely specific to Soviet Russia. In Western Europe in
the early part of the twentieth century, the development of the railway was

largely felt in terms of a transformation of space and a perceived rupture of the "natural" relationship that had existed between the human body and space through more traditional forms of travel during the eighteenth and early nineteenth centuries.[8] Train travel was often seen as dissociating the experience of the body from the experience of travel and reducing space to fleeting visual impressions, divorced from location and deprived of specificity as they rush past the train window. In the words of Wolfgang Schivelbusch: "The train was experienced as a projectile, and travelling on it, as being shot through the landscape—thus losing control of one's senses."[9] Schivelbusch has claimed that the view from the train window blurs the perception of depth in space and produces a "panoramic" impression in which visual stimuli appear to the eye indiscriminately, in a *totality*. "The mobility of vision" produced by train travel, he suggests, meant that "evanescent reality had become the new reality."[10]

Following Schivelbusch, a number of recent film theorists have investigated the relationship between the mobile, panoramic vision of train travel and the development of cinema.[11] The work of these theorists has made a valuable contribution to film theory, seeking a description of cinematic perception that accounts not only for the "gaze," but also for the fluidity and dynamic spatiality of film, and arguing that film re-creates the experience of mobilized vision. This approach has tended to emphasize the predominance of the visual in cinematic representation. Cinema, it is suggested, represents "dematerialized" space— the "evanescent reality" of which Schivelbusch wrote. This emphasis on film as dematerialization fails, however, to account for the mobile *experience* of cinema; and it was this, in the early period at least, that seemed to be cinema's key point of difference. Many early films were travel films, bringing new views of the world to the urban audience. Film was a form of imaginary tourism—a link made most clear in Hale's Tours, which re-created a stationary railway carriage as a cinema and projected images of landscapes, as if through a train window, around the walls. Hale's Tours were the largest chain of theatres exclusively showing films in the United States before 1906.[12] The explicit parallel between film and train travel that they made is revealing; cinema was a means of discovering a new landscape and providing new experiences of the world.

Further consideration of the train metaphor of perception may clarify this. First, it is inadequate to suggest that the perceptual experience of landscape from a train window is a disembodied and totalizing vision in which, as in the panorama, a "complete view" is presented to the spectator in a single moment. It is, instead, predicated on a mobile and contingent vision of space, as each "view" is constantly dissolved into the next view. Perspectival order (the single viewpoint—a feature of the camera obscura model of vision that had predominated in visual representation since the eighteenth century) is disrupted. In its place the train offers a model of vision that is premised on experience—a view that unfolds *in time*. The mobilized body is not necessarily separated from the viewing process. The appearance of the "totality," therefore, continually undermines its own status as totality and is revealed as a fleeting, partial representation, as the landscape "flashes by." It is this version of the perceptual experience of rail travel that I identify in the cinematic adulation of the train in Soviet Russia during the 1920s. The view through the train window seems to actualize the mobile "transition" that Deleuze identified as cinema's visual point of difference (see Chapter 2).

Soviet avant-garde cinema during the 1920s sought to rediscover a physical (sensuous) experience of space, the *oshchushchenie*. This was a key task for the new civilization. Schivelbusch himself makes the interesting suggestion that the development of photography re-created the "intensive experience of the sensuous world, terminated by the industrial revolution."[13] Cinema, which developed out of technologies of vision at the end of the nineteenth century, was at once a representation of the experience of mobile, "deterritorialized" vision, and an attempt to re-create a (or create a new) relationship between the viewing body and the world. This aspect of cinematic representation was of particular importance to many Soviet filmmakers and thinkers, for whom the project of "remaking the world" and of situating a new kind of individual in this new space was of particular social and political importance.

There are, of course, concrete social and political reasons for the status of the train in Soviet Russia. In industrialized Western Europe, the train literally remade the space, imposing new patterns of communication (new maps) on a space that was, by and large, already mapped and traversable.[14] In the Soviet Union (and indeed, in the Russian empire before 1917), the railway was an agent for the *discovery* of space. Thus the opposition of nature and technology that Schivelbusch identifies in the Western European response to train travel, in which the train was perceived to make travel a more unreal, noncorporeal experience, is altered. Furthermore, although the train in prerevolutionary Russia did carry associations of encroaching (and destructive) modernity, in Soviet Russia the machine was perceived as a means by which a new, dynamic relationship between Soviet man and woman (the proletariat) and the material world could be established. Thus the visual experience of train travel was incorporated into a more positive conception of "mobile vision": it provided the conditions for a revolutionary reformulation of the nature of experience. The train was at once a vehicle for the rapid exploration of the vast space of the So-viet Union and a visualization of the new experience of space that Soviet artists sought to demonstrate as the animating condition of the new society.

The train, then, served practical and symbolic functions in the exploratory project. The surviving films from Medvedkin's Film Train, for example, dis-cussed in Chapter 1, reveal how that train was a practical manifestation of Ver-tov's injunctions to represent the real, the fluid, and the momentary: the his-toric present in construction. The train's very motto—"we film it today and show it tomorrow"—emphasized the immediacy of the project. It enabled the filmmakers to engage directly in the process of construction—in the dynamic of the age. Medvedkin's train, furthermore, sought not to bring propaganda from centre to periphery, but to *discover* as much as to teach. Medvedkin's mis-sion statement expressed this reciprocal dynamic, claiming to enlighten and to explore: "I must travel around the whole country, to show more and to find out more" (Figure 27).[15] Trains, then, made possible the key project of the First Plan: the exploration and discovery of the space, and its people.

According to Soviet rhetoric and representation, trains cut new paths through the territory, thus providing structures for *appropriation.* They offered a new experience of the national space to the newly mobile Soviet citizen—the man with a suitcase. In his work on Magnitogorsk, Stephen Kotkin suggests that the enormous labour demands of the First Plan produced a kind of professionally mobile workforce who "were using trains to tour the country."[16] Documentary newsreels presented scenes of workers travelling by train to fulfil the Plan's tar-gets in the provinces. In one film, workers are pictured on a train, reading pam-phlets about trains crossing the nation to take labour to the Donbass.[17] In the first Soviet sound feature film, *Putevka v zhizn'* (*A Path to Life,* 1931), directed by Nikolai Ekk, this link between the train and appropriation was made explicit at the level of plot. The film charts the transformation of homeless children in So-viet Russia in 1923 into model members of the collective through the construc-tion of a communal labour project. The culminating achievement of the new collective is to be the construction of a railway, which will link the commune with the town. Thus the children will be fully integrated into the new Soviet so-ciety by *connection,* integrated into the communicative network upon which the new territory is predicated. The two young heroes of the film, Mustafa and Kol'ka, dream of becoming engine driver and conductor on this new axis of So-vietness.

As the narrative develops, evil elements of the "old" world sabotage the proj-ect. On the very day when the railway is to be ceremonially opened, Mustafa is

Figure 27. "I must travel around the whole country, to show more and to find out more." Aleksandr Medvedkin (front) and the Film Train team on their travels. Courtesy of The Film Museum, Moscow.

killed when saboteurs dislodge the rail tracks, thus breaking the metaphorical connection, the network. In the closing sequences of the film, Mustafa's body is carried, "first, on the first carriage, of the first train," along the triumphal *put'* (path). The message of the film is clear: the construction of the new world will continue nevertheless and is premised on the protection and maintenance of the railway. Thus the film positions the railway at the centre of a narrative in which the formerly marginal find their place in a transformed world. Through the construction of a railway, they *appropriate* a part of that world. In this final sequence, shots of the railway emphasize energy and dynamism. The camera is positioned just above Mustafa's corpse, as the ground rushes beneath it. The train carries the young heroes through a natural world that they view, dynamized, from a new and empowered position, leaning out of the train carriage, looking forward.

The train, then, seemed to encapsulate the revolutionary momentum—the *put'*—of Soviet Russia. Part of a broader cult of technology, the train provides a visualization of the ideological weight of the machine aesthetic during the 1920s. According to the Constructivist architect Moisei Ginzburg, the crucial feature of mechanical movement was that it was defined by a continual striving *in a direction*. Where traditional aesthetics (in architecture in particular) were premised on symmetry, a "balance" of movement, contemporary form would emphasize movement as a *put'*—"in the direction of an axis which is laid out before the movement and which functions as the ideal goal, which is never reached."[18] The sheer fact of movement carried ideological weight, expressed as continual striving toward an unrealizable goal. This vision of the *put'* as a perpetual process was central to the representation of space and time in Soviet Russia of the 1920s. It expressed the dynamism of the age, the creative energy by which the new world was *being built*.

LOOKING DOWN: THE PLANE CONQUERS

This dynamic, exploratory view was the predominant way of looking, and seeing, presented in Soviet film during the 1920s. Even the aerial shot, in its early manifestations, was not aligned with an abstracted, controlling gaze. For Vertov during the 1920s, for example, the aerial perspective was part of the broader investigation of new ways of experiencing space—strategies of appropriation—through film. His use of the aerial shot reproduced the destabilized, mobile viewpoint of the "Cine-eye." The first *Film-Truth* (1922) included aerial shots of Moscow.[19] *Daesh' vozdukh* (*You Give Us Air*, 1924), an educational film about aviation produced by Vertov's group outside the *Film-Truth* series, presented air travel as a gift of technology to the nation, expanding the potential of the Soviet experience. Later, Aleksei Gan wrote a descriptive interpretation of the experience of viewing the thirteenth *Film-Truth*: "And we see airplanes and at the same time watch from them the earth below. But the earth is running, as streets, houses and newspapers shift to another perspective."[20]

The "running," mobile earth Gan described was common in Vertov's early aerial sequences. In the fourteenth *Film-Truth*, the camera films a plane from below as a distant speck in an empty sky before implicitly assuming its viewpoint and exploring the cityscape from above in a series of precarious, highly mobile tracking shots. In the eighteenth *Film-Truth*, the ground seems to rush up from below the carriage of a rapidly descending plane as the film-eye "lands" on Russian territory. To some extent, of course, Vertov's experiments with the aerial shot simply reflected the novelty of new technology and the desire to discover the full cinematic potential of the new medium. I would suggest, however, that the strategy is more significant than this. Vertov refused the monumentalizing potential of the aerial perspective in favour of a vision that was contingent and dynamic. He offered a vision of cinema as "practice," in which the airplane expanded and transforms the perceptual experience of the world.[21]

Shifts in attitudes toward the territory in the course of the 1930s were echoed in a shift in the nature of the cinematic gaze. In Vertov's later film *Kolybel'naia* (*Lullaby,* 1937), tellingly, the aerial shot assumed a different form. *Lullaby,* a sustained hymn to the joys of Stalin's Russia, is framed as a "lullaby" for all the newborn babies who will form the future generation—who will inherit the Soviet promised land. At the film's centre is a lengthy sequence that begins: "You will fly above the earth . . . see everything . . . discover *[uznaesh']* everything." Flight, we understand here, offers an absolute form of knowledge, a totality of control. It is a symbol of conquest. A series of aerial shots succeeds this statement, as planes (piloted by women) seem to fly all over the territory. They are intercut with close-up shots of events all over the nation. The totalizing view of the aerial perspective motivates these shots; it allows us, implicitly, to "discover everything," to encompass the whole *prostor.* During this long sequence, the aerial shot is invariably stable, lacking the dangerous dynamism associated with it in Vertov's earlier films. In addition, the film features a kind of interview with an apparently ordinary woman, who describes the experience of being taken in a plane. The earth, she says, "is wonderfully visible" from up there. Despite her excitement, and the obvious pleasure of the trip, even this interview serves to normalize the sensation of flight: it was not frightening, she claims, for it was as if "you are flying, but cannot feel whether you are flying or not." Thus this film simultaneously exalts and normalizes flight. The aerial gaze is, implicitly, available to all: it represents the totality of knowledge and power that the future generation will inherit.

The aerial view, then, permitted a new kind of relationship with the territory. In real terms, air travel "conquered" the territory; symbolically, the aerial view echoed this dominance (Figure 28). In 1935, for example, Aleksandr Dovzhenko's film *Aerograd* used the aerial perspective to confer a poetic order upon the landscape. *Aerograd* is a striking statement of the poetic centrality of the airplane in Soviet representations of space from the late 1930s. Thematically, it equates air travel with *osvoenie:* the construction of an "aerograd" on the banks

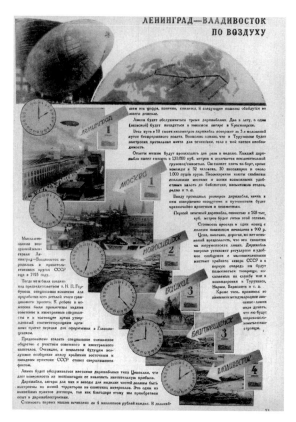

Figure 28. "Leningrad–Vladivostok by air": the plane
conquers space and time. From *Ekran rabochei gazety,* 29 May
1927, p. 13.

of the "great" Pacific Ocean. The opening sequences of the film in particular
provide a strong visual metaphor of conquest. First, the camera tracks the
movement of a plane through the sky before implicitly adopting the aerial view
as the plane progresses east across the taiga toward the ocean.[22] Dovzhenko
uses long tracking shots to emphasize the *neob"iatnyi prostor,* across which the
plane offers new routes. These shots create a sense of boundlessness that is contained within a single moving frame. The *neob"iatnyi prostor* is captured *(osvoen)* within the aerial view, rendered seamless and whole. Ultimately, the point
of view of *Aerograd* is that of de Certeau's voyeur, possessing the landscape. It is
a strategy of assimilation and mapping, mirroring *osvoenie* at a stylistic level.[23]

Through the 1930s, films about air travel developed into a cult of heroism in
which the pilot was increasingly pictured as conqueror, mastering the skies.[24]

In Iulii Raizman's 1935 feature *Letchiki (The Pilots)*, the process of learning to fly echoed the path to consciousness of the young heroine Galia Bystrova (a student at an aviation academy), enabling her to recognize true love. With elevation comes consciousness: raised above the world, Galia can see more clearly. Thus flight became a metaphor for clarity. The aerial view offered an increasingly valorized perspective in which the world was rendered comprehensible and "mapped." A triumphal air show is the site of the narrative denouement of this film (Figure 29) and its final scenes show the protagonists venturing out into the distant reaches of the Soviet *prostor*, their planes implicitly the means by which they will conquer the space.

Yet the image of the pilot as conqueror was only nascent in *The Pilots*. In fact, through a love triangle, this film showcased competing models of heroism (Figure 30). Galia begins the film in love with the dashing and talented pilot Beliaev, whose air acrobatics hold the whole school in thrall. Beliaev, however, lacks discipline—his heroism, though initially undoubted, is that of the reckless individual. It is not, we infer, the heroism of the new Soviet man. Disobeying the rules, Beliaev crashes a plane, is injured, and is banned from further flying (Figure 31). His punishment is administered by the older—and less dashing—head of the aviation academy, Rogachev, who is also in love with Galia. In the course of the film, Rogachev emerges as a low-key kind of hero. He is the wise, moral representative of true Soviet values, and it is he who wins the girl in the end. Galia's path to genuine political consciousness, implicitly achieved by her ascent into the ranks of fully fledged pilot, allows her to see clearly who is the better man for her.

The rejection of Beliaev as extraordinary hero, in favour of a more grounded vision of heroism in the form of Galia and Rogachev, is broadly typical of many films of the early 1930s. *Kryl'ia (Wings)* of 1932, for example, was devoted to the extreme heroism of civil war pilot Sergei Sedov. But Sedov, after the war, has become an "ordinary" Soviet worker, engaged in the task of constructing socialism. He is no extraordinary hero. His heroic exploits reemerge only in battle with his former capitalist enemies at an international air show where he upholds the honour of the Soviet people.[25] The true hero, we understand, is prepared to be ordinary.

In this respect, *Istrebiteli (The Fighter Pilots)*, made in Kiev in 1939, offers a complex vision of the heroism of the pilot and stands at a transitional point in representations of heroism in Stalinist culture. Using the familiar trope of the love triangle, the film follows the fates of three schoolmates, Sergei, Kolia, and Vania. Both men, naturally, are in love with Vania, and both are pilots. They

Figure 29. The air show. Film still from *Letchiki* (Raizman, 1935). Courtesy of B. F. I. Stills, Posters and Designs.

Figure 30. Heroes on parade. Film still from *Letchiki* (Raizman, 1935). Courtesy of B. F. I. Stills, Posters and Designs.

Figure 31. Beliaev's hubris. Film still from *Letchiki* (Raizman, 1935). Courtesy of B. F. I. Stills, Posters and Designs.

compete, therefore, in all areas of their lives. It is Sergei, however, who is the focus—and the hero—of the film, and it is he whom Vania will love. In the early parts of the film, Sergei is shown to be a dashing, skilful, and brave young pilot whose skill in air acrobatics is the joy of the academy. In a revealingly symbolic demonstration of the superiority of the plane over the train, he and Kolia prevent a terrible train crash by flying low enough to warn the driver of blocked rails ahead. They, implicitly, can see all. Such heroism in the sky is confirmed on land when, at a party with his friends, Sergei rescues a small boy from an accident with fireworks. In the course of this act of altruistic bravery, however, his eyes are burned, and he becomes suddenly and dramatically blind while on his next flight. Thus Sergei becomes, of all things, a blind pilot—a curious reworking of the metaphor of flight as clarity of vision. He is unable to fly, of course—symbolically brought to earth, reduced to listening to the distant sound of planes in the sky above. The space of his life narrows—from the freedom of the skies to the constraints of a single room. And in parallel, he rejects Vania's love, feeling himself unworthy of a happy future.

Ultimately, Sergei is saved by a miracle of (Soviet) science; a brilliant "specialist" is able to recover Sergei's sight. In thus regaining a sense that had been lost, he implicitly rediscovers the world: "I never knew how many beautiful things there are in the world," he marvels. He rediscovers, too, his love for Vania—and, ultimately, his destiny as a pilot: at the end of the film, he is back in the sky. Thus, through Sergei's tragedy and (somewhat incredible) salvation, we

Figure 32. "All Hail Soviet Pilots—the Proud Falcons of Our Motherland!" From E. Teiman, ed., *Stalin* (Moscow: Gosudarstvennoe izdatel'stvo politicheskoi literatury, 1939), n.p.

trace the shifting shape of the myth of the pilot in the late 1930s. Through the metaphor of sight, the film can be seen as a modification of the image of the pilot as all-seeing. Sergei implicitly becomes all-seeing only after the loss, and then the regaining, of his sight. Losing his sight, he seems initially to lose his opportunity to be a hero. In the end, however, the film values a different kind of heroism: through trial and hardship, Sergei implicitly gains consciousness. And he is rewarded by a happy ending. The pilot-hero is marked out not only by his (or her) daring, but also by skill (training) and by humility. This was the crucial admixture of Stalinist heroism during this period: after Valerii Chkalov's first long flight from Moscow to Ud Island in 1936, Stalin declared the pilot to be "a concentration of will, character, and the ability to take risks." But, he went on, "bravery and courage are only one side of heroism. The other is ability *[umenie]*" (Figure 32).[26]

Training and humility notwithstanding, however, the glorious exploits of the pilot form the structural centre of these films, and the aerial shot retains its centrality as a controlling gaze. Mikhail Kalatozov's *Valerii Chkalov* of 1941, a film that falls outside the immediate chronological scope of this book, reveals how this growing cult was to develop into a vision of the pilot as increasingly extraordinary. It celebrated Chkalov's most famous flight in 1937, across the North Pole to Vancouver, and pictured air travel as the prerogative of the few: the consolidation of the hero was part of a process of symbolic demobilization of the masses during the 1930s. The single hero—unique and extraordinary—became the representative of the nation.[27] Chkalov is pictured as brave and masterful, and these qualities differentiate him from "common" society: "If I were like everyone else," he exclaims modestly in the film, "I would not have flown in the way that I did." The famous flight over the North Pole provides the central section of the film. It forges a *put'* that is explicitly mapped from Moscow: Kalatozov intersperses aerial shots with maps that demonstrate the flight path. Chkalov's triumphant return to Moscow, after he has conquered the distance, proves that the Soviet *narod* (people) is "great and powerful *[velik i moguch]*."

The consolidation of the myth of the pilot in Soviet cinematography during the 1930s, and the emergent aesthetic of the aerial shot, marked a fundamental shift in the nature of experience that was implicitly available to the mass. Vertov's mobile camera had offered the cinematic "experience" of space to an implied mass, and the view from the train was a view accessible to the ordinary man with a suitcase. The emergence of the aerial shot, by contrast, largely separated the gaze of the pilots from the gaze of those who admired them. The air show—a key feature of the pilot films of the 1930s—made this shift explicit. For these sequences of heroic air display, the camera commonly assumed the position of the spectator on the ground, watching and admiring the performance of the hero. Films, photographs, and paintings pictured the plane from below (Figures 33 and 34). In parallel, the aerial perspective was granted to the extraordinary individual, who looked down on those who admired him and whose controlling gaze was implicitly aligned with the totalizing, heroic vision of *osvoenie*. The aerial view is that of the centre, represented through the single hero-figure. In Vertov's early use of the aerial shot, by contrast, montage dissolved the boundary between the view from below and the view from above. Both points of view were available to all.

CHANGING TRAINS: THE TOURIST GAZE OF THE 1930S

The opposition between plane and train—the aerial shot and the view from the train window—may be linked to a consideration of cinematic techniques

Figure 33. "The Soviet airplane makes regular trips over the high snowcapped peaks of the Caucasian range." From *SSSR na stroike,* 1935, no. 1: n.p.

during this period. A broad generalization might suggest that the aesthetic of the train corresponds more closely to that of montage which predominated in Soviet film of the 1920s, in which the juxtaposition of fleeting images constructed a fragmented and dynamic vision of space. The emergence of the aerial shot was linked to that of the panorama and the creation of more stable landscapes in film of the 1930s.

These two visions—montage and the panorama—correspond to the differentiation between exploration and *osvoenie*. During the 1920s, Soviet avantgarde film in particular represented the experience of seeing as dynamic and corporeal: movement through space. Vertov united cinematic vision with exploration, where the camera was a privileged means of reenvisaging space and experiencing the world anew. The Cine-eye group made explicit the equation between cinema and exploration, describing Il'ia Kopalin, in the credits of a film made in 1926, as a *kino-razvedchik* (film scout). The development of the use of this term is itself revealing; Vertov's early documentaries had no "director" but instead a single "film scout" (often Vertov himself). Toward 1925, the notion of creator/editor began to appear in the credits of *Film-Truth* editions,

Figure 34. Conquering the sky. From *SSSR na stroike,* 1935,
no. 1: front cover.

and the film scouts were reduced to the role of collectors of material. After 1926,
Vertov consistently assumed the role of "director." This shift might be seen to
mirror the more general development that we have identified above. Vertov's
early work, by refusing a single, directorial eye, offered the liberated vision of
cinematography to a wide audience: it was a gaze accessible to all. The emergence of the director reflects the increasing individualization of the cinematic
vision.

In parallel with this consolidation of the controlling gaze, the train in 1930s
cinema lost the dangerous dynamism that it had been granted in films of the
1920s. It became instead a stable space in which Soviet citizens met and con-
versed (and all too frequently sang!) as they travelled across the country. The
speed of train travel—the view from the train window—was obscured by the
creation of the train carriage as a key site of Soviet community. And the space of

the carriage itself was also transformed. In films of the 1920s, the train carriage had served as a microcosmic space for new kinds of social interconnection. In Barnet's *Girl with a Hatbox* and Protazanov's *Aelita,* for example, the train is the site of new and disconcerting social proximity and interaction. In the former, Natasha found that Igor's large and rather dirty boots crushed her hatbox, and in *Aelita,* the protagonists were disconcerted by the proximity of sneezing passengers, whose mucus seemed uncomfortably close. The symbolic "train of revolution" was revealed in these films in its practical manifestation, as a space that brought to the fore the sometimes uncomfortable realities of social change. In films of the later 1930s, by contrast, the carriage was pictured as an idyllic site of traditional values of community.[28] Views from the window became less important than the interior space of the train as a site of community, a domestic, inward-looking site. Ivan Pyr'ev's *Traktoristy* (*The Tractor Drivers,* 1939), for example, opens on a train as three young men, demobilized from the army, discuss their future plans and head to start new lives in different destinations across the territory. They meet and discuss their optimism for the future. And they do not look out of the window.

In Medvedkin's *Novaia Moskva* (*New Moscow,* 1938), similarly, the train journey to the capital acts as a social microcosm in which Moscow is the utopian destination, a powerful space-myth in the minds of the nation. The film's hero, Alesha, summoned to Moscow to demonstrate his technical prowess, sings to the assembled passengers of his dreams of the city: "I see my native capital *[rodnuiu stolitsu].*" The train carriage in films of the late 1930s was a protective microcosm from which views of the Soviet landscape appeared increasingly rarely, and increasingly framed and idealized, tracing an emergent pastoral idyll. In the draft screenplay for *New Moscow,* Medvedkin described the view from the train windows during this journey as a view of "native Russian landscapes *[rossiiskye rodnye peizazhi].*"[29] Landscape (the view) replaced space (the experience). Moreover, Medvedkin's use of the Imperial term *rossiiskii* (not *russkaia*) bears further consideration; the reemergence of *rossiiskii* as a common term under Stalinism accompanied the newly inclusive, Imperial identity. "Socialism in One Country," first articulated as early as 1924 in Stalin's article "October and Trotskii's Theory of Permanent Revolution," was explicitly directed against the vision of international revolution and the workers' International.[30] It replaced this vision of a global, Soviet space with an expanded vision of the Great Russian nationality. In Medvedkin's use, the term serves to generalize the traditional pastoral idyll, rendering it representative of a broader space and thus overcoming difference.

These views of the landscape marked an important shift in attitudes toward the territory—the emergence of what might be called a "tourist gaze."[31] *Puteshestvie po SSSR (A Journey around the USSR)*, a compilation film made in 1937 out of footage collected by Medvedkin's Film Train (see Chapter 1) between 1934 and 1937, clearly demonstrates the emergence of the tourist gaze in Soviet cinema. One part of the film, for example, provides a tour of the Ural region by electric train.[32] The intertitles that accompany the visual images have a clearly touristic tone that differentiates this from the other train films: "Now," we are told, "we will travel along the electrified railway of the Urals." The cinematic gaze is clearly structured as the gaze of the tourist: "let us look around the coal centre of the Urals!" a title enthuses. It is not an *appropriative* gaze, but rather creates a structure of distance. This view of the territory, I would suggest, developed in parallel with *osvoenie*, reifying the periphery, transforming it from a space of experience into a decorative space, implicitly viewed from the centre. In this film, the electric train is presented as the means by which to view the new Soviet territory, and in particular to admire the achievements of Soviet construction. The film pictures Soviet tourism as a curious hybrid of the old and the new, admiring the new *stroiki* (construction sites) alongside the onion-domed churches of old Russia.

The growth of tourism and accompanying reduction of the periphery to a space of leisure is further demonstrated in the 1936 film *Devushka speshit na svidanie (A Girl Hurries to a Rendezvous),* directed by Mikhail Verner. The film's point of origin—its implied centre—is located firmly in Moscow; it opens as two men head away from the city toward the Black Sea for a holiday. The film begins by establishing the central spaces of the city, admiring its widened streets, before moving to a train station. In this film, the train functions as a comic reworking of the dynamic train of earlier cinema. The speed of the moving wheels and the flashes of passing landscape, accompanied by a jaunty musical score, serve here to emphasize impending comic disaster: both men have forgotten their passports. When the protagonists arrive, the resort town of Essentuki is clearly presented as a tourist site: the spectator, in fact, "enters" through the symbolic device of a picture postcard. In the course of the film, which is a farcical comedy of mistaken identity, the city functions principally as a space of leisure. We encounter its parks and its dances, its hotels and its postcard-worthy views. There are no signs of labour in the town and no signs of construction. The peripheral space is thus configured as a playground for the centre, in the nineteenth century literary tradition of the Black Sea resorts, familiar in Chekhov's famous story "Lady with a Lapdog," among others.

Figure 35. Boat *(parokhod)* passing through a lock on the Moscow-Volga Canal (Iakhroma, near Moscow). From *Moskva rekonstriruetsia: Al'bom diagramm, toposkhem i fotografii po rekonstruktsii Moskva,* text by Viktor Shklovskii, design by A. Rodchenko and Varvara Stepanova (1937), n.p.

This shift toward the decorative in attitudes to the territory was part of a broader shift in representations of landscape during the 1930s. The transformation of the space of experience into "landscape" (the view) was part of the consolidating attitude of *osvoenie.* Travel as exploration was gradually replaced by travel as leisure, or tourism. One further means of transport, the *parokhod* (steamboat, or paddle steamer), had an important role to play in this shift, appearing in many films of the 1930s as a symbolically democratic vehicle for mass leisure travel (Figure 35). As early as 1927, in *Two Friends, Their Girlfriend, and a Model,* we see the two young heroes Makhov and Akhov building a scratch paddle boat, which enables them to continue their adventure down the river. Later in the film, the exploratory initiative of the two friends' journey across their local space is balanced by visions of leisure travel, as they relax on a boat on an afternoon day trip, singing songs and both flirting with their love interest, Dasha. In visual terms, the pace of travel offered by the boat offered an alternative relationship with the territory, allowing the landscape to be seen as a "view."

The scenes of leisure in this early film prefigured the emergence of the *parokhod* as a key site of a new kind of travel in films of the 1930s, its leisurely pace symbolically replacing the frenetic energy of the "train of the revolution." In Grigorii Alexandrov's *Volga-Volga,* most obviously, a steamboat provides the thematic centre of the film, which charts the jolly journey of Dunia and her friends along the Volga River and Volga Canal to Moscow. Even in Evgenii Cherviakov's *Zakliuchennye (The Prisoners)* of 1936, which tells a grotesquely idealized tale of the construction of the Belomor Canal by prisoners in a labour camp, the final scene of the film pictures a celebratory journey by paddle steamer down the finished canal. Again, the boat is principally a leisure space, and the views that it affords drift gently by as backdrop to human adventure. In this film, the implicit freedom of the journey by boat is contrasted with the lack of freedom marked by the journey to the north, taken by the prisoners in a closed train at the beginning of the film. Through labour, we infer, and through participation in the collective project of construction, they have won the right to leisure travel.

During the late 1930s, then, tourism and subjugation, intricately connected, increasingly emerged as the only available relationships to the territory. In film, changing modes of transport—the train, the plane, the boat—and their changing representations, echoed shifts in ways of looking at the territory, offering different relationships with the space. The train, during the 1920s, was a symbol of revolution, offering an exciting, mobile experience of the space to a mass population. In parallel, early films used the airplane as a similarly destabilized perspective. In the 1930s, by contrast, the aerial view began to express a relationship of conquest, transforming the dynamic space into a mapped, controllable territory. The train space was increasingly configured as stable, and the dynamic space of exploration was transformed into "landscape," as the tourist gaze emerged.

Chapter 6 Conquest

Сегодня пространство определяет
новую, рождающуюся психику

(Today space defines the new psychology that is being born.)
—*Aleksandr Dovzhenko*

In the final sequences of Grigorii Aleksandrov's film musical *Svetlyi put'*
(*The Radiant Path,* 1940), the heroine, Tania, takes a magical trip across
the Soviet territory in a rather smart flying convertible automobile. She
departs from Moscow on a journey that takes her across a landscape of
wide-open expanses and vertiginous mountain-scapes before returning
to earth—now not only in Moscow, but in the Moscow of the future, in
the new All-Union Exhibition.[1] This journey is Tania's reward: it marks
her transformation from humble servant girl to prize-winning weaver.
Her extraordinary achievements as a member of the labour collective
grant her, we infer, the ability—and the right—to "conquer" the territory and to overcome the quotidian limits of space and time.

Tania's journey demonstrates the emergent tourist gaze of Soviet
cinema. It compresses the diversity and scale of the territory into a

seamless single landscape. The landscape is viewed from above, controlled and domesticated by the aerial view. And in a further twist, the aerial view itself is domesticated through the curious device of the flying automobile, which functions as a rather comfortable touring machine. Tania's experience of the territory is, in many ways, a celebration of the new Stalinist geography, conflating conquest and leisure. On this dream journey, moreover, reality is suspended. Thus, it would seem that our heroine's flying car could take her anywhere at all. So where does she choose as her dream destination? Moscow. And what "world" does the magic car(pet) reveal? Her native land, of course. There is, it seems, nowhere else one would want to go.

Tania's travel choices here echo a key shift in representations of the territory during the 1930s: the Soviet Union began to represent a world in itself. The space that during the 1920s was implicitly *unbounded*—always on the point of transition into the global workers' International—was transformed into a self-contained and bounded state. The popular song "Pesnia o rodine" ("The Song of the Motherland"), written by the composer Isaak Dunaevskii for Aleksandrov's earlier film *Tsirk* (*The Circus,* 1936), assumed the role of an unofficial national anthem, effectively ousting the "Internationale" hymn. The lyrics of "The Song of the Motherland," written by the poet Vasilii Lebedev-Kumach, represented the Soviet Union as a single, unique, and increasingly glorified state: "Wide is my native land," the song begins, "I know no other country where man can breathe so freely."[2] So "wide" and diverse is the territory, the song implies, that it offers all the experiences that anyone could ever need.

The boundaries of this Soviet "world" were increasingly demarcated. The success of the "Socialism in One Country" policy depended on the fierce protection of national borders, confronting the threat of infringement both from within and from without. In 1943, in a culmination of a process of retrenchment that gained added impetus from the Second World War, the "Internationale" was officially replaced as the national anthem by the "Gimn Sovetskogo Soiuza" ("Hymn of the Soviet Union"). The new hymn emphasized the glory of a Soviet Rus', linking prerevolutionary nationality and Soviet brotherhood: "An inviolable union of free republics," it boasted: "Great Rus' has rallied forever."[3] In the course of the 1930s, the border was symbolically reconceptualized as a protective divide from the encroaching evils of the capitalist West. A cult of the border guard *(pogranichnik)* emerged, finding its apotheosis in films such as Vladimir Shneiderov's *Dzhul'bars* of 1935 and in the status of the border guard Karatsiupa ("Hero of the Soviet Union") and his dog Ingus, whose joint portrait appeared on Soviet currency from the late 1930s until 1947.[4] In

Dzhul'bars, a heroic border guard and his faithful hound combat a group of bandits in central Asia. Border insurgents *(narushitely)* were stock villains of Stalinist cinema.[5] In *Doch' rodiny (Daughter of the Motherland)* of 1937, for example, a young girl, Pasha, living on a collective farm in the borderlands uncovers treachery among those in her village. The border, in this film, is the divide between good socialist space and implicitly evil capitalist space. In *Granitsa (The Border,* 1935), directed by Mikhail Dubson, proximity to the Soviet border is an incitement to class consciousness for Jews and workers living in Poland, encouraged to cast off the shackles of oppression. Through the symbol of the border, political and moral values were encoded into territory.

HEROES: THE PERIPHERY AS ADVENTURE SPACE

The border guard was just one of a new pantheon of heroes that emerged during the 1930s. In the culture of the First Plan, the collective had been the primary force, a mass hero. Significant action took place at a microlevel; the ordinary individual, or "little man" *(malen'kii chelovek)* was implicitly conflated with the mass and thus acquired heroic status. Everybody, separately and yet collectively, was taking part in the construction of the new society, moving along the path *(put')* to socialism. The reintroduction of the *propiska* on 28 December 1932, insisting on the registration of all citizens in a single place of residence, marked a key change here—a symbolic attempt to control mobility. Although it was in practice impossible to control population movement through the 1930s (in particular during the widespread famine in the regions during 1932–33, when peasants flocked to find work in urban centres), the law nevertheless represents a key point in the transformation of visions of the Soviet space.

Propiska brought the shared project of exploration to a symbolic end. The power of mobility was symbolically removed from the "little man": henceforward, *osvoenie* was the task of the hero-adventurer. As the 1930s progressed, the collective was replaced by the individual hero, frequently identified by name. The developing myth of the labour hero personified in the record-breaking miner Aleksei Stakhanov in 1935 was part of a process of individuation that shifted the nature of mass participation in the heroics of construction.[6] The changing shape of the hero was evident in cinema, too: many films told of the vital process of "reeducation" *(perevospitanie* or *perekovka* [literally, "reforging"]) through which new, heroic, ideal Soviet citizens were formed out of the malleable raw material of the proletariat. One of the earliest examples of the

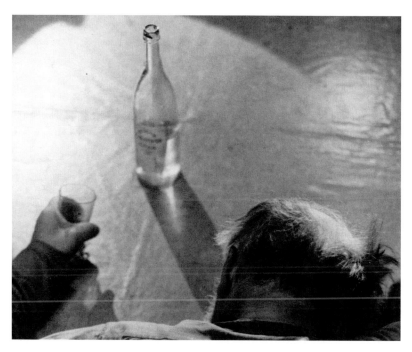

Figure 36. The reeducation of Babchenko. Film still from *Vstrechnyi* (Ermler and Iutkevich, 1932). Courtesy of B. F. I. Stills, Posters and Designs.

new heroism was provided by *Vstrechnyi* (*Counterplan*, 1932), directed by the "brigade" of Friedrikh Ermler and Sergei Iutkevich and hailed as a breakthrough in the search for a model Soviet (Stalinist) film.[7] The film's hero, Semen Babchenko, undergoes an archetypal process of reeducation, transforming himself from an inefficient, drunken old factory worker (Figure 36) into a paragon of industrial efficiency and commitment. Babchenko is just one of a collective of characters in this film, whose interwoven stories seek to present a vision of the shared experience of industrial progress, yet his transformation forms the narrative nexus of the film and prefigures many such transformations in films through the 1930s. Grigori Kozintsev and Leonid Trauberg's popular "Maksim" trilogy, for example, follows the similar transformation of the initially irresponsible, even feckless, Maksim into revolutionary hero.[8] The first film of the trilogy, *Iunost' Maksima (The Youth of Maksim)*, was made in 1934. Later in the decade, in 1938, Iutkevich's *Chelovek s ruzh'em (Man with a Gun)* recounted the (by then well-established) path to political consciousness of the simple-hearted peasant: Shadrin, forced against his will to fight for the Whites during the civil war, is drawn to Bolshevism and has a chance meeting with Lenin himself at party headquarters in St. Petersburg. Through this meeting, and through affiliation with the Bolsheviks, he gains political consciousness, and he becomes in turn a heroic spokesperson for the cause. Yet, like Babchenko, and like Maksim, he remains distinctively ordinary.

These individuals—at once "real" and remarkable—were to encapsulate the new Soviet spirit. The narratives of their lives would serve as prototypes for the Soviet ideal of progress. From the mid-1930s, however, the nature of the hero began subtly to shift. Where Babchenko and Maksim had been ordinary citizens—achievable, positive models for the "little man" to emulate—the hero of High Stalinism was increasingly extraordinary, a "superhero," distinguished by superior personal qualities. The fantastically brave and charismatic Chapaev, in the famous civil war film of the same name, was a prototype for the new mould (Figure 37). Directed by the Vasiliev brothers in 1934, *Chapaev* told the story of a natural leader of men whose energy and foresight inspired men to follow him into battle. Its hero's rough-hewn heroism signalled the emergence of the

Figure 37. Chapaev: A new mould of hero. Film still from *Chapaev* (Vasiliev brothers, 1934). Courtesy of B. F. I. Stills, Posters and Designs.

extraordinary individual as representative of Soviet greatness. Similarly, Erm-ler's two-part epic *Velikii grazhdanin* (*The Great Citizen*, 1937–39) told of the exceptional Shakhov's power to incite loyalty and of his selfless devotion to the cause. Where Chapaev, however, was sometimes dangerously unpredictable, and the film presents his encounter with the "rational" ideals of Soviet leader-ship, the "great citizen" Shakhov experiences no reeducation at all. He is excep-tional from the beginning of the film, and his virtues form the structural centre of the narrative.

The symbol of the "great citizen" was echoed in other heroes, and in a trans-formed relationship with space. As the nature of heroism altered, so the ro-mance and danger of *osvoenie* began to predominate over the practicalities of exploration. The heroism of the pilot, for example, was defined by a controlling perspective on the territory. Romantic visions of trial and conquest—the indi-vidual pitted against the elements—were conflated with the industrialization of the Second and Third Five-Year Plans. The *razvedchiki* of the 1920s were symbolically replaced by the single heroic *geolog* (geologist), romanticized in the popular song that began with the enthusiastic exhortation: "Off you go, Geologist!" The seemingly unglamorous science of geology became the stuff of adventure: one film of 1935 entitled *Zolotoe ozero* (*The Golden Lake*) pictured brave geologists searching for gold in the Altai region and battling with evil bands of gold diggers in league with a Siberian shaman. Similarly, *Lunnyi ka-men'* (*Moonstone*), produced in the same year, told of the discovery and ex-ploitation of a valuable mineral, made possible only under the Soviets.

This idealization of the scientist-adventurer was part of a broader transfor-mation of the "official adventure" genre that had emerged during the First Five-Year Plan. Where earlier tales had focused on the practicalities of exploration, seeking to disseminate ostensibly objective information about life across the territory, later films painted an increasingly romantic vision of the experience of travel. In Boris Barnet's 1935 film *U samogo sinego moria* (*By the Blue Sea*), for example, two motor mechanics encounter a series of physical and emotional trials when sent to work in a distant fishing collective in Soviet Azerbaijan. The beginning of the film makes the adventure genre overt: our heroes are nearly drowned by a storm in the Caspian Sea, and as a title portentously informs us, "for two days their young lives struggled with death." Somewhat miraculously, the "young lives" win the battle against nature and find themselves in a small boat, rescued by the inhabitants of a beautiful island. Even more miraculously, perhaps, one of the pair has managed, throughout the struggle, to retain his jaunty sailor's hat and his accordion—useful accoutrements for a brief sojourn on any semitropical paradise.

Thus begins the adventure of Alesha and Iusuf. Between them, the two men encapsulate the new Soviet "brotherhood": Alesha is blond and transparently Slavic, and Iusuf's physical appearance suggests Central Asian origin. Fetchingly attired in striped naval T-shirts, together they offer a crowd-pleasing vision of physical glamour, a kind of fetish of the healthy Soviet body. And they are perfectly framed by the idealized backdrop of the apparently tropical island in the Caspian Sea on which they find themselves. Their "desert island," however, is by no means deserted; it is, instead, the site of a small fishing collective named "The Flames of Communism" *(Ogni kommunizma)*. And it is to this collective that the young mechanics offer their services. Thus the film maintains a careful—and crucial—balance between the exotic and the practical, between the adventure of construction and its pragmatic import.

Like so many films of the 1920s and 1930s, *By the Blue Sea* is structured around a love triangle, as both men fall for a beautiful young Russian woman, Mashenka (Figure 38). Like Alesha and Iusuf, Mashenka has come to the island to participate in the process of *otkrytie*. Unfortunately, she can love neither of them, for she is already betrothed to another—a distant lover who lives "far away" on the Pacific coast (implicitly also occupied by the grand project of *osvoenie*) and to whom she must be faithful. Faced with the unassailable moral logic of this (compounded with the undoubted worthiness of their rival, who shares their commitment to the project of socialist reconstruction), and thus failed in love, Alesha and Iusuf eventually leave the island to continue their *put'*. They are, it is said, heading "home." Yet we do not know where that home is, and the film ends with an image of their boat heading to sea. Thus although the love narrative evokes a larger space, and a shared project of construction across that space, the film does not offer a clear map of the Soviet territory. It pictures, instead, a vast, amorphous (and rather appealing), adventure space.

By the Blue Sea echoed a broader shift in the representation of the relationship between traveller and native in documentary and feature films of the 1930s. The reciprocal relationship that was, rhetorically at least, the goal of the ethnographic travel films of the late 1920s was replaced by a relationship of benevolence. The principal relationships in this film are between Alesha, Iusuf, and Mashenka—that is, they are between the nonnative *outsiders* who have come to the island to bring aid and support. The native inhabitants have no significant role. And although the film does not make overt a homogenizing dynamic, the representational strategies that Barnet uses tell a somewhat different

Figure 38. Alesha, Iusuf, and Mashenka: a glamorous threesome. Film still from *U samego sinego moria* (Barnet, 1935). Courtesy of B. F. I. Stills, Posters and Designs.

story. In contrast to the robust physicality of these characters, for example, the local population is pictured as supine. The island itself is evoked in visual images that frame and exoticize the periphery as a space of adventure. The territory is configured as a "view," and its inhabitants are part of that view. Thus the "difference" of the periphery is reduced to exotica.

A similarly radial dynamic—extending influence and aid from centre to periphery—is evident in Sergei Gerasimov's 1936 adventure yarn *Semero smelykh (Seven of the Brave),* which follows the Arctic adventures of an expedition of young Komsomol members. The film's central protagonist, Il'ia Letnikov, writes an open letter calling for volunteers for a mission to establish a polar station and spend a year on an Arctic island. From the 409 volunteers who respond to his call, a select group are recruited: meteorologist, pilot, doctor, mechanic, and radio operator. Together with Letnikov himself, who is a geologist, this initial "brave six" offer a roll call of Stalinist heroic professions, tracing the emergence of a new type of professional explorer, who melds scientific expertise with youth and courage.[9] To their group is added a young ruffian who smuggles himself away with them and is eventually granted admission to their group—and thus the opportunity to become a hero himself—by becoming their cook. The narrative of the film charts an extraordinary sequence of exploits as the protagonists demonstrate their extreme bravery, surviving air crashes and avalanches and bringing medical help to the native population. The dynamic here is clear: representatives of the centre support the periphery.

The task of these representatives from the centre, ultimately, is to conquer the inhospitable periphery. In *Seven of the Brave*, as in the opening sequences of Barnet's *By the Blue Sea* and in Dovzhenko's *Aerograd,* the strength of nature is symbolically equal to that of those who conquer it. All three of these films focus, for example, on the power of the ocean. Early in *Seven of the Brave*, we see Letnikov and his comrades standing to attention on the shores of their new, inhospitable adventure space as the ocean crashes around them (Figure 39). The might of nature is conveyed through a steady camera and long, single shots. Throughout the film, the camera emphasizes the scale of the territory and the intractability of the natural elements as the protagonists pit their strengths against that of nature, struggling with snow, ice, and wind (Figure 40). Their

Figure 39. Facing the elements. Film still from *Semero smelykh* (Gerasimov, 1936). Courtesy of B. F. I. Stills, Posters and Designs.

Figure 40. Battling with nature. Film still from *Semero smelykh* (Gerasimov, 1936). Courtesy of B. F. I. Stills, Posters and Designs.

cinematic heroics echo the reality of Soviet *osvoenie:* the "Conquest of the Arctic *[zavoevanie Arktiki]*" was a key Soviet ambition, making new marks on the map of the territory, converting the hostile natural world of the polar circle into social space. Three major expeditions were made into the Arctic region, in 1932, 1933, and 1936, and in 1938, a pocket atlas of the Soviet Union dedicated an entire map to the "Conquest of the Arctic," competitively marking Soviet and foreign expeditions (Figure 41).[10] The hostile physical conditions of the north, moreover, seemed to justify increasingly aggressive vocabulary in relation to the territory: one book, for example, published in 1932 and describing an expedition around the ice-bound northern coast, was entitled *Pobezhdennoe more (The Vanquished Sea).*[11]

The transformation of the wild into the domestic, the antisocial into the social, was central to the project of *osvoenie.* Eventually, in *Seven of the Brave,* the thaw comes, and a ship arrives to carry the young pioneers back to the centre. Letnikov and the glamorous Zhenia, another member of his team, however, have fallen in love and choose to stay on the island until the following winter, vowing to transform the inhospitable north into a Soviet town, to build roads and schools, and thus to complete the process of conquest that they have be-

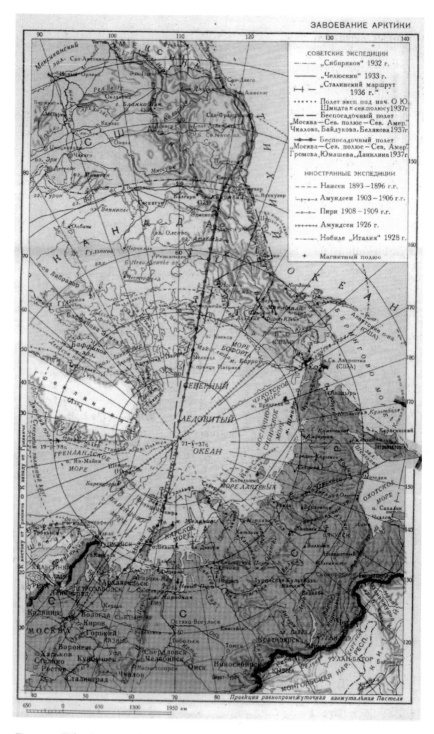

Figure 41. "The Conquest of the Arctic." From *Karmannyi atlas SSSR* (Leningrad, 1939), 5.

gun. The romantic adventures and trials of the winter are thus conflated with construction and habitation.

OSVOENIE: CONQUEST AND CONSTRUCTION

This link between conquest and construction was central to many films during the second half of the 1930s and is fundamental to the paradox of the Stalinist adventure genre. The border was a key site of adventure, yet it was also a space that must be domesticated. In Dovzhenko's *Aerograd* (1935), we witness a similar transition.[12] Set on Soviet Russia's contested border with China (the *granitsa na zamke* [locked border]),[13] the film pictures the borderland as a heroic space of conquest and trial. The key protagonists of the film are former partisan fighters who have lived their lives in the taiga, on Russia's eastern frontier, defending Russian sovereignty over the land. They epitomize a traditional vision of heroism that has folkloric overtones. They know how to "read" the taiga, deal in clear categories of honour and loyalty, and speak in language that seems to have epic, or folkloric, overtones. They are the *bogatyry* (folkloric heroes) of the eastern frontier, defending it from "aliens/strangers *[chuzhye liudi]*" and "saboteurs."

The key tension of the film is located in the relationship between one of these old heroes, Stepan Glushak, and the new Soviet world, tracing his transformation into a Soviet citizen. Glushak is, in the words of his wife, the archetypal "wanderer *[brod'ian]*" and an "old forest dog" (Figure 42). His transformation is brought about, in large part, by his son Vladimir, a pilot, for whom, the old man boasts, "ten thousand kilometres seem no distance at all" and who, with other "young people," is forging a new path to the ocean to build a "frontier city." Ultimately, through the relationship between Stepan and his son, *Aerograd* offers a reconciliation of Soviet *osvoenie* and the more traditional heroics of the partisans. In so doing, it constructs a trajectory that links past, present, and future. Both men—and implicitly both attitudes to the territory—have a role to play in the protection of the Soviet border. Glushak unearths those who seek to sabotage the Soviet project, confronting kulaks and traitors, preparing the way for the construction of the frontier city, the *aerogorod.* The knowledge of the taiga that he and his comrades offer is contrasted with the aerial views of the territory with which the film opens. The experiential knowledge of the old partisan echoes the earlier trope of exploration and *razvedka* in which the space is known through movement. The aerial view, by contrast, is that of the centre and that of *osvoenie.* It seeks to convert the taiga from a land of trial

Figure 42. Stepan Glushak: the "old wanderer." Film
still from *Aerograd* (Dovzhenko, 1935). Courtesy of
B. F. I. Stills, Posters and Designs.

and conquest into habitable and inhabited state territory. After his arrival,
Glushak's son marries and his wife gives birth to a son in the taiga, a clear indi-
cation of the transition from liminal space to social space. The task of the
younger adventurer is not just to explore, but to construct.

The Far East also provided the location for *Komsomol'sk* (1939), directed by
Gerasimov three years after *Seven of the Brave*. Like *Seven of the Brave,* this film
uses real-life adventure as its subject matter: the construction of the frontier
city Komsomol'sk on the banks of the Amur River on the eastern border, begun
in 1932, was a powerful statement of Soviet might, a key act in the project of *osvoenie*. Komsomol'sk, a "city of youth" (named after the brigades of Komsomol
members who headed to the east to build it), was to be a key outpost on the
contested border, and Gerasimov's film focuses on the energy and commitment
of the Soviet workers who construct this new, ideal frontier city. The construc-

tion is pictured as the conquest of real space and time. The reality of the inhospitable space is dissolved into a vision of a conquered, domestic territory that is the city of the future. Throughout the film, the divide between present and future, reality and projection is blurred. The heroine of the film, Natasha, travels from Moscow to join her husband, who is working on the site as an electrical engineer. When she arrives at the construction site, she is met by the young Sergei Chekanov, head of the local Komsomol, who takes her on a tour of the site and presents it to her as an imaginary city. "Here," he claims (somewhat optimistically) "will be the main street . . . here there will be fountains." As they stumble across ditches and piles of rubble, he enthusiastically paints for her a vision of the city that they will become. The divide between present and future is blurred, as Sergei proclaims: "Now we're walking along Lenin Prospect, but there's no asphalt yet." No asphalt, indeed . . . nor, apparently, is there any road at all. Such details are rendered trivial, however, as the spectator is invited to subscribe to a vision that conflates real space and utopian space. The building site *is* the Prospekt Lenina. The future is realized in the ideal of the present: it is just around the corner.

In *Komsomol'sk*, then, we witness the might of Soviet industrial power as it imposes itself upon the physical world and see a "normal" city wrought out of reluctant raw material. This battle between Soviet man and the elements—the conquest of nature—became increasingly important in representations of Soviet construction under Stalin and underpinned a growing mythologization of industry.[14] As nature was transformed, so—implicitly—was Soviet man, reconstructed as conqueror of the elements (Figure 43). Dovzhenko's film of 1932, *Ivan*, set at the Dneprostroi hydroelectric plant, marks a striking early example of this. It represents the monumentality of Soviet construction through long, apparently immobile shots in which nature, industry, and man appear to exist in atemporal harmony (Figure 44). The film begins with an extended panning shot of the *prostor*, as the camera tracks slowly along a river, following the movement of floating ice. This evocation of the impervious, relentless might of nature develops into shots that emphasize the power of the same river: the camera follows the dramatic crashing of water over rocks. Thence the film moves seamlessly to a montage of human labour, intercutting the physical muscle of the Soviet labourer with the natural might of the river. Explosions follow: this cinematic collision of human and elemental forces symbolizes the monumental ambition of the Dnepr construction project—to build a vast dam and to harness the power of the elements.

Later in *Ivan* we witness sequences of moving machines that contrast

Figure 43. "Changing nature, a person changes
himself." Publicity photograph of forced labour
and "reeducation" on the Belomor Canal. From
M. Gor'kii, L. L. Averkbakh, and S. G. Finn, eds.,
*Belomorsko-Baltiisktii kanal imeni Stalina: istoriia
stroitel'stva* (Moscow: Istoriia Fabrik i zavod, 1934), 208.

strongly with scenes familiar from earlier films such as those of Vertov. Here,
the machine is given a stability and strength that render it awe-inspiring. Such
visions of monumental grandeur brought the frantic energy of the 1920s to a
symbolic halt. Vertov's dynamic everyday, epitomized by the ceaseless movement of machines, was replaced by the static and eternal. During the 1920s, the
movement of machines had represented the collective effort of the nation,
moving continually along the *put'* toward an ideal society. The machine of the
late 1930s, by contrast, was a symbol of conquest and of an ideal already
achieved. Ivan Pyr'ev's postwar film *Skazanie o zemle sibirskoi* (*Tale of a Siberian
Land,* 1947), which falls outside the immediate time frame of this book, de-
serves mention here, as it may well represent an apotheosis of this kind of industrial mythologization, transforming the reality of construction into a vision

Figure 44. The cult of industry: building the Dneprostroi hydroelectric plant. Film still from *Ivan* (Dovzhenko, 1932). Courtesy of B. F. I. Stills, Posters and Designs.

of monumental transformation. The film's musician-hero, Andrei, who has abandoned the city and his artistic career and come to Siberia to join in the task of opening it up, composes a Siberian symphony to honour the might and beauty of his adopted homeland and performs it in the city for his former colleagues. As the symphony unfolds, the film offers images of the natural majesty of Siberia, which fuse with monumental-scale visions of the industry with which the Soviets have conquered and transformed the space. Factory chimneys rise into the clouds, smoke harmoniously blending into the sky in a vision of nature and machine united. The fusion of industry with the natural world marks, in a sense, a total domination of nature, according to which the physical world functions as a symbol of Soviet achievement. The power of nature is an index of the power that has tamed it. Vast construction projects served as metonymic indices of the vast power of Stalin (Figure 45).

This process of what might be called *stabilization* was part of a broader shift in the representation of technology. The impersonality of the machine, a symbolic *perpetuum mobile* of progress during the 1920s, was tempered by a process

Figure 45. Stalin at the Rionges plant. From E. Teiman, ed., *Stalin* (Moscow: Gosudarstvennoe izdatel'stvo politicheskoi literatury, 1939), n.p.

of humanization, a closer relationship with the human hand. The cult of the machine was replaced by a cult of the shock-worker, of individuals celebrated for their exemplary production records: this cult focused, then, not on the machine itself, but on what man or woman could achieve through the machine. In Aleksandrov's *The Radiant Path,* for example, the heroic Tania is pictured demonstrating her skills as a prize-winning weaver, skilfully handling the huge mechanized loom. Like Vertov's images of his colleague and partner Svilova, her hands working the editing equipment in *Man with a Movie Camera* (1929), images of machines increasingly featured a human hand, controlling technology (Figure 46). The machine served the body. This was, implicitly, a key Soviet achievement: in Kozintsev and Trauberg's *The Youth of Maksim,* for example, a disjunctive relationship between the body and the machine served as a symbol of prerevolutionary oppression, as an unsafe factory floor led to fatal accidents for workers. Through revolution, we understand, the worker enters a new, positive, *appropriative* relationship with the machine. During the 1930s, this relationship was often expressed as a kind of domestication of technology.

Figure 46. Taming the machine: woman and machine. From
SSSR na stroike, 1933, no. 7: n.p.

These "friendly" machines existed side by side with the magnificent, semi-
mythical machine in Soviet representations of industry. From the First Five-
Year Plan onward, countless journals and newspapers encouraged and dissemi-
nated a cult of industrialization. Chief among these was the large-format,
glossy *SSSR na stroike (USSR in Construction),* the first issue of which was produced in January 1930 by the State Publishing organization. With Iurii Pi-
atakov (Deputy Minister for Heavy Industry) as its nominal editor and an editorial team that included Maksim Gor'kii, the journal was produced monthly
and served as an illustrated glorification of industrial achievement.[15] It was
published in four languages—English, French, and German in addition to
Russian—and served to publicize abroad Soviet achievement. *USSR in Con-*

struction used still photography (often by the former Constructivist Rod-chenko) as the chief medium for the representation of industrialization, seeking to provide an "artistic representation *[khudozhestvennoe izobrazhenie]* of our construction": it acknowledged the need to aestheticize present reality.

The introductory mission statement of the first edition of *USSR in Construction* defined the task of film and photography as the provision of "a systematic reflection of the dynamics of our construction."[16] This appears, in retrospect at least, ironic: in practice, the photographic images used in the journal transformed the "dynamic" machines of construction into static, monumental temples to achievement. The journal mirrored the developing aesthetic of *osvoenie* during the first half of the 1930s, in which the grand scale began to dominate the small. It anticipated later Stalinist representations of industry and industrialization that emphasized buildings over individuals, large tasks over small. One 1930 edition, for example, glorified "the Soviet Union's capital cities" (Moscow, Kharkov, Tbilisi, Stalinabad, Ashkhabad, and Samarkand) as grand-scale public spaces.[17] In many of the journal's photographic spreads, celebrating large-scale construction projects, the photographic point of view emphasized the grandeur of industrialization. Images were clearly framed and centred, the viewpoint stable (Figure 47). The frame functioned as limit, creating a perspectivally or geometrically ordered space. In this respect, Rodchenko's involvement in the production of *USSR in Construction* is revealing: his published photographs here were in striking contrast with much of his earlier work, produced during the 1920s in collaboration with Constructivist groups and Vertov. In the earlier work, the camera was used to represent precisely the contingency and fluidity of the present moment and the process of construction. The photographic frame appeared to be a permeable limit. The camera captured fragments of a dynamic reality, emphasizing unusual perspectives and transient glimpses of a mobile world, echoing the cinematic aesthetic propounded by Vertov and the Cine-eye group. In *USSR in Construction,* by contrast, that world was pictured as static and eternal.

The monumentalization of industry during the 1930s was a symbol of the Soviet ideal realized. In 1936, Stalin announced that the USSR was no longer *na stroike* (in construction) but that it had "*been realized* [*uzhe osushchestvleno;* emphasis in original]."[18] The dynamic "open system" of cultural images during the 1920s, in which everything was in the *process* of change, was replaced by a "closed system." There was nowhere else to go, and time came to a symbolic halt.[19] Stalinist representations existed out of history and place, abstracted from context. This was echoed in a shift in filmic time. In Gerasimov's enthusi-

Figure 47. Framing the machine. From *SSSR na stroike*,
1930, no. 1: 9.

astic evocation of the future city in *Komsomol'sk*, for example, the conflation of
present and future seems to suspend historic time: the ideals of the future are
implicitly realized in the Stalinist present. The *put'* of the 1920s, characterized
by a positive dynamism, the perpetual striving toward an unrealizable goal, was
replaced by a vision of a permanently perfect present. In the words of a documentary film "newspaper" of 1933, "the good life is already no longer a dream
for us."[20]

This shift is made particularly clear in the oeuvre of Vertov—and in particular through a comparison of the 1934 film *Tri pesni o Lenine (Three Songs of
Lenin)* with his earlier work. *Three Songs of Lenin* was made in honour of the
tenth anniversary of Lenin's death and is organized as three separate "songs"
that combine to form a visual and aural elegy. In the opening sequences of the

film, the motif of the song is as a key metaphor: everywhere, the titles proclaim, people sing songs. Song (like film) is unbounded—"no one knows the authors," yet the songs are carried from settlement to settlement and country to country (Figure 48).

The pace and technique of *Three Songs of Lenin* are in striking contrast with the rapid montage of Vertov's earlier films. In the first and second songs especially, the pace of the film is strikingly slow. In the first, the camera moves deliberately around the space of a building, apparently a mosque, articulating the height and depth of the building through lengthy panning shots, moving at unexpected angles up and down the tall columns of the building before moving outside into an "Eastern" space. This vertical axis of camera movement remains important throughout the film. Later, for example, when the viewer is taken to see a factory, the camera begins at the top of a tower and moves, in a single shot, down the tower and across the façade of the building before entering the building and exploring the factory floor.

The use of this vertical spatial movement has an important effect on the film. It replaces the forward motion of the *put'*, which we associate with Vertov's earlier work, with an alternative axis. The temporal momentum of the film is not one of forward motion. Time seems to stand still. The principal movement in the film is upward—it is, implicitly, movement out of time, within the realized idyll of the present. In the third song, this hymn to the present becomes overt. In contrast to the past tense of the previous songs, which praise Lenin's glorious founding of the Soviet state, the third song moves firmly into the present tense as "we conquer *[zavoevyvaem]*." The forward march of Vertov's 1926 *Forward March, Soviet!* is replaced by the upward gaze. There is nowhere left to go, for the future is already achieved: "life has become cheerful and joyful." "If only Lenin could see our county now" an intertitle declares. The vertical axis thus articulates the end of time as movement forward and replaces it with a vertical movement that endows the present with almost mythical grandeur.[21]

The film's celebration of ambitions achieved is further manifest in an important rhetorical shift. Eight years earlier, Vertov's 1926 film *A Sixth of the World* had directed itself at the Soviet viewer with an urgent "You!" In that film, as I have suggested, the titles served as a form of interpellation, drawing peasant and worker (in all the different parts of the Soviet Union) into the collective project of the construction of socialism. In contrast, *Three Songs of Lenin* speaks not to the ordinary man or woman but *as* the ordinary man or woman: "My collective farm," the titles proclaim: "My country . . . My earth." This shift is revealing. The project of agitation and persuasion is, implicitly, completed. In-

Figure 48. "From country to country . . . From settlement to settlement." Film stills from *Three Songs of Lenin* (Vertov, 1934). Courtesy of B. F. I. Stills, Posters and Designs.

stead of a call to arms, this film is a celebration of victory. The recipient of the message has become the bearer of the message, joining in the hymn to "my" country. There is a further subtlety here, however. The use of the singular personal pronoun *moi* (my) in place of the plural *nash* (our) is specific to the first song of the trilogy. Both the second and third songs shift toward the more familiar "our" of 1930s rhetoric: "We loved him as we love our steppe." Thus, through the movement from "I" to "we," the film enacts a universalizing process that transforms the particular into the general: every "me" is part of the general "we." Difference is elided in the creation of a single, homogenous national subject.

MOSCOW: FILLING IN THE EMPTY CENTRE

Three Songs of Lenin has much in common with Vertov's later film *Lullaby.* Both films are structured as praise of the achievements of the present, in which "all paths have been opened." In both, crucially, montage is used to construct an inclusive "created geography," linking city and country, centre and periphery, factory and agriculture. In both, Moscow is given a central role, intercut with various peripheral spaces, all of which are inhabited, or conquered *(osvoen)*. The third song to Lenin, for example, begins by locating itself in Moscow, in "the great stone city," and articulates an overtly radial structure of influence (Figure 49). Moscow, as the burial place of Lenin, is the mythical centre. Where the montage of *A Sixth of the World* emphasized difference in its picture of an alternative kind of empire, the energy of these later films moves toward sameness. In *Three Songs of Lenin,* for example, comrades across the entire territory are shown mourning Lenin at the same time: through montage, Vertov is able to suggest that as the bells ring in the Kremlin, they are heard in Central Asia. "Moscow time" is national time: the entire space shares a single moment, and distance is overcome.

Vertov's metaphor of Moscow time was drawn from reality. After all, if space could be conquered, so too could time. Although Greenwich mean time had been adopted immediately after the revolution, on 1 June 1919, bringing the Soviet Union in line with international time, an edict of 16 June 1930 went one step further than that, designating *Moskovskoe vremia* (Moscow time) as a mean time for the vast nation and thereby marking the city as the temporal centre. The centralization of time symbolized by Moscow time was, in a sense, an attempt to realize, in real time and space, the simultaneity of experience represented by Vertov in *Three Songs of Lenin.* It was a drive toward homogenization.

Figure 49. Moscow: "The Great Stone City." Film stills from *Three Songs of Lenin* (Vertov, 1934). Private collection.

Placing Moscow symbolically at the centre of the space was an unambiguous rejection of the fantasies of the Urbanists and Disurbanists (see Chapter 1). By the end of the First Five-Year Plan, a restructuring of spatial hierarchies marked the effective end of the drive to the periphery. The linear, horizontal spatial formation represented by the antiurban movement was firmly rejected. In a sense, of course, this was simply an acknowledgement of reality: while Urbanists and Disurbanists alike were railing against the metropolis, the metropolis had in fact been growing inexorably. Between 1926 and 1939 the urban population grew by at least thirty million, and during the First Five-Year Plan the population of cities grew by 44 percent.[22] The major trajectory of the mobile population was, apparently, toward the city. Reconciliation with the city was thus politically pragmatic. In 1929, Nadezhda Krupskaia wrote against the Disurbanists in *Pravda,* stating that urban centres could and should function as organizing centres for the new society.[23] From October 1930, a clear campaign against the "visionary" planners was in evidence. The anti-urban ideal of "Chaianovism" (see Chapter 1) became a political crime. Eventually, Disurbanism was officially recognized as anti-Soviet: Okhitovich was excluded from the party in 1934 and eventually arrested. In 1930, one I. Chernia, a frequent spokesman of the party line in this debate, stated that "the concentration of the proletariat in a defined space . . . is *absolutely vital* in these conditions [emphasis in original]."[24] The city took centre stage.

From the early 1930s, Moscow became the focus of architectural fantasy. The battle to create the great centre—to "fill in" the centre that had been metaphorically emptied by the centrifugal spin of the 1920s and the Cultural Revolution—had begun. As the centre of the Soviet space, the chaotic urban structure of Moscow was to be remade to suit its status as the capital of the socialist world (Figure 50). In the words of Lazar Kaganovich, who was the commissar in charge of the city's reconstruction, Moscow was to become a city "worthy of the country, and worthy of the proletariat."[25] In February 1931, an open design competition for a Palace of Soviets *(Dvorets sovetov)* was proclaimed. This monumental new building was to be the centrepiece of the city, and of the nation.[26] June 1931 saw the beginning of construction of the Moscow-Volga Canal, and work on the Moscow metro began in 1932.

In March 1932, a committee was appointed to organize the preparation of a master plan for the reconstruction of the city. Competing visions of the city were tested and debated over several years until finally, a party-government resolution of 10 July 1935 revealed the shape of the new city: an enormous, metropolitan centre organized on radial principles, with Red Square as its centre (Fig-

Figure 50. "We are mobilizing all forces to fulfil the Stalin Plan for the reconstruction of Moscow." Stalin and Kaganovich above the city. From *Moskva rekonstriruetsia: Al'bom diagramm, toposkhem i fotografii po rekonstruktsii Moskva,* text by Viktor Shklovskii, design by A. Rodchenko and Varvara Stepanova (1937), n.p.

ures 51 and 52). The General Plan echoed the historical, radial structure of Moscow, with its emphasis on a central point: a utopian node or omphalos.[27] But it was otherwise to alter the cityscape entirely, transforming the narrow streets of the old centre into vast boulevards or parade routes *(magistrales),* sweeping past imposing façades. The scale (or lack of scale) of the plan is testament to its monumental ambitions: if scaled, Gor'kii Street would in places run to 125 metres in width.

In this vision of Stalinist Moscow, the ordering principle of space was transformed. The monumental space of the city was structured not according to use, but as façade. It was an ideologically constructed *public* space, designed to accommodate the displays of citizenship and participation upon which the new society was founded. The chaos and dynamism that had characterized the urban experience during the 1920s were to be eradicated (Figure 53). The area extending from Red Square to the projected Palace of Soviets was the centre of this performance space, and, after a long competition, a choice was made for the design of the palace itself (Figure 54). Awe-inspiring in its scale and solidity,

Figure 51. Cover of the published book *General Plan for the Reconstruction of Moscow (General'nyi plan Moskvy)* (Moscow: Moskovskii rabochii, 1936).

the proposed building was crowned by an enormous statue of Lenin, emphasizing the visual dominance of the building as the panoptic centre of the newly organized space. The symbolism here was clear: the great departed leader was afforded a uniquely powerful gaze from the centre, out across the entire territory.

Lenin's anticipated visual dominance over the city, and the nation as a whole, echoed Moscow's symbolic dominance over the territory. The city's new transportation systems offered an alternative conception of travel that emphasized the majesty of Soviet power, *conquering* the space.[28] Symbolically at the centre of the national territory, Moscow was to be the "port of five seas," and a documentary film of that name produced in 1933 celebrated this monumental ambition (Figures 55, 56, and 57). The Moscow-Volga Canal, opened in 1935, was the

Figure 52. "Scheme for the planning of Moscow" (The General Plan, 1935). Private collection.

first of a proposed network of canals that would link the capital to all of the five seas and oceans surrounding the enormous territory. Thus the Bolsheviks would, it was proclaimed, correct the "error of nature" that had left the capital "deprived of a powerful water artery" (Figure 58).[29] The opening of the Moscow-Volga Canal was heralded by a film directed by Vladimir Erofeev entitled *Put' otkryt (The Way Is Open),* which lingered lovingly over the classical elegance of the magnificent locks that were built along the length of the canal and admired the monumental statues that presided over the canal's entrance into the capital.

Figure 53. Eradicating urban chaos. The foldback section of the photographs reveals the chaos of the city before reconstruction. From *Moskva rekonstriruetsia: Al'bom diagramm, toposkhem i fotografii po rekonstruktsii Moskva,* text by Viktor Shklovskii, design by A. Rodchenko and Varvara Stepanova (1937), n.p.

Figure 54. Model of the Palace of Soviets. Final approved
project by Vladimir Gel'freikh and Vladimir Shchuko.
Photograph courtesy of Jana Howlett. Private collection.

The classical architecture of the canal system was echoed in the magnificence
of the Moscow metro, the opening of which was a high point in the city's grand
transformation. The metro was a defiant statement of Soviet mastery not only
over space *above* ground but below ground as well, celebrated as the workers'
underground kingdom. It was much more than an urban transport system: it
was a national myth, and even those unlikely ever to travel on it were invited to
rejoice in the simple fact of its existence. Throughout the decade, the transformation of Moscow was the subject of huge propaganda campaigns: everyone
was to be proud of the centre and to participate symbolically in its reconstruction. In the words of a pamphlet produced in celebration of the reconstruction,

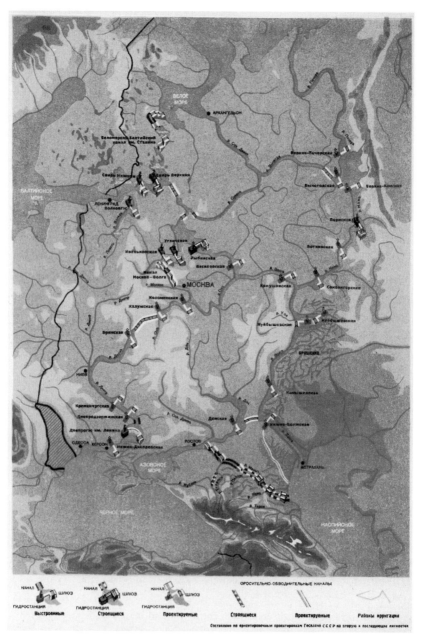

Figure 55. "Moscow—Port of Five Seas." From *Moskva rekonstriruetsia: Al'bom diagramm, toposkhem i fotografii po rekonstruktsii Moskva,* text by Viktor Shklovskii, design by A. Rodchenko and Varvara Stepanova (1937), n.p.

Figure 56. Creating the canal network. Film still from *Port piati morei* (Lemberg, 1933). Private collection.

Figure 57. A monumental dam on the new canal system. Film still from *Port piati morei* (Lemberg, 1933). Private collection.

Figure 58. Building the Moscow-Volga Canal. Photograph
courtesy of Jana Howlett. Private collection.

"as Moscow is rebuilt, so the whole country is rebuilt."[30] In the journal *Around
the World,* weekly stories charted the rebuilding of the city.[31] In parallel, the infrastructural project of *radiofikatsiia* (radiofication), installing radio lines across
the nation since the early 1920s, ensured that the voice of Moscow spoke out
across the territory, offering symbolic participation—through the centre—in
the collective life of the nation. In the words of a school geography text of 1936,
Moscow was the "centre of the Soviet rail network . . . and also the centre of the
radio and air networks" and was soon to become "the greatest city in the
world."[32]

The geography of Stalinist films reflected this centralization of the national
space. Aleksandrov's *The Radiant Path,* for example, opens to its heroine doing
the housework as the voice of Moscow ("Moscow talking" *[govorit Moskva]*) in-
structs her in daily exercise. Moscow time regulates Tania's day. In *Seven of the
Brave,* the protagonists' adventure is anchored by radio contact to Moscow,

which functions as a guarantor of safety and order. As both symbol and reality, Moscow was rebuilt. It became the narrative telos of socialist Realism. Inhabitants of the provinces dreamed of a journey to Moscow, and this journey frequently functioned as the triumphant finale of cinematic narrative—it was the ultimate reward, granted to model citizens for the overfulfilment of production targets. Events at the periphery found justification in recognition from the centre. The train in 1930s cinema had either its origin in or its destination as Moscow, firmly consolidated at the centre of the national space.

The cinematic city itself was mapped through grandiose central spaces, in particular the key area around the Kremlin, Red Square, and the new Moscow hotel. Alexandrov's *Tsirk* (1936), for example, centred on the view of the Kremlin from the heroine's window in the hotel Moskva. As the construction of the Palace of Soviets failed to materialize during the late 1930s, this area was increasingly configured as the grand centre of the city: it was the subject of Iurii Pimenov's famous painting of 1937 "Novaia Moskva" ("New Moscow," Figure 59), which glamorized the new capital. In Aleksandrov's *Volga-Volga* (1938), the arrival of the barge carrying the heroine Dunia Petrova and her group of folksingers to Moscow offered an alternative view of the capital, approached along the Moscow-Volga Canal and then along the Moscow River. The boat travels through magnificent locks, arriving at the grandiose "river station" *(rechnoi vokzal),* which formed a key point of entrance to the city (Figure 60). From the decks of the barge, the travellers are afforded marvellous views of their capital. Dunia's journey to the city along the canal exemplifies how the Stalinist territory was pictured as knowable and mapped: even the waterways have clear road (river) signs at their junctions that guide the way through the territory before eventually announcing one's arrival at Moscow. The adventurous expedition offered to the *razvedchiki* of the First Five-Year Plan is here domesticated into a mere excursion.

Thus the lived city of the 1920s was transformed into a city that was on display, framed for an admiring audience.[33] Documentary films of Moscow during the 1930s make this transformation clear, presenting the city as a stable, framed, and monumental space. Boris Nebylitskii's trilogy of city films, for example—*Moskva* (1937), *Nasha Moskva* (*Our Moscow,* 1938), and *Moskva segodnia* (*Moscow Today,* 1944)—indicate a broad representational shift. Gone was the dynamic urban space of Barnet's *House on Trubnaia Square* or of Vertov's *Forward March, Soviet!* In its place, Moscow emerges as a visible, public space in which collective behaviour was prescribed. It is surely significant, moreover, that *The Devil's Wheel* and *Bed and Sofa,* films that pictured the city (Leningrad

Figure 59. The glamour of the capital. *Novaia Moskva* (Pimenov, 1937). Courtesy of the State Tret'iakov Gallery, Moscow.

and Moscow, respectively) as a fluid, transgressive space, were banned in 1936.[34] The nature of the urban centre was transformed.

One of the most interesting films of or about Moscow during the 1930s was made by the former director of the Film Train, Aleksandr Medvedkin. Medvedkin's *Novaia Moskva (New Moscow)* of 1938 is ostensibly a paean to the reconstruction of Moscow. The opening sequences of the film are firmly implanted within the dominant spatial hierarchies of the Soviet Union: in a rural setting, "three thousand kilometres from Moscow," echoes of modernization are felt: a man is having his beard cut off (a symbol of modernization since Peter the Great), and a hydroelectric power station is to be built by a young Soviet-style hero, Alesha. In addition, Alesha has made a "moving" scale model of Moscow and is now headed to the city with his grandmother to exhibit it. His honour is the pride of the village: the periphery defines itself according to recognition from the centre.

Figure 60. Arriving at the *Rechnoi Vokzal* (River Station), Moscow. From *Sovetskaia arkhitektura za XXX let RSFSR* (Moscow: Iszatel'stvo akademii arkhitektury SSSR, 1950), n.p.

A thematics of urban space orders the narrative of *New Moscow:* it is not only *in* the city, it is *about* the city. Alesha's "living" moving model of Moscow functions as a *mise-en-abîme* of a Moscow that, quite literally, *moves,* forcibly propelled into its great transformation. The arrival in Moscow of Alesha and his grandmother (together with their new friend Olga, a swineherd) takes place within familiar urban settings, the mythical centre of the city. On arrival, the grandmother is taken by car on a route that reveals the Bol'shoi theatre and key central areas: the sites of the monumental centre in construction, revealing a cityscape laid out for a tourist gaze.

In contrast with the static urban façades that confront the eye here, however, trolley buses and pedestrians crossing the frame create a sense of dynamism and metropolitan energy. Medvedkin emphasizes fluidity and contingency over the monumentality of the public sphere, offering a picture of lived space that contrasts with the monumental space common to later Socialist Realist films. This Moscow is fluid and chaotic and as such recalls the *bytovye* films of the 1920s.

The dynamism of this city, however, is more extreme and is rooted in a particular historical reality. Moscow is literally made mobile by the film—it is represented in the very process of transformation. An artist, Fedia, is trying to paint a scene of Moscow but is unable to do so because the cityscape is changing before his eyes. Buildings are pulled down before he has a chance to "fix" them in paint, and he is reduced to trying to capture "the Moscow that is disappearing [ukhodiashchaia Moskva]." "I only need two days!" he cries desperately, but the buildings move as he paints them. Elsewhere, two women are at home, when suddenly buildings move outside their window. It is, it turns out, their apartment block that is moving, lifted and carried to an alternative location.

This apparent fantasy was founded in reality: during the rebuilding of Gor'kii Street, in accordance with the grand ambitions of the General Plan, more than fifty buildings were quite literally moved to facilitate the widening of the street and the creation of a unified façade (Figures 61 and 62).[35] The publicity that these removals acquired was unprecedented, celebrating the power of Stalinist Russia to, quite literally, remake the world and create a new landscape. Another film of 1939, *Shumi, gorodok (Cause a Stir, Little Town),* showed a small regional town outside Moscow trying to emulate the capital. They, too, want to transform their townscape by moving whole buildings, asserting that "if Moscow can do it, so can we." Moscow, as always, was a model for national endeavour, and its reality was more fantastic than any imagination could dream up. In Medvedkin's city, however, this extraordinary reality was curiously normalized: the moving houses that initially shock the two female inhabitants do not interrupt conversation for long, merely requiring that they protect houseplants from damage.

Medvedkin's most direct engagement with the myth of the new Moscow takes place toward the end of the film, when Alesha and his partners are gathered to present their cinematic vision of the future capital to an assembled audience of dignitaries. A disaster occurs: the film is placed in the projector the wrong way, and instead of the glorious achievements of socialism rising from the ruins of old Moscow, the audience sees these great buildings collapsing and old Moscow returning. Demolished cathedrals spring up from the rubble and the Soviet ideal is destroyed. The audience is hysterical with laughter; Alesha is frantic. Finally, however, the situation is saved, and the film is put in correctly. Zoia, Alesha's newfound love (whom he has met in the capital), introduces the film as it should be: "Fulfilling the Stalin plan for the reconstruction of Moscow," she announces proudly, "Moscow Bolsheviks have carried out a colossal task. Our beloved Moscow has been transformed into the most magnificent

Figure 61. Widening Moscow's streets. From *Moskva rekonstriruetsia: Al'bom diagramm, toposkhem i fotografii po rekonstruktsii Moskva,* text by Viktor Shklovskii, design by A. Rodchenko and Varvara Stepanova (1937), n.p.

Figure 62. Plan showing the widening of Gor'kii Street and other central Moscow streets. From *Moskva rekonstriruetsia: Al'bom diagramm, toposkhem i fotografii po rekonstruktsii Moskva,* text by Viktor Shklovskii, design by A. Rodchenko and Varvara Stepanova (1937), n.p.

capital. Great Stalin made this plan for reconstruction happen. . . . Look what we have done to the town in the past three years alone." Accompanied by Zoia's words, the image of old Moscow, wooden and haphazard, is transformed. Gor'kii Street is widened, houses moved, bridges built, new canals filled with water. This, it is claimed, is the Moscow of "today."

Then follows a vision of Moscow *as it will be:* the present is blurred with the future, as the great work of construction exists as history in the making. New residential areas will spring up, connected by an ever-expanding metro, with new rail routes cross the city and territory. The decorated city will acquire a "fairy-tale beauty," conflating fantasy and reality. And finally, the new Palace of Soviets, rising from a newly constructed series of magistrales and public squares, looms into the sky as planes fly overhead (Figure 63). This was a controlling vision of space in which, as Medvedkin wrote in the screenplay for the film, "Moscow—new, shining, pure and limitless—stretches out to the horizon."[36]

This majestic vision came too late for the censors, however. The film was banned before its release, accused of weak dramaturgy and an excess of directorial fantasy.[37] It would seem that the striking image of the socialist utopia collapsing, the transformation of the centre into periphery, the capital into provincial town, was enough to condemn the film. In fact, Medvedkin's ironic subversion of the myth of Moscow's monumental public space is consistent throughout the film. Three Moscow spaces figure: the "central" area, the metro, and the space of the first All-Union Agricultural Exhibition. All are transformed into sites of chaos, disorientation, and adventure. The space of the exhibition in particular fulfils a curious function. Much of the film takes place on "Carnival Night," a title emblazoned by lights (electrical power) above the city skyline (the heads of Lenin and Stalin are also emblazoned in these *lampochki Il'icha*). Within the film's narrative, the exhibition space functions as a classical liminal site of carnival, in which masks and costumes permit transgression and shifting identity. Zoia cannot tell her two suitors (of whom Alesha is one) apart as both are dressed as white bears; Alesha's grandmother is lost and found. Chaos reigns. We are reminded of Mikhail Bakhtin's conception of *carnival* (in literary genres) as a transgressive and subversive site of pleasure, where "centrifugal" forces are dominant.[38] For Medvedkin, the exhibition space offered an alternative vision of space from that presented by the monumental public sphere of central Moscow.

In giving the exhibition space a starring role in his film, Medvedkin was by no means unique. The first agricultural exhibition of 1923 had been the subject of a documentary film by Vertov's Cine-eyes group (the seventeenth *Film-Truth*); it emphasized the role of the exhibition in achieving the *smychka* and stressed the involvement of all the peoples of the Soviet Union in the great process of transformation. It also included an extraordinarily detailed animated map of the exhibition and shot of all pavilions. In 1941, Ivan Pyr'ev's *Svinarka i*

Figure 63. Alesha's film of "Moscow as it will be." Film stills from *Novaia Moskva* (Medvedkin, 1938). Private collection.

pastkukh (The Swineherd and the Shepherd)—starring, like *New Moscow,* a glamorous and worthy young swineherd(ess)—used the exhibition as a meeting place, the site of a Romantic encounter between citizens from opposite ends of the Soviet territory. As such it maintained Vertov's image of the exhibition as a space of interconnection but transformed that *smychka* into a romantic encounter. Moscow enables the encounter: it is the central and unifying space of a diverse territory. The exhibition compressed and contained the diversity of the territory—and of the "Union"—within its boundaries, as a simulacrum of the real space of the nation.[39] Tania's magical journey in *The Radiant Path* ends, revealingly, not in the traditional centre of the city, but at the All-Union Exhibition itself: as such, it is a fitting end to her leisurely voyage of visual *osvoenie.*

RURAL IDYLLS: THE PERIPHERY TAMED

Although the thematic focus of *New Moscow* is, obviously, the city, its second key space is Alesha's village, which he is to transform by the construction of a majestic hydroelectric power station. The central love story between Alesha and Zoia founders on a confrontation of centre and periphery. While Zoia wishes never to leave Moscow (the perfect urban space), Alesha will not stay: he is bound to return to the village, where his technical skills are much needed. A happy ending is achieved when Zoia, equipped with "ladies'" swamp boots (difficult to find in Moscow department stores, it seems), finally decides to follow Alesha "as far as the edge *[krai].*"[40] She is too late to join him at the station, however, and tragedy is only just averted by new technology (after all, "what are planes for?") such that she is able to arrive at the village (now a construction site) before him. Her journey is tracked by aerial shots of the vast and empty Soviet landscape, and her arrival at the periphery is framed within the rhetoric of *osvoenie*: "beyond the river," a title says, "a beautiful little socialist town was developing."

The myth of the centre, after all, depended on an equally clearly articulated myth of the periphery, or province. As the centre was consolidated, so the glories of the *prostor* were increasingly represented within an idealized framework. Images of the periphery were filtered through the centre. In *Tale of a Siberian Land,* for example, Andrei's Siberian symphony is performed in the city. In *Volga-Volga,* Dunia composes a song about the glories of the Volga River and takes it to Moscow. As the barge enters the city, everybody seems to be singing about the glories of the province. A clear axis of centre-periphery relations is thus established. The real space of the province is transformed into a symbolic image bank through which the centre is consolidated and Soviet identity constructed.

Yet, as *New Moscow* makes clear, the real work of *osvoenie* was to be done beyond the capital, in the farthest reaches of the *prostor*. Siberia, in particular, occupied a key place in a growing mythology of the periphery. Konstantin Iudin's 1939 film *Devushka s kharakterom (A Girl with Character)* offered a clear statement of an axis that ran from Moscow to the romantic plains of Siberia. Its heroine, Katia, a young woman from Siberia, sets off to her local administrative centre to file a complaint. By accident, through a case of mistaken identity, she finds herself on a nonstop train to Moscow and decides to take her complaint there instead. Waiting for the complaints procedure to be resolved, she takes on work in the city, first in a fur boutique and later in a record factory. Never fully in thrall to the capital, however, she serves instead as a voice of the periphery, extolling the virtues of Siberia, where landscape and people are "strong and beautiful." Such is her zealous enthusiasm for the place that she induces many young women she encounters to head off on the *put' na Vostok* (the journey to the East) in search of husbands. The final scene in the film shows Katia and her band of converts leaving Moscow by train, headed for home, and singing songs that extol the beauty of Siberia.

In contrast to the journey to Moscow, this film pictured a trajectory out of the city: the *put' na Vostok*.[41] This journey to the periphery was a reworking of the populist movement "to the people" during the nineteenth century.[42] And like the Populists, *A Girl with Character* mythologized the periphery as the site and source of an elusive "authenticity" or good life, which served ultimately to consolidate the centre. Like Pyr'ev's *A Tale of a Siberian Land,* in which Andrei's experience of the "journey to the East" was majestically repackaged as a symphony for the urban centre, here Siberia was extolled as the provider of good husbands for Moscow girls. The film pictured a clear axis from monumental centre to beautiful natural landscape, or site of adventure. The centre was defined by its hold over the territory. Other spaces—the ordinary space of exploration that was open to all during the 1920s—were symbolically elided.

This mythologization of the periphery went hand in hand with an idealization of the village in the second half of the 1930s, and with the creation of what might be called a Stalinist "pastoral." The changing shape of the village in cultural production during the 1920s and 1930s reveals complex and fluctuating attitudes to the peasantry. During the 1920s, cinematic images had focused on exploring village life, exposing backwardness and neglect. The village was the breeding ground of what Lenin called the "remnants *[ostatki]*" of old-Russian backwardness, and the very mystery of the peasant that, in the nineteenth century, had represented the "mystery" of the Russian soul was reconfigured as an obstacle to progress.[43] In symbolic terms, the village was dark and awaited the illumination—both metaphorical and practical—of electrification, and of Soviet enlightenment *(prosveshchenie)*. Vertov's twenty-first *Film-Truth,* produced in 1924, encapsulates this view of the village, showing village life to be removed from socialism, calling for urgent transformation.

Collectivization, initiated in 1928, was a huge-scale drive to illuminate the dark corners of peasant Russia and to transform the peasantry into the proletariat (see Chapter 1). It sought to replace the village by the collective farm *(kolkhoz).* In the course of the 1930s, a new, idealized vision of the (collectivized) village emerged. Sheila Fitzpatrick describes this idealized *kolkhoz* as a "Potemkin village": describing the world not as it was, but as it would be. It was, she points out, an invention of propaganda, which existed side by side with the reality of the hungry, drab, and demoralized villages of the 1930s.[44] Film had a key part to play in the creation of this Potemkin village. In the films of the First Plan, many documentaries and features showed the new village emerging out of the dark, neglected corners of the Soviet space, contrasting visions of the villages before and after collectivization. Eisenstein and Alexandrov's 1928 film *General'naia liniia (The General Line),* for example, traced the transformation of a village from a sinister, backward space into a model collective farm, in which machine and man work in harmony—a transformation expressed visually as a movement from darkness into light.

Toward the end of the First Plan, the "ideal" collective farm was increasingly represented as a dream realized, and the new village became a common setting for feature film. In this respect, *Derevnia (The Village),* a feature-length documentary produced in 1930 by Il'ia Kopalin (former member of Vertov's Cine-eye group), marked a transitional point.[45] In it, a mix of "real" and "idyll" demonstrated the emerging fictionalization of the collectivization process. A title ostentatiously proclaims that the film is "built from documentary material, recorded in the ordinary conditions of the village" and that the collective farm represented is—as the subtitle of the film notes—"typical of many." Where many earlier documentary films emphasized *local* identity (see Chapter 1), here specificity is reduced to archetype, and the "documentary" images of the film provide the framework for a developing myth of rural life. Kopalin blends "real" images of the backwardness and decay with which collectivization has to struggle with the developing symbolism of the rural idyll, in which white-shirted peasants march across wide panoramas of the Russian landscape (dotted with birch forests and wide rivers). Traditional folk songs provide a perpetual backdrop. The propagandistic representational process is explicit: "See how we live!" a title announces. The ravaged Soviet countryside is transformed into a harmonious vision of a nurturing earth in which the human body and nature work together.

By the mid-1930s, this new vision of the village was consolidated as an idealized site of the new rural community. In a sense, this marked a return to the myth of the provincial idyll, familiar in nineteenth-century literature and visual art. The Russian village was traditionally the locus of cultural values of *narodnost'* (an almost untranslatable term that locates "national" identity in the *narod* [people, or folk]) and idealism: the peasant is blessed with the elusive *russkaia dusha* (Russian soul), and the village is the site of a lost provincial idyll.[46] In the Soviet version of the idyll, these values were once again evoked, but within a new framework. Alesha's village in *New Moscow,* for example, is a revealing hybrid of old and new—at once a repository of traditional, implicitly "old-Russian" values of community and simplicity and a rapidly modernizing workers' settlement *(poselok)* that exemplifies the power of Soviet *osvoenie.* The emergence of the village idyll was marked also by the appearance of landscape. The village was commonly situated within a pastoral, "Russian" landscape, identified by wide-open spaces (the *prostor*), birch trees, and (invariably) a river. The iconography of this Soviet-Russian landscape seems to owe much to the nineteenth-century landscapes of painters such as Ivan Shishkin and the other *Peredvizhniki* (itinerant) painters who sought in rural Russia an image of national essence. It was the creation, in effect, of a single, archetypal landscape, which compressed the problematic diversity of the territory into a universal backdrop.

The emergence of landscape in Soviet cinema marked, moreover, an important shift in attitudes to the national space—what Bakhtin might describe as a rupture between space and action. Tracing a history of literary genre according to the representation of space and time (the "chronotope"), Bakhtin suggests that the appearance of landscape in textual description meant that "nature itself ceased to be a living participant in the events of life." Space, formally "active," became "horizon"(seen) and background (setting). Nature was reduced to "picturesque remnants." In Bakhtin's words, "Then nature became, by and large, a 'setting for action,' its backdrop; it was turned into landscape."[47] In the

Soviet context, the emergence of landscape marked the transformation of space into "background." As such, it accompanied the shift from exploration to *osvoenie*. The space of exploration and experience that had predominated during the 1920s and into the First Plan was reconfigured as knowable and controllable. It became a "view." And the simple-hearted peasant was part of that view, mapped into the landscape. The relationship between the individual and space was transformed. Films of the 1920s had eschewed landscape in favour of representing a physical experience of space, the *appropriation* of that space. With the development of the pastoral idyll, the "little man" was increasingly represented as a decorative figure on the new Stalinist landscape.

In parallel, what might be called a "folklorization" of the village took place in Stalinist cinema during the second half of the 1930s, exemplified in the film musicals of Aleksandrov and Pyr'ev, in which Soviet villagers uniformly danced and sang their way through a realized utopia. Aleksandrov's *Volga-Volga* (Figure 64) and Pyr'ev's *Bogataia nevesta* (*The Rich Bride*, 1937) epitomize this genre: the ideal collective farm was at once an efficient Soviet agricultural producer and the locus of "authentic" national identity, expressed in colourful "folk" costumes and national dances and song. The dark image of the peasant as representative of the uncontrollable and unknown was transformed; the new countryside was peopled by simple, pure folk who overfulfilled agricultural quotas and amused themselves in the evening with folk dances. In Pyr'ev's *The Tractor Drivers,* for example, farm workers sing songs that simultaneously glorify the Russian countryside and Soviet might as they rhythmically scythe the fields. The extraordinary personal qualities of the hero of the film are guaranteed by his ability to dance the traditional Cossack dance better than his peers.[48]

The clear-cut moral categories of folklore were also a useful foundation for the simple messages of Stalinist propaganda. In contrast to this ideal peasant, for example, some films offered a polar opposite in the form of the kulak. The darker side of peasant traditionalism was exaggerated into a trope of anti-Sovietness: those who opposed collectivization were depicted as greedy, obscurantist, and often simply evil. In Ermler's rural melodrama of 1934, *Krest'iane* (*The Peasants),* greed and selfishness bring a young kulak to murder his pregnant wife when she, infected by Soviet ideals, dreams of raising their baby in a collective. In less sinister but no less striking terms, Medvedkin's extraordinary comedy of 1935, *Schast'e (Happiness),* offered a clear dichotomy of kulak and collective farm worker. Ostensibly a satire on the difficulties the peasant faces in abandoning dreams of wealth upon entering the Soviet system, *Happiness*

Figure 64. Singing Sovietness. Advertising still from *Volga-Volga* (Alexandrov, 1938).
Courtesy of B. F. I. Stills, Posters and Designs.

traced the transformation of its hero, Khmyr', from hapless peasant into model
member of his collective.[49]

Medvedkin made two feature films before *New Moscow* and both use a semi-
folkloric rural space as their setting. His use of folkloric archetypes stands, however, in stark contrast to the hybrid "pastoral" of other films. In *Happiness,* the
folkloric tradition is evident in the establishment of location: it is set in a name-
less rural space that is not positioned within geographical space. This lack of
concrete location is typical of the folkloric genre. The Russian folktale habitu-
ally opens with an unequivocal statement of the refusal to name its space: "In
some kingdom, in some nation," etc.[50] Folkloric space is unmapped: it is a
space of action; and it is emphatically not "landscape." As the folkloric theorist
Vladimir Propp wrote in his structuralist account of the folktale: "There is no
attempt to describe landscape. Forest, river, sea, steppes and city walls are men-
tioned when the hero jumps over or crosses them, but the narrator is indiffer-
ent to the beauty of the landscape."[51] The space of *Happiness* is unmapped, and
it exists only as a space of action. In contrast to the pastoral aesthetic of Pyr'ev's

agricultural musicals, for example, in this film there are no "views," and there is no landscape. Rejecting the "view," Medvedkin offers a more active relationship between the individual and space. In addition, the film reimagines the pastoral as the site of the absurd and extraordinary. The appearance of the Baba Iaga–like figure of the local witch and the archetypal corrupt clergy of Russian *bytovoi fol'klor* (folklore of the everyday), for example, serve to undermine the pastoral perfection of the rural idyll.[52]

This reimagining of the Stalinist pastoral was continued in Medvedkin's second film, *Chudesnitsa* (*The Miracle Worker*, 1936). Here, he re-created the apparently static folkloric space of *Happiness* but adorned it this time with greater attention to landscape: the film opens with a pastoral and archetypal scene of birch trees and fields. The folkloric space of the film was thus situated within the pastoral aesthetic of the 1930s and inflected by it. In addition, *The Miracle Worker* was Medvedkin's first sound film, and as such aired many of the folk ballads that became representative of the pastoral idyll. The film is set in a collective farm, which is in a relationship of "socialist competition" *(sorevnovanie)* with its neighbouring farm. Within this ostensible subscription to the norms of the Stalinist narrative, and its imaginary geography, however, the film maintained elements of the absurd.

The "folklorization" of the village in Stalinist film of the late 1930s was, in effect, a sanitization of the reality of rural life. It is here that the particularity of the Medvedkin vision was crucial. In *Happiness* and, to a lesser extent, in *The Miracle Worker*, he debunked the region as site of organic Russianness, creating instead a vision of the periphery as the site of the peculiar and particular. Medvedkin's folklore was a popular folklore, sharply differentiated from the political manipulation of the genre, which sought to appropriate regional and folkloric space to a centralized and centralizing structure. As such, it stood outside the project of Stalinist "mapping"—indeed, it can be seen as a rejection of it. After all, the use of folkloric archetypes and decoration in Stalinist culture was, in many ways, a transformation—even a deformation—of the coordinates of early Russian folklore. In parallel with the exoticization of ethnic otherness, which reduced real difference to its cipher, the folklorization of the collectivized village was a means of domesticating the "ungraspable." It tamed the obstreperous peasant and framed the vast *prostor* as a picturesque landscape. But it rejected the space and time of the folkloric world picture, and it is this that Medvedkin's films sought to retain.

The implications of these parallel and opposing folkloric visions are far-reaching. In 1937, Bakhtin wrote of the spatiotemporal coordinates of folkloric texts. Written just as the Stalinist folk-pastoral hybrid was consolidated, his observations seem to offer a curious repudiation of that false folklore, and a commentary on the shifting shapes of Soviet time and space. Folkloric time, Bakhtin suggests, "is a time maximally tensed toward the future." In it, "all labour processes are aimed forward" and characterized by growth and production. The present moment is defined by a "general striving ahead," but time itself is not divided into the precise categories of present, past, and future. In place of these temporal categories the folkloric chronotope offers a "time that is profoundly spatial and concrete."[53] It is lived in the present, embedded in the experience of space.

This description of folkloric time and space seems to echo my description of the early Soviet imaginary geography. During the 1920s and into the First Plan, Soviet time had been "maximally tensed toward the future." Past, present, and future were fused in productive momentum: the dynamism of the present was expressed in a trope of mobility, which sought to create a new relationship between the individual and space. The early Soviet *put'* was the primary symbol of progress defined not by its end goal (which was by definition never reached) but by perpetual movement. And this enacted an *appropriation* of space for the ordinary man and woman. In Stalin's Russia, by contrast, the end goal was, rhetorically at least, reached, and utopia was realized *(osushchestvleno)*. This demanded a reenvisaging of the nature of the *put'* and, in parallel, a rethinking of the nature of spatiotemporal experience. Through the microcosm of the transformation of folkloric time and space, we have a glimpse of how this change took place. As the folkloric space of experience was replaced by a folk "landscape," the dynamic of exploration came to a symbolic end.

Afterword Mapped?

исследование мира всё равно
что творчество нового мира

(The investigation of the world is the same as the creation of a new world.)
—*Andrei Platonov*

The old Soviet passport is a document of "hyphenated" identity. With categories of citizenship (of the Soviet Union), nationality (the infamous "fifth point" that insisted on a statement of "ethnic" origin and that included the category of "Jew"), and place of residence, it is symbolic testament to the layering of personal and public identities that constituted the Soviet "self," from the supranational, through the national, and finally to the local. The roots of this matrix of "Sovietness" lie in the complexities of the period of "mapping" that we have explored. The cultural texts of early Soviet Russia sought to create a context for citizenship, to link the individual and the collective within a shared conception of time and space. For today's media age, the Soviet case provides a useful study of identity formation. Sovietness was a cultural construct that owed its shape and impact to an extraordinary project of mass media representation. During the first decade after the revolution, processed images of the new Soviet identity collided with older, lived identities; the national collided with the local; the imaginary map of the new world met with the lived space of the old. The imaginary geography of Imperial Russia—premised on a disjunctive relationship between lived identity and mapped identity, and on a curious hybrid of mythical *neob"iatnost'* and pragmatic conceptualization—was reinterpreted and reshaped to meet the demands of the revolutionary age.

Above all, the formation of the new imaginary geography was a process of incorporation, an attempt to link local and national spaces, centre and periphery, as a single whole. From 1917 until 1935, as we have seen, centrifugal and centripetal ideals of spatial organization coexisted in descriptions of the territory. Exploration and conquest *(osvoenie)* were, ultimately, part of a single project. During these early years, however, we can trace the contours of alternative conceptions of "national" identity in Soviet Russia. Within the emphasis on interconnection and participation that structured the rhetoric of industrialization and modernization during the 1920s lurked an apparently paradoxical focus on localness. The ideal of the new Soviet supranational identity was premised on a decentred vision of the territory, in which citizenship was mediated via the local space, as part of a network *(set')* of interconnected spaces.

This vision of the new Soviet workers' International was, in a sense, an early statement of the ideals of global identity that now recur in the twenty-first century, picturing a world without borders, united by common concerns. In its own time, however, this vision of decentred spatial organization was frustrated by the practicalities of state building. The ideals of heterogeneity collided with the practical advantages of homogeneity in the creation of a unified Soviet state. By the second half of the 1930s, for reasons at once pragmatic and symbolic, the centripetal model of Soviet space was firmly established and the space was "mapped."

The frontispiece map of the 1934 volume edited by Maksim Gor'kii in celebration of the opening of the Baltic–White Sea Canal, offers a clear vision of the dream geography of Stalin's Russia (Figure 65).[1] This "map" is, as it proudly declares, "not like other maps." It is a pictorial representation of space as power, in which Lenin's call for a map as an educational document finds a curious realization. Here, Moscow is the red star at the centre of the Soviet space, from which the all-seeing Stalin—perched, implicitly, in his office-eyrie—looks out across a domesticated *prostor*. The land that was ripe for exploration and exploitation in the late 1920s is here imagined as already exploited, transformed

Figure 65. Map of the USSR in 1931. From M. Gor'kii, L. L. Averbakh, and S. G. Finn, eds., *Belomorsko-Baltiiskii kanal imeni Stalina: istoriia stroitel'stva* (Moscow: Istoriia Fabrik i zavod, 1934). insert. Courtesy of the Russian State Library, Moscow.

into a benevolent provider of supplies for Moscow. In the depths of Siberia, for example, "it turns out the wheat can grow." On the northern coast, icebreakers are making the sea navigable. Benign Soviet influence extends from the capital into the farthest, darkest corners of the territory, and the borders of the Soviet Union are clearly drawn.

The radial (centripetal) vision of space implied by this symbolic map provided the predominant model for the maps—real and imaginary—produced during the second half of the 1930s. In 1935, the Commissariat for Internal Affairs assumed control of national cartography. The map was an important ideological document of state power, expressing control over the territory. In 1938, a set of ten standardized maps of the Soviet Union was produced for the purpose of being hung in schools across the nation, ensuring that a shared knowledge of the territory was provided as a foundation for good citizenship in the future. Three million copies of these sets were produced. As a symbolic climax of the process, after the suffering and victories of the Second World (or "Great Patriotic") War, the largest map of the Soviet Union was produced between 1946 and 1947. It was much praised for the extraordinary cartographic detail of the territory that it provided and won the Gold Medal of the Soviet Geographical Society in 1947. It was to be hung, symbolically, at the very centre of the territory: in the Historical Museum on Red Square.

The pictorial certainties of the ideological space of the Belomor Canal map, then, mark the beginning of the resolution of the period of intense spatial flux that this book has explored. Between 1920 and 1935, the coordinates of Sovietness were fluid and unfixed. From 1935, they began to solidify, and by the beginning of the war in 1941, Sovietness was an identity to be reckoned with, the rallying point of patriotism. In the late Stalin period, the map was a document of power (Figure 66).[2] Yet within the ostensible transparency of the "conquered" space during the 1930s, and until Stalin's death, there lurked yet another and more sinister spatial history. There were the "closed cities" of Soviet Russia, to which travel by foreigners was not permitted; more disturbingly still, there were officially "secret" cities, and spaces, often linked with the arms and nuclear industries, which appeared on no public maps of the territory. These were inhabited spaces, home to many, and yet they remained officially "unmapped"—curious hybrids of official and unofficial topography. In parallel, the gulag—the labour camps upon which so many of those grand construction projects of the Stalinist period depended—left no traces on public maps of the territory. Vast tracts of apparently uninhabited territory were in fact peopled by prisoners of the gulag. The territory was "conquered" and domesticated by grand construction projects, certainly. But it was also lived and experienced under duress. For many labour prisoners, the gulag space became a de facto home. Yet these lived spaces were at the same time secret spaces—unmapped, and "ungraspable." Perhaps, then, the category of *neob"iatnost'* was merely relocated and reinterpreted during the Stalin period? Maps were ideological documents that served, ultimately, to leave the territory largely unknown and unknowable.

Under Nikita Khrushchev, during the first period of "de-Stalinization" in the late 1950s, these hidden worlds began to be discovered. In many cases, the sites of former labour camps formed the basis for new settlements, forming new, official maps on the territory. As this alternative history and geography were exposed, knowledge of the territory was shown to be unreliable, and the map was thrown into flux. Official and unofficial topography diverged, as the lived, private space was increasingly revealed as the only reliable locus of identity. Doubt reentered the discourse of Soviet space, unsettling the certainties of the ideological map. Nearly forty years later, with the collapse of the Soviet Union in 1991, such certainties suffered another—and this time fatal—blow. Still more new marks on the map emerged. As the Union disintegrated, moreover, the territory was fundamentally destabilized—its borders contested, and its coher-

ПОД ВОДИТЕЛЬСТВОМ ВЕЛИКОГО СТАЛИНА—ВПЕРЕД К КОММУНИЗМУ!

Figure 66. "Under the Leadership of Great Stalin—Forward to Communism!" Boris Berezovskii, Mikhail Solov'ev, and Ivan Shagin, 1951. Courtesy of The Hoover Institution.

ence as an ideological "empire" destroyed, apparently for good. Russia, formerly the centre of the empire, was left stranded and uncertain in the midst of a *prostor* that was once again uncertain, and unmapped. Cityscapes were transformed by the destruction of monuments to the old regime. Streets were renamed. Moscow—once the majestic centre of the conquered territory—became merely the chaotic urban metropolis at the centre of a radically reduced state. In the cultural texts of early *glasnost'*, it was revealed not as monumental centre, but as the hiding ground of urban underworlds and (once again) as a lived space of gritty disorder. Social and political uncertainties were mapped onto spatial uncertainties.[3]

The process did not end there, however, and Russia's imaginary map has many stages yet to live. In the Moscow of the late 1990s, for example, the rebuilding and remodelling of the cityscape by Mayor Iurii Luzhkov was celebrated as an assertion of national might—an attempt to reconstruct the city, this time in a commercial context. In the new millennium, Moscow begins to emerge as a new kind of megalopolis, where the certainties of Sovietness are superseded by the uncertainties of capital. In a final irony, the ambitions of the socialist workers' International find a curious realization in capitalist globalization. The dream of the electrical network has become the reality of the new global *set'*: the World Wide Web. Thus history seems to repeat itself. In post-Soviet Russia—in an ironic reworking of the revolutionary project—history is being rewritten through the remodelling of space.

Notes

INTRODUCTION: PROJECTING

1. See Fredric Jameson, "Cognitive Mapping," in *Marxism and the Interpretation of Culture,* edited by Gary Nelson and Laurence Grossberg, 347–60; and *The Geopolitical Aesthetic.* Jameson describes the experience of space as a dual experience of the "here and now" and the "mental map of the social and global totality we all carry around in our heads." He suggests that no social or political project can be successful without providing a "map" of that social and spatial totality within which the individual subject is to be inserted.

2. Walter Benjamin, "Moscow," in *Reflections: Essays, Aphorisms, Autobiographical Writings,* edited by Peter Demetz, 118. RSFSR: Russian Soviet Federated Socialist Republic. The USSR was formed in December 1922.

3. "Model' mira," *Vokrug sveta,* 23.

4. This term is drawn from a synthesis of diverse sources. See, for example, Derek Gregory, *Geographical Imaginations.*

5. Isaak Babel', "Neft'," in *Sochineniia,* 226.

6. Anthony Smith, *National Identity,* 9, defines a common understanding of a "homeland" as a prerequisite for national identity.

7. With these caveats, I will use the term *national space* in the course of this book as a convenient shorthand through which to explore precisely the complexities of the shifting representation of the Soviet territory as homogeneously national or non-national.

8. Aleksandr Blok, *Zapisnye knizhki,* 83.

9. Vasilii Kliuchevskii, *Sochineniia,* 70.

10. Nikolai Berdiaev, *Sud'ba Rossii,* 65. Berdiaev (1874–1948) was a "Christian Marxist" living in exile in Paris from 1922. He produced the famous text *Russkaia ideia: osnovnye problemy russkoi mysli XIX veka i nachala XX veka* (Paris, 1946).

11. Berdiaev, *The Origin of Russian Communism,* translated by R. M. French, 9.

12. Berdiaev, *Sud'ba Rossii,* 65.

13. See Lidia Sazonova, "Ideia puti v drevnrusskoi literature," 471–88.

14. Nikolai Gogol', "Mertvye dushi: tom pervyi," in *Sobranie sochinenii,* 249.

15. See *Prostranstva Rossii: khrestomatiia po geografii Rossii,* edited by D. N. Zamiatin, for a collection of Russian writings on space/territory.

16. The first *chertezhy* (sketches, or maps without degree grid) of the *russkaia zemlia* were produced during the sixteenth and seventeenth centuries, marking rivers, lakes, wells, and adjacent towns. The first atlas of Siberia was produced in 1701 by S. V. Remezov. For a brief history of Russian geography, see A. A. Grigor'ev, "Russian Geography," in *Soviet Geography: Accomplishments and Tasks,* edited by I. P. Gerasimov and G. M. Ignat'ev, translated by Lawrence Ecker, 9–13. On prerevolutionary work of the Geographical Society, see Nathaniel Knight, "Science, Empire and Nationality: Ethnography in the Russian Geographical Society, 1845–1855," in *Imperial Russia: New Histories for the Empire,* edited by Jane Burbank and David L. Ransel, 108–41.

17. *Entsiklopedicheskii slovar'* (St. Petersburg, 1895), vol. 15 (a): 633–40.

18. Further discussion of *osvoenie* is offered in my article "Borders: The Aesthetic of Conquest in Soviet Cinema of the 1930s," *Journal of European Studies.*

19. The "totalitarian" model of historiography of the Soviet period is represented by writers such as Adam Ulam, *Stalin: The Man and His Era* (Boston: Beacon Press, 1989), and Robert Tucker, *Stalin as Revolutionary 1879–1929,* who emphasize the power of Stalin as an individual. Administrative historians such as E. H. Carr, *The Bolshevik Revolution, The Interregnum 1923–24,* and *The Russian Revolution from Lenin to Stalin 1917–1929,* focus on the concentration of power in the central state apparatus.

20. Definitions taken from *Slovar' sovremennogo russkogo literaturnogo iazyka,* 1078. The earlier term *osvoiti* is attested to in historical dictionaries as early as the twelfth century, when it appears to have been used in both senses. See *Slovar' drevnerusskogo iazyka po pis'mennym pamiat'nikam,* edited by I. I. Sreznevskogo, 2 (1902): 714.

21. The precise meaning of *osvoit'* seems to have varied according to region. In general, however, it was an assimilative movement in which the local population was to be subjected to Imperial, colonizing power. Some commentators suggest that the term *osvoenie* was used to suggest a more peaceful process of colonization in contrast to the military emphasis of terms such as *pokorenie* (subjugation) and *zavoevanie* (conquest). See, for example, David N. Collins, "Subjugations and Settlement in Seventeenth- and Eighteenth-Century Siberia," in *The History of Siberia: From Russian Conquest to Revolution,* edited by Alan Wood, 37. Etymologically, of course, *osvoenie* expresses *assimilation* as much as conquest. In the Soviet context, both *osvoenie* and *zavoevanie* were used, and increasingly interchangeably.

22. The semiotician and cultural historian Vladimir Toporov, drawing on suggestion rather

than evidence, suggests that linguistically, the prefix *o (o-svoenie)* implies an encircling, assimilative gesture, premised on the notion of containment within borders, and defines *osvoenie* as "circling around the territory along its perimeter: an act of assimilating the centre." Vladimir Toporov, "Prostranstvo," in *Mifi narodov mira v dvukh tomakh,* edited by S. A. Tokarev, 2: 341. Although the etymology of the prefix *o* is more precisely to be understood as indicating a process of transformation/becoming, Toporov's suggestion has interesting resonance for my purposes.

23. Michel Foucault, *Discipline and Punish: The Birth of the Prison,* translated by Alan Sheridan, 201.

24. Foucault, "Space, Knowledge, Power," in *The Foucault Reader: An Introduction to Foucault's Thought,* edited by Paul Rabinow, 252.

25. Foucault, *Discipline and Punish,* 195–228.

26. Henri Lefebvre, *The Production of Space,* translated by Donald Nicholson-Smith, 165. For these purposes, I focus on the term *dominated* space. Lefebvre uses a further term, *abstract* space, to describe the domination of space in contemporary capitalist society, arguing that it is space which exists in opposition to lived experience. I prefer "dominated," as it expresses a more political dimension, which can be linked to Foucault's "carceral regime" descriptions and which expresses the conquering dimension that I am concerned to identify in Soviet space.

27. Lefebvre, *The Production of Space,* 372.

28. Katerina Clark, *The Soviet Novel: History as Ritual,* 93–114.

29. Karl Marx and Friedrich Engels, *Communist Manifesto: Socialist Landmark,* edited by Harold J. Laski, 131. More recently, Marxist theorists have suggested that the success of the capitalist system depends on this uneven, hierarchical organization of space. See, for example, Edward Soja and Costis Hadjimichalis, "Between Geographical Materialism and Spatial Fetishism: Some Observations on the Development of Marxist Spatial Analysis," *Antipode: A Radical Journal of Geography;* Derek Gregory, *Geographical Imaginations,* provides a detailed analysis of the development of human geography in relation to contemporary social theory, demonstrating the relationships and differences between key thinkers who have engaged the spatial question. Also, David Harvey, *Consciousness and the Urban Experience: Studies in the History and Theory of Capitalist Urbanization.*

30. Studies on Socialist Realism and High Stalinist culture include Boris Groys, *The Total Art of Stalinism: Avant-Garde, Aesthetic Dictatorship, and Beyond,* translated by Charles Rougle; *The Culture of the Stalin Period,* edited by Hans Günther; and Régine Robin, *Socialist Realism: An Impossible Aesthetic,* translated by Catherine Porter.

31. Vladimir Papernyi, *Kul'tura Dva.*

32. Clark, *Petersburg: Crucible of Cultural Revolution,* 281.

33. Karl Marx, "Critique of Hegel's Dialectic and General Philosophy (Economic and Philosophical Manuscripts of 1844)," in *Karl Marx: Selected Writings,* 104–18. The term *sensuous* will be used henceforward according to the New Oxford Dictionary of English definition as "relating to/affecting the senses (not the intellect)." In this respect, I will also use "sensory" and "sentient."

34. Marx, "Private Property and Communism (Economic and Philosophical Manuscripts of

1844)," in *Karl Marx: Selected Writings,* 97. Susan Buck-Morss, *Dreamworld and Catastrophe: The Passing of Mass Utopia in East and West,* 119, discusses the status of Marx's "Philosophical Manuscripts" in Soviet Russia.

35. Marx, "Private Property and Communism," 99–100.

36. Marx, "Private Property and Communism," 100.

37. Italics will be used henceforward to signal my use of this term *appropriation,* referring to the set of interrelated concepts that I define here.

38. Susan Buck-Morss, *Dreamworld and Catastrophe: The Passing of Mass Utopia in East and West,* 119.

39. Sheila Fitzpatrick, defining the period of the First Five-Year Plan as "Cultural Revolution," has argued for what might be called a "revolution from below" historiography, which breaks down the dichotomy of state and society common to the "totalitarian" model: see *Cultural Revolution in Russia,* edited by Sheila Fitzpatrick. With the other contributors to this seminal volume of essays (including Gail Lapidus, Katerina Clark, Moshe Lewin, and S. Frederick Starr), Fitzpatrick explored the social consequences of the new policies Stalin's government adopted between 1928 and 1932. The volume suggested that "Cultural Revolution" was a process generated and sustained as much by forces in society as by a central state authority. This represented a significant historiographic revision, shifting the focus away from the centre and revealing more complex relationships between state and society; it has had significant effect on the new generation of "revisionist" historians, who argue that it was a key achievement of the state to create social structures that acted to consolidate and sustain the new regime. Representations of space were part of this process. See, for example, *Bolshevik Visions: First Phase of the Cultural Revolution in Soviet Russia,* edited by William Rosenberg and Lewis Siegelbaum; *Social Dimensions of Soviet Industrialization,* edited by Rosenberg and Siegelbaum; *Bolshevik Culture: Experiment and Order in the Russian Revolution,* edited by Abbot Gleason, Peter Kenez, and Richard Stites; Stephen Kotkin, *Magnetic Mountain: Stalinism as a Civilization;* and Fitzpatrick, *Everyday Stalinism: Ordinary Life in Extraordinary Times: Soviet Russia in the 1930s.*

40. Oksana Bulgakova, "Sovetskoe kino v poiskakh 'obshchei modeli'," in *Sotsrealisticheskii kanon,* edited by Hans Günther and Evgenii Dobrenko, 156.

41. N. F. Preobrazhenskii, "Predislovie," *Khronika.* Preobrazhenskii was president of the Moscow Cinema Committee (Moskinokomitet) from its formation (as a subdivision of Narkompros) in spring 1918.

42. For more detail on this subject see, in English, Jay Leyda, *Kino: A History of the Russian and Soviet Film,* 132–39; Richard Taylor, *The Politics of the Soviet Cinema 1917–1929,* and, for an account of film as propaganda under Stalin, *Film Propaganda: Soviet Russia and Nazi Germany;* also Viktor Listov, *Lenin i kinematograf, 1917–24* and *Istoriia smotrit v ob"ektiv.*

43. The trains were organized by the Otdel agitpar-poezdov (Department of Agit-trains) under vtsik (Vserossiiskii tsentral'nyi ispolnitel'nyi komitet). For a detailed history of the *agitpoezda,* see Listov, *Istoriia,* 199–213.

44. *SK,* 1925, nos. 2–3: 56.

45. See Taylor, *The Politics of Soviet Cinema,* 64–86, for a discussion of the formation of Sovkino, and pp. 87–101, for a detailed examination of the ways in which Sovkino and parallel organizations sought to organize production and distribution in Soviet cinema.

46. ODSK: Obshchestvo druzei sovetskogo kino. Leonid Sukharebskii, *Nauchnoe kino.*

47. Aleksandr Katsigras, "Kino i derevnia: kino-obshchestvennost' i zadachi Sovkino v derevne," *SK,* 1927, no. 3: 8. Katsigras, a Narkompros functionary, was instigator of the *kinofikatsiia* project in 1924.

48. "ODSK: kinofikatsiia derevni i obshchestvennost," *SK,* 1927, nos. 5–6: 24–25.

49. *Puti kino: Vsesoyuznoe partiinoe soveshchanie po kinematografii,* edited by B. S. Olkhovyi, 429–44, extract reprinted as "Party Cinema Conference Resolution: The Results of Cinema Construction in the USSR and the Tasks of Soviet Cinema," in *The Film Factory: Russian and Soviet Cinema in Documents 1896–1939,* edited by Richard Taylor and Ian Christie, 210. The quotation is taken from A. I. Krinitskii's (head of Agitprop Department of the Central Committee) report to the First All-Union Party Conference on the Cinema, March 1928, which was also cited in a summary of the conference resolutions, "Ideologicheskie kino-direktivy," *SK,* 1928, nos. 2–3: 3–5 (4).

50. See, for example, *SK,* 1925, no. 1.

51. The cinema press between 1925 and 1928 was full of discussion of how to implement *kinofikatsiia* more successfully. See, for example, M. Grinevskii, "Kino i derevnia (kino-telega)," *SK,* 10–12, and the column entitled "Po provintsii," *SK,* 1927, nos. 2, 24–25, which recount the experience of travelling with a *peredvizhnik.*

52. "O kinofikatsii derevni," *SK,* 1928, nos. 2–3: 6.

53. See "Party Cinema Conference Resolution," 211.

54. See Listov, *Istoriia,* 129, for evidence that Vertov was not the only director responsible for *kinonedelia.*

55. Figures from the catalogue of the *Rossiiskii gosudarstvennyi arkhiv kinofotodokumentov* (All-Russian State Archive of Film-Photo Documents, RGAKFD).

56. *SK,* 1925, nos. 2–3: 53.

57. Adrian Piotrovskii, "Platforma Petrova-Bytova i sovetskaia kinematografiia," *Zhizn' iskusstva,* reprinted as "Petrov-Bytov's Platform and Soviet Cinema," in *The Film Factory,* 262–64. Piotrovskii was a writer, critic, and theorist and artistic director of Leningrad studios between 1928 and 1937. He was author of the screenplay for the 1926 film *Chertovo koleso.* Pavel Petrov-Bytov, author of the article (cited below) to which Piotrovskii was responding, was a film director.

58. Pavel Petrov-Bytov, "U nas net sovetskoi kinematografii," *Zhizn' iskusstva,* reprinted as "We Have No Soviet Cinema," in *The Film Factory,* 259–62.

59. *SK,* 1925, nos. 2–3: 51. Piotrovskii's article was a response to this initial statement. See Denise Youngblood, *Movies for the Masses: Popular Cinema and Soviet Society in the 1920s,* for discussion of the ideology/entertainment debate and viewer preferences.

60. Dziga Vertov, "Kinoglaz," *Stat'i, dnevniki, zamysly,* edited by Sergei Drobashenko, 90.

61. See Youngblood, *Movies for the Masses,* 19–21.

62. See Richard Taylor, "Ideology as Mass Entertainment: Boris Shumiatskii and Soviet Cinema in the 1930s," in *Inside the Film Factory: New Approaches to Russian and Soviet Cin-*

ema, edited by Richard Taylor and Ian Christie, 193–217, and "'A Cinema for the Millions': Soviet Socialist Realism and the Problem of Film Comedy," *Journal of Contemporary History.*

CHAPTER 1. CONNECTING

1. It was followed in February 1918 by the more developed *Dekret Vserossiiskogo tsentral'nogo ispolnitel'nogo komiteta (VTSIK) o sotsializatsii zemli* (Decree of the All Russian Executive Committee on the Socialization of Land).

2. *Komgosoor (Komitet gosudarstvennykh sooruzhenii),* 9 May and 18 June 1918. Cited in Margarita Astaf'eva, "Razvitie teoreticheskoi mysli i printsipov Sovetskogo gradostroitel'stva v pervye poslerevoliutsionnye gody, 1917–25," 28. The committee comprised architects, planners, and technicians and included the influential prerevolutionary architects Ivan Zholtovskii, Aleksei Shchusev, and Sergei Shestakov, all of whom came to particular prominence later as proponents of a new style of architecture under Stalin.

3. Lenin replied to Krzhizhanovskii's electrification proposals with immediate enthusiasm: see V. I. Lenin, Letter to Krzhizhanovskii, 26 December 1919, *Polnoe sobranie sochinenii,* 51: 105. Other writings and letters by Lenin on electrification include *PSS,* 40: 62–63, 41: 395–96. On the formation of Gosplan, see Lenin, "Doklad vserossiiskogo tsentral'nogo ispolnitel'nogo komiteta i soveta narodnykh komissarov o vneshnei i vnutrennei politike (VTSIK)," *PSS,* 42: 128–62.

4. See Roger Pethybridge, *The Social Origins of Stalinism.* According to Max Vasmer, *Russisches etymologisches Wörterbuch,* 3: 273, the term *plan* emerges in the Russian language in 1704 in association with the modernizing ambitions of Peter the Great. It acquired iconic status during the Soviet period, particularly under Stalin.

5. Friedrich Engels, cited in *SA,* 1930, nos. 1–2: 56.

6. Leonid Sabsovich, *Gorod budushchego i organizatsiia sotsialisticheskogo byta,* 18. Sabsovich was an economist in Gosplan who came to particular prominence in the late 1920s when this small book launched him as one of the initiators of the debate between Urbanists and Disurbanists. The phrase "victory over distance" occurred in many other contexts during the period.

7. GOELRO: Gosudarstvennaia komissiia po elektrifikatsii Rossii. G. M. Krzhizhanovskii was an engineer and a member of the Bolshevik party serving in the Electrical Trust of the Supreme Economic Council. In December 1919, during a fuel crisis in Moscow, Lenin received a copy of his work. G. M. Krzhizhanovskii, "Oblastnye elektricheskie stantsii na torfe i ikh znachenie dlia tsentral'nogo promyshlennogo raiona Rossii," *Trudy soveshchanii po podmoskovnomu ugliu i torfu.*

8. Ruth Roosa, "The Association of Industry and Trade, 1906–1914," cited in Anne D. Rassweiler, *The Generation of Power: The History of Dneprostroi,* 23. See also Roosa, "Russian Industrialists and State Socialism," *Soviet Studies.* Krzhizhanovskii wrote his first proposals for electrification as a civil servant in the Imperial ministries.

9. Krzhizhanovskii, *Ob elektrofikatsii: rech' na 8-m S'ezde Sovetov,* 9.

10. See Jonathan Coopersmith, *The Electrification of Soviet Russia,* 157–67, for a detailed discussion of these debates.

11. These comprised the Central-Industrial area, the North-West, the Urals, Donetsk, the West, the Middle-Volga, Siberia, and the Caucasus. It should be noted that these were in fact the traditional industrial centres.

12. I. I. Skvortsov-Stepanov, *Elektrifikatsiia R.S.F.S.R. v sviazi s perekhodnoi fazoi mirovogo khoziaistva,* 176.

13. *Plan elektrifikatsii RSFSR: vvedenie k dokladu,* 142.

14. *Plan elektrifikatsii,* 217.

15. Lenin, "Doklad VTSIK," *PSS,* 160.

16. The source of this expression is difficult to trace, as it was in common use. See, for example, the photograph from the journal *Prozhektor* titled "Zasiiala lampochka Il'icha," reproduced in *Oktiabr'skie Stranitsy (1917–1941),* edited by V. S. Listov and G. A. Ambernadi, 158.

17. Lenin, "Doklad o rabote VTSIK i sovnarkoma na pervoi sessii VTSIK," *PSS,* 40: 109.

18. Lenin, "Doklad VTSIK," *PSS,* 160–61.

19. Lenin, Preface to Skvortsov-Stepanov, *Elektrifikatsiia R.S.F.S.R.,* x. In some editions of this pamphlet, the introduction is attributed to N. Lenina (Nadezhda Krupskaia).

20. Lenin, *PSS,* 55: 159.

21. Lenin, *PSS,* 55: 158.

22. Lenin, "Letter to A. I. Rykov and I. I. Radchenko," 28 October 1920, *PSS,* 51: 320.

23. See R. W. Davies, "The Soviet Economy in Turmoil," in *The Industrialization of Soviet Russia,* for further discussion.

24. Mikhail Okhitovich, "O sotsialisticheskoi planirovke rasseleniia," *SA,* 1930, no. 6: 1.

25. "Puti na karte SSSR."

26. See, for example, *Pervaia piatiletka v SSSR* (1929), RGAKFD I-13973.

27. Sergei Tret'iakov, "Chem zhivo kino," *Novyi LEF,* 28. Tret'iakov (1892–1939) was a writer (playwright and essayist) and critic associated with *LEF* and *Novyi LEF.* He was chairman of the Artistic Council of the first Goskino studio in 1925.

28. See, for example, *Magnitostroi* (1930), RGAKFD I-3319.

29. "Obzor pechati," *Voprosy kommunal'nogo khoziaistva,* 76.

30. *Pusk Dneprostroia* (special edition, 10 October 1932, 8 p.m.). See Aleksandr Medvedkin, "Chto takoe kinopoezd?," in *Iz istorii kino: dokumenty i materialy,* 45.

31. *Desiat' let plana GOELRO: Kino-illiustratsiia k dokladu t. Krzhizhanovskogo* (1930). This film was billed as "a cinematic illustration of the paper of Krzhizhanovskii," accompanying Krzhizhanovskii's celebrationary presentation: Krzhizhanovskii, *Desiat' let Goelro: rech' na torzhestvennom plenume mosoblispolkoma i mossoveta 25 Dek. 1930.*

32. Cited in Geoffrey Hosking, *A History of the Soviet Union,* 160.

33. Figures from Chris Ward, *Stalin's Russia,* 40.

34. Between 1927 and 1929, a gradual shift in attitudes of central government toward the peasantry occurred. See Moshe Lewin, *The Making of the Soviet System: Essays in the Social History of Interwar Russia,* 100. Molotov, speaking at the Central Committee plenum of November 1929, forecast the socialization of several million households by March 1930 despite the fact that 90 percent of peasants at that time lived and worked in traditional communities. Targets were progressively increased.

35. Stalin published his famous article "God velikogo pereloma," celebrating the twelfth an-

niversary of the revolution, in *Pravda* on 7 November 1929. I. Stalin, "God velikogo pereloma," *Sochineniia,* 12: 118–31.

36. See Kathy Frierson, *Peasant Icons: Representations of Rural People in Late 19th Century Russia,* for the historical background to this view of the peasant.

37. See especially Lynn Viola, *The Best Sons of the Fatherland: Workers in the Vanguard of Collectivization.*

38. See, for example, *Za sotsialisticheskuiu derevniu* 24 (1931), RGAKFD I-2365 a; also 18 (1931), RGAKFD I-3848.

39. The first phase of collectivization came to a dramatic end on 2 March 1930 when Stalin published his famous criticism of overzealous officials and called for the restoration of the "voluntary principle" of collectivization: Stalin, "Golovokruzhenie ot uspekhov: k voprosam kolkhoznogo dvizheniia," *Sochineniia.* Official figures stated that 50 percent of households were collectivized by February 1930, overfulfilling Molotov's predictions. Henceforth collectivization slowed, and the figures of newly collectivized households dropped significantly between March and May of 1930, from an estimated fifteen million in March, to around six million in May, remaining at that figure for the rest of the year. See Ward, *Stalin's Russia.* See Maurice Hindus, *Red Bread,* 147, for an account of peasant reactions to Stalin's letter, telling of chaos and confusion in the villages. Hindus was an American who lived in Russia during the First Five-Year Plan.

40. Sergo Ordzhonikidze, "O razvitii chernoi metallurgii, (Otchetnyi doklad narodnogo komissariata tiazheloi promyshlennosti, na plenume TsK VKP (b))," in S. M. Ordzhonikidze, *Stat'i i rechi,* 412.

41. For a discussion of the spatiotemporal coordinates of the Russian prerevolutionary imagination, see Vladimir Toporov, *O mifopoeticheskom prostranstve,* and L. I. Sazonova, "Ideia puti v drevnrusskoi literature."

42. The *mir* was more or less destroyed by the violent transformations of 1930, and in January 1930, an effective end was put to those schemes that had sought to rationalize the *mir* as the basis for a new socialist agriculture.

43. *Za sotsialisticheskuiu derevniu* 15 (1931), produced by Soiuzkinozhurnal, RGAKFD I-2356.

44. Officially, the train was called *Kino-fabrika poezd tresta Soiuzkinokhroniki* and changed its name in 1933 to *Kino-fabrika poezd imeni K. V. Voroshilova.*

45. Richard Taylor, "An Interview with Alexander Medvedkin," in *Inside the Film Factory: New Approaches to Russian and Soviet Cinema,* edited by Richard Taylor and Ian Christie, 169.

46. Seventy-two short films were made on the train in the single year 1931–32, when Medvedkin was its commander. Most of these films were considered lost until 1989, when nine were discovered in an unexplored archive. The surviving train films produced by the *Kino fabrika-poezd tresta Soyuzkinokhroniki* over its full period of operation are located in the RGAKFD: *Gazeta n. 4* (1932), directed by Nikolai Karmazinskii; *Kak zhivesh', tovarishch' gorniak?* (1932), directed by Nikolai Karmazinskii; *Za naivazhnyi . . . Kribassa* (1932) (in Ukrainian), directed by G. Piotrovskii; *Da, zveno* (1932); *Veitlus: opyt luchshikh vsem kolkhozam* (1932); *Pis'mo kolkhoznikam* (1932), cinematography by E. Lifshitz; *Tovarishch' Prokuror: kino ocherk* (1933), directed by S. Bubrik, plan by N. Safronov; *Pusk Dneprostroia,* special edition, 10 October 1932, 8 p.m.; *Zveno pobedy* (1933), directed by S.

Bubrik. A later Film Train film is also preserved: *Puteshestvie po SSSR, 1934–1937,* directed by S. Bubrik. This film uses material from a series of earlier journeys, including *Elektrofikatsirovannaia doroga Urala,* shot during the first "transport expedition" along the Perm railway line (see Chapter 5). In 1933, the train was renamed in honour of Voroshilov, then Peoples' Commissar for Military and Naval Affairs. Voroshilov had been head, with Budennyi, of the Konarmia regiment for whom Medvedkin worked as propaganda officer. For a full filmography and bibliography of Medvedkin, and of the work of the train, see Aleksandr Deriabin, "Ves' Medvedkin: filmografiia," *Kinovedches-kie zapiski.*

47. Medvedkin, "Chto takoe kinopoezd?," 30–31.

48. The first, called the "transport expedition/trip *[transportnyi reis]*" by Medvedkin, focused on transportation issues in the Ekaterinburg and Ural area for three months over the autumn and winter of 1931–32. The train followed the railway network, seeking to teach local peasants how to repair tracks and maintain the system in poor weather conditions. Subsequent trips were made to mining areas, first the Kribass and later the Donbass, aiming to increase the distribution *(razgruzka)* of coal. In addition, a special trip was made in honour of the opening of the Dneprostroi hydroelectric power station in 1932, and the "military" expedition focused on improving conditions and morale in the armed forces.

49. Taylor, "An Interview with Alexander Medvedkin," 169.

50. Medvedkin, "Chto takoe kinopoezd?," 28.

51. Medvedkin, "Chto takoe kinopoezd?," 28.

52. The need to communicate was paramount. The train made Ukrainian titles for films in the Ukraine, such as *Kak zhivesh', tovarishch gorniak?*

53. Medvedkin, "294 dnia na kolesakh," 37. N. A. Izvolov suggests similarly that the effect of self-recognition on Medvedkin's viewers must have been dramatic, blending familiarity with strangeness, recognition with transformation: Izvolov, *Fenomen kino: istoriia i teoriia,* 247.

54. Medvedkin, "294 dnia na kolesakh," 37. Also "Chto takoe kinopoezd?," 34.

55. The first film to use the camel was *Verbliud na PRZ* (1931), shot during the Dnepetrovsk transport trip. The film is not preserved, but Medvedkin's screenplay is in the *Fond Medvedkina.*

56. *Dvenadsat' udarnykh reisov,* 12.

57. Medvedkin, "Chto takoe kinopoezd?," 37.

58. Medvedkin, "Chto takoe kinopoezd?," 35, recounts how forty-nine thousand miners were "served" by the train during a three-month trip to the Kribass region. See Medvedkin, "294 dnia na kolesakh," for further viewing statistics.

59. *Temp,* 7 December 1932. Fotoarkhiv, no. 128.

60. *Dvenadsat' udarnykh reisov,* 29.

61. Louis Althusser, *Essays on Ideology,* 47.

62. Jacques Lacan, "The Mirror Stage as Formative of the Function 'I'," in *Ecrits. A Selection,* edited by Alan Sheridan, 1–7.

63. Stephen Kotkin, *Magnetic Mountain: Stalinism as a Civilization,* 98.

64. Lewin, *The Making of the Soviet System,* 220.

65. The root of this term is *brodiaga* (vagrant) and *brodit'* (to wander or roam).

66. The term *poselok* developed specifically in tandem with industrialization during the nineteenth century and is strongly differentiated from village *(derevnia/selo)* or even settlement *(poselenie)*. *Poselok* describes a nonrural, nascently urban space.

67. S. A. Besserov, "Problema prostranstva v perspektivnom plane," *Planovoe khoziaistvo.*

68. *SA*, 1930, no. 4: cover.

69. Catherine Cooke, "The Town of Socialism," is one of few architectural historians to have recognized the revolutionary global significance of Soviet urban planning debates.

70. Another group, the ARU (Ob"edinenie arkhitektorov-urbanistov) headed by Ladovskii, was also influential. Debates were frequent and involved diverse groups, which will not be discussed here. For further detail, see especially V. I. Khazanova, *Sovetskaia arkhitektura pervoi piatiletki: problemy goroda budushchego.*

71. The OSA (Ob"edinenie sovremennykh arkhitektorov), led by the Constructivist architects Moisei Ginzburg and the Vesnin brothers (Aleksandr, Viktor, and Leonid), included among its members the Constructivist theorist Aleksei Gan, Aleksandr Pasternak, Mikhail Barshch, Ivan Burov, and Ivan Leonidov. Like many avant-garde groups in the Soviet Union during the 1920s, it united figures from varied disciplines: sociologists, technicians, and artists worked with architects and urban planners.

72. Leonid Sabsovich, *Sotsialisticheskie goroda*, 30.

73. Sabsovich, *Sotsialisticheskie goroda*, 30.

74. Sabsovich, *Gorod budushchego*, 18.

75. Mikhail Okhitovich, "Sotsialisticheskoe rasselenie," *Vestnik Kommunisticheskoi Akademii*, and "K probleme goroda," *SA*.

76. Okhitovich, "Zametki po teorii rasseleniia," *SA*, 12.

77. Okhitovich, "Zametki po teorii rasseleniia," 9.

78. Okhitovich, "Zametki po teorii rasseleniia," 14.

79. Okhitovich, "Zametki po teorii rasseleniia," 14.

80. "Poiasnitel'naia zapiska k smete na ustroistvo tipovoi zhiloi iashcheiki po proektu Gosplana RSFSR," *SA*, 1930, no. 6: 6.

81. Velemir Khlebnikov, "My i doma," *Sobranie proizvedenii*, 279.

82. Okhitovich, "K probleme goroda," 134. There is evidence of a film made by the Disurbanists and shown in the Communist Academy in March 1930 as part of a debate "on the planning of the socialist town." In discussion, the film was criticized by Miliutin, then representative of the State Commission for the Building of New Towns, for an unrealistic representation of the possibilities of mobility in the new space. Habitation and production were so distant from one another, he pointed out, that an "insane speed" would be necessary to transport the worker efficiently from home to work. Furthermore, the film was accused of representing a world in which the individual would in effect *create* paths through the space. This was neither possible nor practical, Miliutin maintained: the rational organization of space would restrict individual mobility, constructing single, direct routes. Miliutin's criticisms of this film pinpoint exactly the extent to which the Disurbanist vision was one of movement and dynamism. It sought to enable the perpetual *exploration* of the space. See "Iz referirovannoi stenogrammy diskussii o planirovke

sotsialisticheskogo goroda, sostaiavsheisia v Komakademii, 20 i 21 maia 1930 g.," *Vestnik Komakademii,* 145.

83. N. Osinskii (V. V. Obolenskii), *Avtomobilizatsiia SSSR,* 22. Osinskii was Head of the Central Statistical Bureau.

84. Osinskii also published *Amerikanskii avtomobil' ili rossiiskaia telega: stat'i.*

85. Anatole Kopp, *Ville et révolution (architecture et urbanisme soviétiques des années vingt),* 181.

86. Okhitovich, *SA,* 1930, no. 6: 1.

87. The plan was produced by Ginzburg and Barshch. "Zelenyi gorod: sotsialisticheskaia rekonstruktsiia Moskvy," *SA,* 17–32.

88. "Zelenyi gorod," 18.

89. "Zelenyi gorod," 16–17.

90. The *Slovar' sovremennogo russkogo literaturnogo iazyka,* 11: 394, describes *privol'e* as *otkrytoe prostranstvo* (open space).

91. See *Iz istorii sovetskoi arkhitektury, 1917–1925 gg.: dokumenty i materialy,* edited by K. N. Afanas'ev, 33–36, and Khazanova, *Sovetskaia arkhitektura pervykh let Oktiabria,* 51–53, for excerpts and analysis of the *Privol'e* plan.

92. Cited by Cooke, "The Town," who speaks of the inadequacy of Khazanova's reference to "rumour" in this respect. For further discussion of utopian proposals during the 1920s, see Richard Stites, *Revolutionary Dreams: Utopian Vision and Experimental Life in the Russian Revolution,* and S. Frederick Starr, "Visionary Town Planning during the Cultural Revolution," in Sheila Fitzpatrick, *Cultural Revolution in Russia 1928–31.*

93. Aleksandr Chaianov (Ivan Kremnev), *Puteshestvie moego brata Alekseia v stranu krest'ianskoi utopii,* Part 1. Chaianov (1888–1939) was an agrarian economist who wrote sociopolitical texts proposing a peasant economy based on traditional structures of kinship and community. Chaianov, *Osnovnye idei i metody obshchestvennoi agronomii.* He also wrote a number of tales and short novels, sometimes under pseudonyms, of which this is the best known. See Rashit Iangirov, "Iz istorii odnoi kinoutopii," *Kinovedcheskie zapiski,* for an account of Chaianov's fictional work, in particular his connections with cinema.

94. Chaianov, *Puteshestvie,* 12, 16, 48, 46.

95. Okhitovich, "Zametki po teorii rasseleniia," 13.

96. "Zelenyi gorod," 23.

97. Okhitovich, "K probleme goroda," 134.

98. Between 1926 and 1927 in *SA* the group developed and refined the "functional method" formulated by Ginzburg in his book of 1924 *Stil' i epokha.* See, for example, Ginzburg, "Konstruktivizm kak metod laboratornoi i pedagogicheskoi raboty," *SA.* The ideas in this piece are well summarized in tabular form by Cooke, "The Town," 58, and reprinted in Cooke, "'Form Is a Function X': The Development of the Constructivist Architect's Design Method," *Architectural Design,* 43.

99. This term was coined by Nikolai Chuzhak: see Hans Günther, "Zhiznestroenie," and Irina Gutkin, "From Futurism to Socialist Realism," in *Creating Life: The Aesthetic Utopia of Russian Modernism,* edited by Irina Paperno and Joan Delaney Grossman, 185. It was commonly used during the period.

100. Ginzburg, "Tselevaia ustanovka v sovremennoi arkhitekture," *SA*.

101. On the influence of Ford, Taylorism, and Gastev, see especially Stites, *Revolutionary Dreams,* 149. Also, Rolf Hellebust, "Aleksei Gastev and the Metallization of the Revolutionary Body," *Slavic Review*. In 1928, *Sovremennaia arkhitektura* published the diploma thesis of Nikolai Krasil'nikov, who sought to produce a mathematical and scientific theory of architectural form that would organize the built environment in such a way as to optimize and rationalize the time needed for movement in daily activity.

102. Okhitovich, "K probleme goroda," 134.

103. This is, in a sense, an early statement of globalization and of more "post-modern" theories of space and mass communications technology that theorists such as Paul Virilio have explored. Virilio, *War and Cinema: The Logistics of Perception,* and *The Vision Machine*.

104. Ginzburg, *Stil' i epokha,* 99.

CHAPTER 2. FEELING

1. Moisei Ginzburg, *SA*.

2. Dziga Vertov, "Kinoki. Perevorot," reprinted in *Stat'i, dnevniki,* 54.

3. Vertov, "Kinoki," 53.

4. Vertov, "Kinoki," 53.

5. Aleksei Gan, *Konstruktivizm,* 56.

6. Vladimir Maiakovskii, "Kino i kino," *Kino-fot,* reprinted in *PSS,* 7: 29.

7. Rudolf Arnheim, *Film as Art*. Walter Benjamin, "The Work of Art in the Age of Mechanical Reproduction," in *Illuminations: Essays and Reflections,* edited by Hannah Arendt, 217–53; Siegfried Kracauer, *Theory of Film: The Redemption of Physical Reality* (this book is a synthesis of theories developed in earlier articles and in the book *From Caligari to Hitler*); André Bazin, *What is Cinema?,* selected and translated by Hugh Gray.

8. For more detailed analysis see Colin McCabe, "Theory and Film: Principles of Realism and Pleasure," in *Film Theory and Criticism: Introductory Readings,* edited by Gerald Mast, Marshall Cohen, and Leo Braudy, 79–93, who traces the development from Bazinian Realism toward the conception of the cinema as structured around the "gaze" and psychoanalysis, which was influenced by Jacques Lacan. Dudley Andrew, in *The Major Film Theories: An Introduction* and *Concepts in Film Theory,* provides a more general account of the history of film theory.

9. Erwin Panofsky, "Style and Medium in the Motion Pictures," in Mast, Cohen, and Braudy, eds., *Film Theory and Criticism,* 236.

10. Panofsky, "Style and Medium," 247.

11. Yuri Tsivian, *Early Cinema in Russia and its Cultural Reception,* translated by Alan Bodger, 202.

12. Tsivian, *Early Cinema,* 160.

13. Béla Balázs, "The Close-up," in Mast, Cohen, and Braudy, eds., *Film Theory and Criticism,* 260; *Character and Growth of a New Art*. See also Balázs, "Novye fil'my. Novoe zhizneoshchushchenie," *SK*.

14. Kracauer, *Theory of Film,* 40.

15. Miriam Bratu Hansen, "The Mass Production of the Senses: Classical Cinema as Vernacular Modernism," in *Reinventing Film Studies,* edited by Christine Gledhill and Linda Williams, 341–42.

16. Hansen, "The Mass Production," 342.

17. Benjamin, "The Work of Art," 237.

18. Benjamin, "The Work of Art," 240.

19. L. Shipulinskii, "Dusha kino," in *Kinematograf: sbornik statei,* 8.

20. See Tsivian's CD-ROM, *Immaterial Bodies: Cultural Anatomy of Early Russian Films.*

21. Lev Kuleshov, "Moi opyt," in *Sobranie sochinenii v trekh tomakh,* edited by A. Khokhlova, 1: 171.

22. Vertov, "Kinoki," 54.

23. Kuleshov, "Iskusstvo, sovremennaia zhizn' i kinematograf," *Kinofot.* Reprinted in English in Richard Taylor and Ian Christie, eds., *The Film Factory: Russian and Soviet Cinema in Documents 1896–1939,* 68–69.

24. Susan Buck-Morss suggests that the "paradox" of montage is "that which it shows us is both given (in the pieces of the film) and constructed (in the juxtaposition that gives these pieces meaning)." Buck-Morss, "The Cinema Screen as Prosthesis of Perception: A Historical Account," in *The Senses Still: Perception and Memory as Material Culture in Modernity,* edited by Nadia Seremetakis, 47.

25. Buck-Morss, "The Cinema Screen," 46.

26. Louis Delluc, "Photogénie" (Paris: Editions de Brunoff, 1920), reprinted in Delluc, *Ecrits cinématographiques,* edited by Pierre Lherminier, 1: 33–77.

27. Jean Epstein, "Photogénie and the Imponderable," in Richard Abel, *French Film Theory and Criticism: A History/Anthology 1907–1939,* 2: 189.

28. Ian Christie, "Myths of Total Cinema," *After-Image.*

29. For a discussion of this, see Mikhail Iampol'skii, *Vidimyi mir: ocherki rannei kinofenomenologii,* 5.

30. Epstein, "The Senses 1 (b)," *After-Image.* Reprinted in Abel, *French Film Theory,* 1: 245 (page citations are to the reprint edition).

31. Lui Deliuk, *Fotogeniia,* translated by T. I. Sorokin. For references to Epstein, see V. Pozner, "Frantsuzskii kinematograf v 1924 godu (pis'mo iz Parizha)," *Kino-zhurnal ARK,* 28. The general currency of the term *photogenic (fotogenichnyi)* is evidenced in the popular 1924 film comedy *Papirosnitsa ot Mosselproma (The Cigarette Girl from Mosselprom)* when an infatuated cameraman spots a glamorous young cigarette seller on the streets of Moscow and declares "what a photogenic *[fotogenichnoe]* face!" It is first listed in a dictionary only in 1937, however, and then in a *Slovar' inostrannykh slov.* See *Slovar' sovremennogo russkogo literaturnogo iazyka,* 15: 1528.

32. "Kartiny, kotorye nam pokazyvaiut," *Kino.* For references to the release of the films, see *Kino i vremia: biulleten' Gosfil'mofonda,* 2: 371, 372.

33. Vsevolod Pudovkin, "Fotogeniia," *Kino-zhurnal ARK.* This issue also carried a review written by L. Rosental' of Delluc's book. The subsequent edition of the journal carried an article written in response to Pudovkin: Leo Mur, "Fotogeniia," *Kino-zhurnal ARK.*

34. Pudovkin, "Fotogeniia," 10.

35. Cited in Iampol'skii, "'Smyslovaia veshch' v kinoteorii Opoiaza," in *Tynianovskii sbornik: tret'i tynianovskie chteniia,* edited by M. O. Chudakova, 109–20.

36. Epstein, "The Senses 1 (b)," 246.

37. Karl Marx, "Private Property and Communism," 101.

38. Sergei Eisenstein, "Towards a Materialist Approach to Film Form," in *An Eisenstein Reader,* edited by Richard Taylor, translated by Richard Taylor and William Powell, 57.

39. Eisenstein, "Towards a Materialist Approach," 55.

40. Eisenstein, "October: Beyond the Played and the Non-played," in Taylor, *An Eisenstein Reader,* 773–79.

41. Eisenstein, "October," 76. For a fuller discussion of debates about "played *(igrovoe)*" and "unplayed" films see Liudmila Dzhulai, *Dokumental'nyi illiuzion: otechestvennyi kino-dokumentalizm—opyty sotsial'nogo tvorchestva,* 24–30. Also see, in English, Graham Roberts, *Forward Soviet!*

42. Eisenstein, "October," 76.

43. Iampol'skii, *Vidimyi mir,* offers a detailed account of the influence of photogénie on Formalist film theory.

44. Viktor Shklovskii, *O teorii prozy,* 12.

45. Boris Eikhenbaum, "Problemy kino-stilistiki," in *Poetika kino,* edited by Boris Eikhenbaum, 23.

46. Eikhenbaum, "Problemy," 44.

47. Aleksei Gan, *Konstruktivizm,* 64, 61, 62.

48. Shklovskii, "Semantika kino," in *Za 60 let: raboty o kino,* edited by E. Levin, 32.

49. Eikhenbaum, "Problemy," 15.

50. A five-volume collection of Bergson's writing was published in Russia between 1913 and 1914: *Anri Bergson: Sobranie sochinenii,* edited by M. I. Semenov. Translations of individual works appeared earlier than this and continued to be published in new editions through the 1920s. See James Curtis, "Bergson and Russian Formalism," *Comparative Literature,* for an analysis of the influence of Bergson on the Formalists more generally, and Hilary L. Fink, *Bergson and Russian Modernism, 1900–1930,* for a comprehensive history of Bergson's influence in Russia.

51. Henri Bergson, *Matter and Memory,* translated by N. M. Paul and W. S. Palmer, 197.

52. Shipulinskii, "Dusha kino," 14.

53. Bergson, *L'évolution créatrice,* 330–31. Bergson's conception of movement as heterogeneous and indivisible was set out in *Matter and Memory* in 1896.

54. Shklovskii, *Literatura i kinematograf,* 25.

55. Shklovskii, *Literatura i kinematograf,* 24.

56. Gilles Deleuze, *Cinéma 1: The Movement-Image,* translated by Hugh Tomlinson and Barbara Habberjam, 2.

57. Deleuze, *Cinéma 1,* 22.

58. Deleuze, *Cinéma 1,* 24.

59. Vlada Petric, *Constructivism in Film: The Man with the Movie Camera, a Cinematic Analysis,* 7.

60. Vertov, "My. Variant manifesta," in *Stat'i, dnevniki,* 49.

61. This is a very simplified description of Eisenstein's montage. See *Sergei Eisenstein: Selected Works: Volume 1, Writings, 1922–34,* edited and translated by Richard Taylor, which traces the development of Eisenstein's thought from the "Montage of Attractions" toward intellectual montage. See also, for example, Jacques Aumont, *Montage Eisenstein.*

62. Vertov, "Kinoki," 53.

63. Petric, *Constructivism in Film,* 4.

64. It is this phenomenological aspect of Marx that has influenced philosophers such as Maurice Merleau-Ponty. For Merleau-Ponty, "man is in the world, and only in the world does he know himself." Maurice Merleau-Ponty, *The Phenomenology of Perception,* translated by Colin Smith, xi.

65. Gan, *Da zdrastvuet demonstratsiia byta,* 14.

66. Vertov, "Ot 'kinoglaza' k 'radioglazu' (iz azbuki kinokov)," *Stat'i, dnevniki,* 112.

67. Mikhail Bakhtin, "Forms of Time and the Chronotope in the Novel," in *The Dialogic Imagination: Four Essays by Mikhail Bakhtin,* edited by Michael Holquist, translated by Michael Holquist and Caryl Emerson, 84–259. In Bakhtin's discussion of the *put'* as a narrative structure, the emphasis on *process* over defined aim is informative.

68. Roman Jakobson, *Language in Literature,* edited by Krystyna Pomorska and Stephen Rudy, 30. See also *Russian Art of the Avant Garde: Theory and Criticism,* edited by John E. Bowlt, 205–54, for expressions of this dynamic in the visual arts.

CHAPTER 3. DECENTRING

1. The early FEKS (Fabrika ekstsentricheskogo aktera) comprised Grigorii Kozintsev and Leonid Trauberg, with Sergei Yutkevich, Georgii Kryzhitskii, and the cameraman Andrei Moskvin. The films produced by the group were *Pokhozhdeniia Oktiabriny* (1925), *Chertovo koleso* (1926), *Shinel'* (1926), *SVD (Soiuz Velikogo Dela)* (1927), and *Novyi Vavilon* (1929). After 1929, Kozintsev and Trauberg's next film, *Odna* (1931), marked an aesthetic transition that Kozintsev himself described as a shift toward the representation of a "hero of our time," leading eventually to the Maksim trilogy (see Chapter 6). Grigorii Kozintsev, *Sobranie sochinenii v piati tomakh,* I: 364.

2. David Burliuk, Aleksandr Kruchenykh, Vladimir Maiakovskii, and Viktor Khlebnikov, "Poshchechina obshchestvennomu vkusu," in Vladimir Maiakovskii, *PSS,* 13: 244–45.

3. Kozintsev, "Kliuch k faktam," from *Ekstsentrizm,* 9–10.

4. For Eisenstein's formulation of the "montage of attractions," see "The Montage of Attractions," 29–34, and "The Montage of Film Attractions," 35–52, in *An Eisenstein Reader,* edited by Richard Taylor.

5. Naum Kleiman, "Ekstsentricheskoe i tragicheskoe," 133.

6. Kozintsev, *Glubokii ekran,* I: 91.

7. Kaufman was Vertov's brother and cameraman on most key films. See the special edition of *Iskusstvo kino,* 1997, no. 8, dedicated to films of and about Moscow, for further discussion of images of the city, in particular, R. Iurenev, "Tri Moskvy Il'i Kopalina," 69–74.

8. Writing from Berlin in 1929, Vertov expressed his dismay at suggestions that the "Cine-eye" was influenced by Ruttman's film. He was at pains to emphasize that the "symphony

of a city" idea had been present in the *kinok* group's films from the beginning: Dziga Vertov, "Pis'mo iz Berlina," *Stat'i, dnevniki,* 120–22.

9. Georg Simmel, "The Metropolis and Mental Life," in *Simmel on Culture,* edited by David Frisby and Mike Featherstone, 175.

10. Charles Baudelaire, "A une passante," *Les Fleurs du mal et autres poèmes,* 114.

11. Richard Sennet, *Flesh and Stone: The Body and the City in Western Civilization,* 256.

12. For a general discussion of the role of the city in Russian history and culture, see *The City in Russian History,* edited by Michael F. Hamm and David M. Bethea, *The Shape of Apocalypse in Modern Russian Fiction.*

13. See Iurii Lotman, "Simvolika Peterburga i problema semiotiki goroda," *Vnutri mysliashchikh mirov: Chelovek, tekst, semiosfera, istoriia,* 275–96.

14. Sennet, *Flesh and Stone,* 310

15. See Julian Graffy, "Moscow (Urban Legends: Ten Cities that Shook Cinema)," *Sight and Sound,* 26–29, for further discussion of this and other *bytovye* films of Moscow.

16. See Ian Christie, "Down to Earth: *Aelita* Relocated," in *Inside the Film Factory,* edited by Taylor and Christie, 80–102.

17. Walter Benjamin, "Moscow," 108.

18. Maiakovskii, "Misteriia-buff: geroicheskoe, epicheskoe i satiricheskoe izobrazhenie nashei epokhi: vtoroi variant," in *PSS,* 2: 248.

19. See Svetlana Boym, *Common Places: Mythologies of Everyday Life in Russia,* for illuminating discussion of the history of *byt.*

20. Maiakovskii, *PSS,* 2: 73. See Boym, *Common Places,* and Victor Buchli, *An Archaeology of Socialism,* 55–62, for further discussion of the dangers of decoration. Also Olga Matich, "Remaking the Bed: Utopia in Daily Life," in *Laboratory of Dreams: The Russian Avant-garde and Cultural Experiment,* edited by John E. Bowlt and Olga Matich, 59–81.

21. Ermler's films during the 1920s and 1930s were *Kat'ka—bumazhnyi ranet* (1926) (codirected with Eduard Ioganson), *Parizhskii sapozhnik* (1927), *Dom v sugrobakh* (1928), *Oblomok imperii* (1929), *Vstrechnyi* (1932), *Krestian'e* (1934), and *Velikii grazhdanin* (1938–40). See Denise Youngblood, *Movies for the Masses: Popular Cinema and Soviet Society in the 1920s,* 139–53.

22. See Julian Graffy, *Bed and Sofa,* for further discussion of this film.

23. Iurii Tsivian, *Istoricheskaia retseptsiia kino: kinomatograf v Rossii 1896–1930,* 392–419, offers a detailed analysis of the montage of *Oblomok imperii.*

24. See Sigmund Freud, "The Uncanny," in *Art and Literature: Jensen's Gradiva, Leonardo da Vinci and Other Works,* 335–77.

25. Benjamin, "Moscow," 124.

CHAPTER 4. EXPLORING

1. E. Finn, "Chuzhaia rodina," *Vokrug sveta.*

2. *Vokrug sveta,* 1931, no. 4: 1.

3. "Vtoroi v mire," *Vokrug sveta,* 1.

4. "Tak rastut goroda," *Vokrug sveta,* 20.

5. *Vokrug sveta,* 1928, no. 1: 1.

6. The circulation of *Vokrug sveta* rose from 150,000 in 1928 to 300,000 in 1931. From 1928 it was issued weekly.

7. "Na zabroshennoi stantsii," *Vokrug sveta,* 10; "Po taige—po porogam."

8. "Vakhshkaia Dolina," *Vokrug sveta.*

9. I. Lesnovskii, "Kama-pechora!," *Vokrug sveta.*

10. M. Il'in, "The Scouts of the Five Year Plan," in *New Russia's Primer: The Story of the Five Year Plan,* translated by George S. Counts and Nucia P. Lodge, 21. Il'in was a frequent contributor to *Vokrug sveta.*

11. "Razvedchiki piatiletki," *Vokrug sveta.*

12. Il'in, *New Russia's Primer,* 21.

13. L. N. Godunova, "Organy upravleniia muzeinym delom v SSSR, 1917–1941gg.," *Muzeinoe delo v SSSR: Muzeinoe stroitel'stvo v SSSR, sbornik nauchnykh trudov,* compiled by L. I. Arapova and L. N. Godunova, 27. The term *kraevedenie* (from *krai*—region / area and *vedenie*—study) is difficult to translate, incorporating all forms of local study—geological, ethnographic, scientific. It has been translated as "home lore"—a term that is useful in emphasizing the *local* emphasis of the initiative. See Iu. K. Efremov, "Local Studies and Geography," in *Soviet Geography,* edited by I. P. Gerasimov and G. M. Ignat'ev, 382.

14. TSBK: Tsentral'noe Biuro Kraevedeniia. A. V. Ushaov, "Nauchno-issledovatel'skaia rabota muzeev istoricheskogo profilia, 1917–1959gg.," *Muzeinoe delo,* 46. See also N. P. Antsiferov, *Antsiferovskie chteniia: materialy i tezisy konferentsii (20–22 dekabria 1989 g.),* edited by A. I. Dobkin and A. V. Kobak, for further discussion of *kraevedenie.* On prerevolutionary work of the Geographical Society, see Nathaniel Knight, "Science, Empire and Nationality: Ethnography and the Russian Geographical Society, 1845–1855," in *Imperial Russia: New Histories for the Empire,* edited by Jane Burbank and David L. Ransel.

15. *Ves' SSSR: spravochnik-putevoditel',* edited by D. F. Sverchkova.

16. See, for example, "Ul'tra-goluboi ugol': novyi istochnik energii," *Vokrug sveta;* "Elektricheskaia strana," *Vokrug sveta.*

17. RGAKFD: *Nauchno-populiarnye fil'my,* 1924–30. See also *SK,* 1927, no. 4: 15, for a list of twelve *nauchno-populiarnyi* films produced in 1926. Titles include *Water and Nature, Aviation,* and *Black and White Diamonds.*

18. *Chto dolzhen znat' rabochii i krest'ianin o SSSR* (1928), directed by A. Bushkin. The film has not been preserved. See *Sovetskie khudozhestvennye fil'my: annotirovannyi katalog,* edited by A. V. Macheret, 1: 310.

19. Cited in K. A. Salishchev, "Cartography," in *Soviet Geography: Accomplishments and Tasks,* edited by I. P. Gerasimov and G. M. Ignat'ev, 46.

20. Lenin, letter to G. E. Zinoviev, 24 April 1921, *PSS,* 52: 163–65.

21. "Model' mira," *Vokrug sveta.*

22. *Soiuzkinozhurnal* 47 (1929).

23. Il'in, *New Russia's Primer,* 26.

24. Antsiferov, *Kak izuchat' svoi gorod: v plane shkol'noi raboty.*

25. The *uezd,* an ancient administrative unit, was retained in Soviet Russia until 1929, providing a local organizational focus.

26. In addition to *Turksib,* see also *Pervomaiskii podarok trudiashchimsia strany* (1930); *Turk-*

sib (1930), directed by Ermolaev, cinematography by Kozlov; *Turksib otkryt: kino-ocherk* (1930), directed by G. Room, Vostokkino. Vostokkino was organized 26 March 1928 to provide films in those eastern republics that had no regional film studio.

27. *Pervomaiskii podarok trudiashchimsia strany.*

28. *Giganty raportiruiut.*

29. "Beg paravoza," *Vokrug sveta.*

30. *Sol' Svanetii (Shvante)* (1930), directed by Mikhail Kalatozov. In this film, Kalatozov used some footage from an earlier film of Svanetia, directed by Zheliabushski, director of the comedy *Papirosnitsa ot Mossel'proma: Svanetiia (serdtse gor) (Svanetia [Heart of the Mountains]).* For a contemporary review of *Sol' Svanetii,* see *Proletarskoe kino,* 1931, no. 4: 55. This anonymous reviewer ("S.A.") refers to the director throughout as Kalatozishvili.

31. Dziga Vertov, "O 'kinopravde,'" *Stat'i, dnevniki,* 78.

32. vskhv: Vserossiiskaia sel'skokhoziaistvennaia vystavka. Vertov, "O 'kinopravde,'" 78. *Kinopravda* 17 (1923), directed by Dziga Vertov, with Ivan Beliakov, Mikhail Kaufman, and Elizaveta Svilova.

33. Vertov, "Iz istorii kinokov," *Stat'i, dnevniki,* 116.

34. Yuri Slezkine, "The USSR as a Communal Apartment, or How a Socialist State Promoted Ethnic Particularism," *Slavic Review.*

35. See Francine Hirsch, "The Soviet Union as a Work in Progress: Ethnographers and the Category *Nationality* in the 1926, 1937 and 1939 Censuses," *Slavic Review,* for a detailed study of the "ethnographic" identification of "nationality" between 1925 and 1940.

36. Hirsch, "The Soviet Union," 257.

37. *Sovetskoe iskusstvo,* 1925, no. 3: 74–77.

38. Vertov, "Ot 'kinoglaza' k 'radioglazu,'" *Stat'i, dnevniki,* 112.

39. "Nam nuzhno znat' svoiu stranu."

40. "Etnografiia i kino," *SK,* 12.

41. *Kinematograf ("zhivaia fotografiia"): ego proiskhozhdenie, ustroistvo, sovremennoe i budushchee obshchestvennoe i nauchnoe znachenie,* accompanying *Vokrug sveta,* 1909, 108.

42. *SK,* 1927, no. 4: 12.

43. Leonid Sukharebskii, "Nauchnye kino-ekspeditsii i ikh zas"emka," *SK.* This article details projects sponsored by Gosplan, the state planning authority.

44. M. Veremienko, "O kul'turfil'me," *SK.*

45. Shneiderov went on to be a key player in the development of the genre of filmic *kraevedenie.* See *Kinoslovar' v dvukh tomakh,* edited by S. I. Iutkevich and S. Ginzburg, 2: 951. The *Velikii perelet* film was organized by Proletkino.

46. Kh. Khersonskii, "Put' na Vostok: 'Velikii perelet,'" *ARK,* 22. For further discussion of *Velikii perelet,* see Vladimir Shneiderov and Georgii Blium's article, "Kak snimalsia 'Velikii perelet,'" *ARK.*

47. "Kino-ekspeditsii," *SK.*

48. See, in particular, James Clifford, *The Predicament of Culture: Twentieth Century Ethnography, Literature, and Art,* and *Writing Culture: The Poetics and Politics of Ethnography,* edited by James Clifford and George E. Marcus.

49. J. L. Black, "Opening up Siberia: Russia's 'Window on the East,'" in *The History of*

Siberia: From Russian Conquest to Revolution, edited by Alan Wood, 61–62. See also Knight, "Grigor'ev in Orenburg, 1851–1862: Russian Orientalism in the Service of Empire?," *Slavic Review.*

50. "Kino-ekspeditsii," *SK.*

51. "Etnografiia i kino," *SK,* 12.

52. "Etnografiia i kino," 12.

53. See, for example, *Krasnaia panorama,* 1928, no. 8: 15.

54. "God sredi lesnogo naroda," *Vokrug sveta.*

55. See, for example, "S kino-apparatom po Buriatii," *SK,* and "Zadushevnoe slovo o puteshestvii vokrug sveta," *SK.*

56. Vladimir Erofeev, "Kino-industriia v Germanii," *SK.*

57. *Za poliarnym krugom* (1927), *Krysha mira* (1927), *Serdtse Azii* (1929), *K schastlivoi gavani* (1930), *Daleko v Azii* (1931), *V ussuriiskom taige* (1938), *Geroicheskii perelet* (1938), and *Liudi moria* (1939). Erofeev also made a film in honour of the opening of the Volga-Moscow Canal, *Put' otkryt* (1934), and two films of Moscow parades that emphasize national unification: *Olimpiada isskustv* (1930) and *Stalinskoe plemia* (date unknown). Erofeev's first film, titled *Za poliarnym krugom (Beyond the Polar Circle)* in 1927, was a montage of footage produced during an expedition in which he did not take part. See *Vladimir Alekseevich Erofeev (1898–1940): Materialy k 100-letiiu so dnia rozhdeniia,* edited and with an introduction by A. Deriabin, for a filmography.

58. Erofeev, "Iz dnevnika Pamirskoi ekspeditsii," *SK.*

59. Erofeev, *Po "kryshe mira" s kino-apparatom (puteshestvie na Pamir),* advertisement for Molodaia gvardiia, inside front cover.

60. Erofeev, *Po "kryshe mira,"* 110

61. Erofeev, *Po "kryshe mira,"* 185.

62. "Razvedchiki piatiletki," *Vokrug sveta,* 16.

63. Edward Saïd, *Orientalism.* Saïd suggests that Western states exoticize and "reify" the Oriental "other" as a means of consolidating their national selfhood and superiority.

CHAPTER 5. TRAVELLING

1. See Mary-Anne Doane, "' . . . When the direction of the force acting on the body is changed': The Moving Image," *Wide Angle,* and Laurence Kardish, *Junction and Journey: Trains and Film.*

2. See Yuri Tsivian, *Early Cinema in Russia and Its Cultural Reception,* 137–47, and "K simvolike poezda v rannem kino," *Trudy po znakovym systemam,* for a discussion of the train myth in early Russian cinema.

3. Viktor Shklovskii, "'Velikii Perelet' i kinematografiia" (1925), in *Za 60 let,* 76.

4. Sergei Tret'iakov, "Skvoz' neprotertye ochki," *Novyi LEF,* 20.

5. Tret'iakov, "Skvoz' neprotertye ochki," 23.

6. Michel de Certeau, *The Practice of Everyday Life,* translated by Steven Rendall, 92.

7. de Certeau, *The Practice of Everyday Life,* 101.

8. See Wolfgang Schivelbusch, *The Railway Journey: The Industrialization of Time and*

Space in the Nineteenth Century, translated by Anselm Hollo. John Ruskin was one of the most celebrated opponents of the railway, claiming that it destroyed the natural experience of "beauty."

9. Schivelbusch, *The Railway Journey*, 54.

10. Schivelbusch, *The Railway Journey*, 64.

11. In particular, Giuliana Bruno, *Streetwalking on a Ruined Map: Cultural Theory and the City Films of Elvira Notari;* Anne Friedberg, *Window Shopping: Cinema and the Postmodern.*

12. See Raymond Fielding, "Hale's Tours: Ultra-realism in the Pre-1910 Motion Picture," in *Film before Griffith*, edited by John L. Fell, 116–30.

13. Schivelbusch, *The Railway Journey*, 63.

14. In the United States, of course, the train occupies an important and distinct place in cultural mythology, tied in interesting ways to a project of spatial "conquest" that may be compared with that of Russian and Soviet *otkrytie*. A sustained comparison of the creation of the imaginary maps of these two vast territories would yield much but is not my project here.

15. Iakov Tolchan recalls this as Medvedkin's mission in an interview with Chris Marker in *The Last Bolshevik*, 1992. Tolchan (1901–1995) worked with Vertov on *A Sixth of the World* and travelled with Medvedkin on the train at its inception. He committed suicide in 1995.

16. Stephen Kotkin, *Magnetic Mountain: Stalinism as a Civilization*, 97.

17. *Soiuzkinozhurnal* 41 (1931), RGAKFD I-2217. Also *Organizovanno nabirat' rabochuiu silu* (1930), RGAKFD Ref I-2235 "b," in which workers are recruited and crowd onto trains headed for *stroiki;* and *Soiuzkinozhurnal* 18 (1931), RGAKFD I-2195.

18. Moisei Ginzburg, *Stil' i epokha*, 104.

19. The aerial shots documented short fund-raising flights over the city.

20. Aleksei Gan, "Kinopravda: trinadtsatyi opyt," *Kinofot.*

21. In Western modernist literature the plane was a symbol of liberation and transgressive experience, offering alternative narrative and viewing positions. See Gillian Beer, "The Island and the Aeroplane: The Case of Virginia Woolf," in *Nation and Narration,* edited by Homi K. Bhabha, for a discussion of the ways in which the airplane transformed perceptions of the world, "erasing" borders.

22. See my article, "Borders," for further discussion of this film.

23. Evgenii Dobrenko, "Seiatel' vetra: 'tvorimoe prostranstvo' Aleksandra Dovzhenko," *Iskusstvo kino*, 60.

24. Scott W. Palmer, "Aviation and Cinema in Stalin's Russia: Conformity, Collective, and the Cultural Revolution," offers a study of aviation and cinema in Stalinist Russia from the perspective of individuality/collectivity. Sheila Fitzpatrick, *Everyday Stalinism: Ordinary Life in Extraordinary Times: Soviet Russia in the 1930s,* 71–74, discusses the significance of the pilot and other heroes in Stalinist culture.

25. *Kryl'ia* (1932), directed by I. Kravchunovskii, screenplay by A. Filimonov, cinematograpy by A. Urnis. Rosfil'm (Moscow). The film has not been preserved. Details in *Sovetskie khudozhestvennye fil'my,* 1: 460. For a review of the film, see *SK*, 1932, nos. 3–4.

26. I. V. Stalin, speech reprinted in *Pravda,* 14 August 1936, 1.

27. Katerina Clark has discussed the significance of the hero in Stalinist culture: the pilot was a central figure. See Clark, *The Soviet Novel: History as Ritual*, 124–41.

28. These images of community represent, in a sense, a secular reformulation of the ideal of *sobornost'*. This term was used to describe the particularities of the prerevolutionary peasant commune in Russia, emphasizing spiritual unity within the community, and frequently was used in a looser sense by Slavophile writers to define the distinctiveness of the Russian national character against the individualism of the West. See Kathy Frierson, *Peasant Icons: Representations of Rural People in Late 19th Century Russia*, 101–15, for a detailed account of the heritage of *sobornost'* and images of communality.

29. *Veselaia Moskva*. Stsenariia (rabochii variant), *Fond Medvedkina*.

30. Stalin, "O dvukh osobennostiakh oktiabr'skoi revoliutsii, ili Oktiabr' i teorii permanentnoi revoliutsii Trotskogo," *Sochineniia*.

31. John Urry, *The Tourist Gaze*.

32. This adapted the earlier film, made during Medvedkin's time on the train but not directed by him, titled *Electrifitsirovannaia doroga Urala*, shot during the first transport expedition along the Ural railway.

CHAPTER 6. CONQUEST

1. A permanent home for the All-Union Agricultural Exhibition (VSKHV: Vsesoiuznaia sel'sko-khoziaistvannaia vystavka) was built in 1939. In 1958 it was transformed into VDNKH (Vystavka dostizhenii narodnogo khoziaistva SSSR [the Exhibition of the Achievements of the National Economy of the Union of Soviet Socialist Republics]).

2. Lebedev-Kumach became a popular Socialist Realist poet. See V. I. Lebedev-Kumach, *Vpered k pobede! Pesni i stikhi*.

3. After long debate, the music of this original Soviet anthem has recently been adopted as the anthem for Vladimir Putin's twenty-first-century Russian federation.

4. "Karatsiupa, N. F.," in *Sovetskii entsiklopedicheskii slovar'*, 1911.

5. Gasan Guseinov, *Karta nashei rodiny: ideologema mezhdu slovom i telom*, 12, offers an explanation of this and other related terms in Soviet culture. Other films dealing with the theme were *Na granitse* (1938), *Granitsa na zamke* (1938), and *Rodina* (1940).

6. The record-breaking production of a miner in the Donbass region, A. Stakhanov, gave rise to a cult of the heroic worker, the "Stakhanovite."

7. For an example of the positive reviews of this film, see I. Grossman-Roshchin, in *Proletarskoe kino*, which praises the film for its representation of "simple fact."

8. *Iunost' Maksima* (1935), *Vozvrashchenie Maksima* (1937), and *Vyborgskaia storona* (1939).

9. See Irina Gutkin, *The Cultural Origins of the Socialist Realist Aesthetic, 1890–1934*, 106–30, for a discussion of literary models of the "New Soviet Man."

10. *Karmannyi atlas SSSR* (Leningrad, 1939).

11. M. Ezinger, *Pobezhdennoe more: ocherk karskikh ekspeditsii*, 7 (from the foreword by P. G. Smidovich).

12. On *Aerograd*, see Evgenii Margolit, "Perechitivaia istorii sovetskogo kino," in *"Close-up": isotiko-teoreticheskii seminar vo VGIKe*, edited by A. S. Troshin, 188–202.

13. This was a common term used to describe the eastern border. See, for example, Nikolai

Kostarev, *Granitsa na zamke,* and the title of the later feature film *Granitsa na zamke* (1938).

14. Mark Bassin, "The Greening of Utopia," in *Architecture and Empire in Russia,* edited by James Cracraft and Dan Rowlands. See also Katerina Clark, *The Soviet Novel: History as Ritual,* 93–114.

15. Editors also included A. B. Khalatov, Mikhail Kol'tsov, F. M. Konar, and S. B. Uritskii.

16. *SSSR na stroike,* 1930, no. 1: 3. Films such as *Turksib* were praised for their fulfilment of this task.

17. "7 soiuznykh sovetskikh stolits," *SSSR na stroike,* 1930, nos. 7–8: 5.

18. I. V. Stalin, "O proekte konstitutsii Soiuza SSSR," in *Sobranie sochinenii,* edited by Robert McNeal, 1: 182.

19. For discussion of the mythic and cultic quality of Stalinist cinema, see Richard Taylor, "Red Stars, Positive Heroes and Personality Cults," in *Stalinism and Soviet Cinema,* edited by Richard Taylor and Derek Spring, 69–89.

20. *Sotsialisticheskaia derevniia: Kino zhurnal* 24 (1933).

21. Vertov's overt replacement of montage with slow-paced, panoramic takes that swing in disconcerting directions nevertheless retains the unsettling energy that defined his earlier films. Ostensibly conforming to the visual economy of Socialist Realism, he offers further exploration of the myriad possibilities of cinematic vision.

22. Moshe Lewin, *The Making of the Soviet System: Essays in the Social History of Interwar Russia,* 219.

23. Nadezhda Krupskaia, "Goroda budushchego," speech to the first Moscow *oblast'* of the Komsomol.

24. I. Chernia, "Na zemliu!," in *Revoliutsiia i kul'tura,* 40.

25. Cited in S. M. Kravets, *Arkhitektura Moskovskogo metropolitena imeni L. M. Kaganovicha,* 3.

26. See Karl Schlögel, "The Shadow of an Imaginary Tower," and Igor A. Kazus, "The Competition for the Country's Supreme Building," in *Naum Gabo and the Competition for the Palace of Soviets, Moscow, 1931–1933;* Alexei Tarkhanov and Sergei Kavtaradze, *Architecture of the Stalin Era,* 25–38, also has a useful overview of the various project proposals for the Dvorets sovetov.

27. V. L. Orleanskii, *Planirovka i rekonstruktsiia Moskvy,* discusses the validity of this radial organization at length.

28. Viktor Makhaev, "Obraz puti v sovetskoi kul'ture i arkhitekture (arkhitektura obshchestvenno-transportnykh kompleksov 1930–50-x gg.)," undertakes a sustained analysis of Stalinist architecture (transport systems) as the creation of a monumental cult of travel that was premised upon spatial domination.

29. *Arkhitektura kanala Moskva-Volga,* 5.

30. Orleanskii, *Planirovka i rekonstruktsiia Moskvy,* 83.

31. See, for example, "Prevrashchenie goroda," *Vokrug sveta.*

32. N. N. Baranskii, *Ekonomicheskaia geografiia SSSR: uchebnik dlia 8-go klassa srednei shkoly,* 142.

33. Evgenii Dobrenko has argued that cinematic images of space in feature films of the 1930s

represented the periphery as a more active and self-sufficient space than the centre. Moscow, he suggests, although certainly the symbolic *oikos* and *telos* of all narratives, is an always absent space. When it appears, it is no longer the site of significant action, but a monumental symbol. This analysis is supported in images of the city in films from 1935. Dobrenko, "Do samykh do okrain," *Iskusstvo kino.*

34. *Repertuarnyi ukazatel'* (Moscow: Kinofotoizdat', 1936), cited by Peter Kenez, *Cinema and Soviet Society, 1917–1953,* 144.

35. Greg Castillo, "Gorkii Street and the Design of the Stalin Revolution," in *Streets: Critical Perspectives on Public Space,* edited by Zeynip Çelik, Diane Favro, and Richard Ingersoll, 57–70, discusses in considerable depth the rebuilding of Gor'kii Street, organized by Arkadii Mordvinov, who was rewarded for his achievement by a position on the Supreme Soviet and other unprecedented honours.

36. As he clarifies in the screenplay for the film, Medvedkin used the winning design of Iofan and Gelfreich for this representation. *Veselaia (Novaia) Moskva.* "Stsenariia," 195.

37. See *Iz'iatoe kino: katalog sovetskikh igrovykh kartin, ne vypushchenykh vo vsesoiuznyi prokat no sovershennykh v proizvodstve ili iz'iatykh iz deistvuiushchego fil'mofonda v god vypuska na ekran 1924–1953,* edited by Evgenii Margolit and Viacheslav Smyrov, 63.

38. Mikhail Bakhtin, *The Dialogic Imagination: Four Essays by Mikhail Bakhtin,* edited by Michael Holquist, translated by Michael Holquist and Caryl Emerson, 212. The Bakhtinian "carnival" is an overused term, the appropriation of which tends to obscure Bakhtin's original meaning. See Gary Saul Morson and Caryl Emerson, eds., *Mikhail Bakhtin: Creation of a Prosaics,* especially pp. 89–96, for a clear exposition of the genesis and development of the term in Bakhtin.

39. Castillo, "Peoples at an Exhibition: Soviet Architecture and the National Question," *South Atlantic Quarterly* (special issue: *Socialist Realism without Shores,* edited by Thomas Lahusen and Evgeny Dobrenko), discusses the architecture of the exhibitions from the point of view of Soviet nationalities policy within a colonialist perspective, tracing the increasing reduction of national particularity to decoration and the creation of a homogenous "Stalinist" style.

40. The notion of *krai (na kraiu)*—the "edge" of space—recurs in descriptions of space through the Soviet period.

41. See Bassin, "Russia between Europe and Asia: The Ideological Construction of Geographical Space," *Slavic Review.*

42. See Kathy Frierson, *Peasant Icons: Representations of Rural People in Late 19th Century Russia,* 38–47.

43. See Frierson, *Peasant Icons.* Also Donald Fanger, "The Peasant in Literature," in *The Peasant in Nineteenth Century Russia,* edited by Wayne Vucinich, 231–62. Frierson discusses positive and negative myths of the peasant.

44. Sheila Fitzpatrick, *Stalin's Peasants: Resistance and Survival in the Russian Village after Collectivization,* 262. Prince Potemkin, favourite minister of Catherine II, draped façades of ideal villages along the banks of the river for his monarch's trip through the Russian South to give Catherine the illusion that she presided over an empire of pastoral harmony and contented peasants.

45. Kopalin began his cinematic career with Dziga Vertov and the *kinoki,* but the style of *Derevnia* is a marked departure from the *kinok* aesthetic.

46. *Narodnost'* (national/folk identity) developed in the nineteenth century in particular as a term that described a "national" identity which was defined *outside* the twin poles of autocracy and orthodoxy and which located its source in the *narod*—in the ordinary people (the peasantry). *Narodnost'* was configured as "authentic" Russian identity. It was also used by writers and critics such as Aleksandr Pushkin himself, and later Vissarion Belinskii and others, to describe the engagement of literature in "real" (that is, nonelite) Russia.

47. Bakhtin, "Forms of Time and the Chronotope," in *The Dialogic Imagination: Four Essays by Mikhail Bakhtin,* edited by Michael Holquist, translated by Michael Holquist and Caryl Emerson, 217, 144, 217.

48. See Maia Turovskaia, "I. A. Pyr'ev i ego muzikal'nye komedii. K probleme zhanra," *Kinovedcheskie zapiski,* and Masha Enzensberger, "'We were born to turn a fairytale into reality': Grigori Alexandrov's *The Radiant Path,*" in Taylor and Spring, eds., *Stalinism and Soviet Cinema,* 97–109. Enzensberger's title is taken from the popular song "The Aviators' March": "My rozhdeny, chtobi skazky sdelat' byl'iu." See *Mass Culture in Soviet Russia: Tales, Poems, Songs, Movies, Plays, and Folklore, 1917–1953,* edited by James van Geldern and Richard Stites, 257–58.

49. See Richard Taylor, "An Interview with Alexander Medvedkin," in *Inside the Film Factory: New Approaches to Russian and Soviet Cinema,* edited by Richard Taylor and Ian Christie, 172–73.

50. A. N. Afanasiev, *Russkie narodnie skazki,* edited by A. Chach. Other examples abound: "V odnoi derevne . . ." (48), "V odnom meste . . ." (184), "V etakikh mestakh, v etakikh bol'shikh derevniakh . . ."(305), etc.

51. Vladimir Propp, "Folklore and Reality," in *Theory and History of Folklore,* edited by Anatoly Liberman, translated by Ariadna Y. Martin and Richard P. Martin, 21. Translated from Propp, *Folk'lor i deistvitel'nost': Izbrannye stat'i,* edited by B. N. Putilova, 12.

52. Baba Iaga is a recurrent figure in Russian folktales. She is most often a witch figure, who lives in a hut "on chicken legs" and intervenes in the folk hero's journey or quest.

53. Bakhtin, "Forms of Time and the Chronotope," 207, 208.

AFTERWORD: MAPPED?

1. *Belomorsko-Baltiiskii kanal imeni Stalina: istoriia stroitel'stva,* edited by Maksim Gor'kii, L. Averbakh, and S. Finn.

2. V. M. Sukhodrev, Sostavlenie, *Oformlenie I podgotovka k izdaniiu uchebnykh kart.*

3. Gasan Guseinov, *Karta nashei rodiny: ideologema mezhdu slovom i telom,* tracks the shifting certainties of the Soviet imaginary map, with particular focus on the more recent period.

Glossary

byt the "everyday," everyday life

bytovoe adjective from *byt* (everyday)

chuzhaia rodina an alien native land

Gulag the Soviet labour camp system

kinofikatsiia cinefication (the distribution of cinematic equipment and films across the country)

kinoki Dziga Vertov's "Cine-eye" group

Kinonedelia *Film Week* (film series produced by the Cine-eye group)

Kinopravda *Film-Truth* (film series produced by the Cine-eye group)

kolkhoz collective farm

Komsomols urban communists

lampochki Il'icha Lenin's little light bulbs (slogan from the electrification propaganda)

malen'kie liudi "little people," that is, ordinary people, the masses

meshchanstvo petty bourgeoisness

nauchno-populiarnyi popular-scientific (film, literature, etc.)

neob"iatnyi prostor boundless space

novyi byt the "new everyday life" that revolution would create

obrabotka processing (term used by Constructivist theorists to refer to the industrialization of art)

oshchushchenie feeling or sensation

osvoenie mastery, conquest

ostatki remnants (the remnants of old systems or old classes)

otkrytie opening up (the opening up of uninhabited/inhospitable parts of the territory)

propiska the system of internal passports that registers each citizen as a resident in a particular region

prostor wide open space

put' journey or path

razvedchik scout (military reconnaissance)

razvedka reconnaissance or prospecting

rodnaia zemlia native land or earth

set' network

smychka joining or linking (the economic linking of town and countryside)

sy're raw materials, natural resources

tekuchest' fluidity (energy, dynamism)

velikii perelom Great Leap Forward

vol'ia will, freedom (distinguished from *svoboda,* which indicates freedom from restraint)

prostranstvo space

zavoevanie conquest

Filmography

Details are given as available.

Aelita. Directed by Iakov Protazanov. Screenplay by Fedor Otsep and Aleksei Tolstoi. Cinematography by Iurii Zheliabuzhskii and E. Shoneman. Mezhrabpom-Rus', 1924.

Aerograd. Directed and screenplay by Aleksandr Dovzhenko. Cinematography by Eduard Tisse. Mosfil'm and Ukrainfil'm, 1935.

Aleksandr Nevskii. Directed by Sergei Eisenstein with D. Vasiliev. Screenplay by P. Pavlenko. Cinematography by E. Tisse. Mosfil'm, 1938.

Arsenal. Directed and screenplay by Aleksandr Dovzhenko. Cinematography by Daniil Demutskii. Mosfil'm, 1928.

Aviomarsh. Directed by Mikhail Kaufman. Soiuzkinokhronika, 1934.

Beregi zdorov'e. Directed by Aleksandr Medvedkin. Gosvoenkino, 1929.

Berlin: Symphony of a Great City. Directed by Walter Ruttman. 1927.

Bogataia nevesta. Directed by Ivan Pyr'ev. Screenplay by Evgenii Pomeshchikov and Vladimir Dobrovol'kii. Cinematography by Vladimir Okulich. Ukrainfil'm, 1937.

Bol'shaia zhizn'. Directed by Leonid Lukov. Screenplay by Pavel Nilon. Cinematography by Ivan Shekker. Kievskaia kinostudiia, 1938.

Bronenosets Potemkin. Directed by Sergei Eisenstein and Grigorii Aleksandrov. Screenplay by Nina Agadzhanova. Cinematography by Eduard Tisse. Goskino (First Factory), 1925.

Byt krest'ian. From 1926. Documentary film series.

Byt rabochikh. From 1926. Documentary film series.

Chapaev. Directed and screenplay by Georgii and Sergei Vasiliev. Cinematography by Aleksandr Sigaev and A. Ksenfontov. Lenfil'm, 1934.

Chastnaia zhizn' Petra Vinogradova. Directed by Aleksandr Macheret. Screenplay by L. Slavin. Cinematography by E. Slavinskii. Moskinokombinat, 1934.

Chelovek iz restorana. Directed by Iakov Protazanov. Screenplay by Oleg Leonidov and Iakov Protazanov. Cinematography by Anatolii Golovnia and K. Vents. Mezhrabpom-Rus', 1927.

Chelovek s kino-apparatom. Directed and screenplay by Dziga Vertov. Assisted by Elizaveta Svilova. Cinematography by Mikhail Kaufman. VUFKU (Kiev), 1929.

Chelovek s ruzh'em. Directed by Sergei Iutkevich. 1934.

Chertovo koleso. Directed by Grigorii Kozintsev and Leonid Trauberg. Screenplay by Adrian Piotrovskii. Cinematography by Andrei Moskvin. Leningradkino, 1926.

Chlen pravitel'stva. Directed by Aleksandr Zarkhi and Josef Heifits. Screenplay by Katerina Vinogradskaia. Cinematography by Aleksandr Ginzburg. Lenfil'm, 1940.

Chudesnitsa. Directed and screenplay by Aleksandr Medvedkin. Cinematography by Igor Gelein. Mosfil'm, 1936.

Da, zveno. Kino-fabrika-poezd tresta Soiuzkinokhronika, 1932.

Daesh vozdukh. Directed by Dziga Vertov. Cinematography by Mikhail Kaufman. Soiuz-kino, 1924.

Daleko v Azii. Directed by Vladimir Erofeev. 1931.

Derevnia. Directed by Ilia Kopalin. Soiuzkino, 1930.

Desiat' let plana GOELRO: Kino illiustratsiia k dokladu t. Krzhizhanovskogo. 1930.

Deti bol'shogo goroda. Directed by Evgenii Bauer. 1914.

Devushka s kharakterom. Directed by Konstantin Iudin. Screenplay by G. Fish and I. Skliut. Cinematography by T. Lebeshev. Mosfil'm, 1939.

Devushka s korobkoi. Directed by Boris Barnet. Screenplay by Valentin Turkin and Vadim Shershenevich. Cinematography by Boris Frantsisson and Boris Fil'shin. Mezhrabpom-rus', 1927.

Devushka speshit na svidanie. Directed by M. Verner. Screenplay by A. Zorich. Cinematography by A. Bulinskii. Belgoskino, 1939.

Dezertir. Directed by Vsevolod Pudovkin. Screenplay by Nina Agadzhanova and M. Krasnostavskii. Cinematography by Anatolii Golovnia. Mezhrabpomfil'm, 1933.

Doch' rodiny. Directed by V. Korsh-Sablin. Screenplay by I. Zel'tser. Cinematography by B. Riabov and E. Shapiro. Belgoskino, 1937.

Dom na Trubnoi. Directed by Boris Barnet. Screenplay by Bela Torich, Anatolii Mariengof, Vadim Shershenevich, Viktor Shklovskii, and Nikolai Erdman. Cinematography by Evgenii Alekseev. Mezhrabpom Rus', 1928.

Dom v sugrobakh. Directed by Friedrikh Ermler. Sovkino, 1928.

Dubrovskii. Directed and screenplay by A. Ivanovskii. Cinematography by A. Sigaev. Lenfil'm, 1935.

Dva druga, model', i podruga. Directed by Aleksei Popov. 1928.

Dzhul'bars. Directed by V. Shneiderov. Screenplay by G. El'-Registan. Cinematography by A. Shelenkov. Mezhrabpomfil'm, 1936.

Garmon'. Directed by Igor Savchenko. Screenplay by A. Zharov and Igor Savchenko. Cinematography by Evgenii Shneider and Iurii Fogelman. Mezhrabpomfil'm, 1934.

Gazeta n. 4. Directed by Nikolai Karmazinskii. Kino-fabrika-poezd tresta soiuzkinokhronika, 1932.

General'naia linia (Staroe i novoe). Directed and screenplay by Sergei Eisenstein and Grigorii Aleksandrov. Cinematography by Eduard Tisse. Sovkino, 1929.

Geroicheskii perelet. Directed by Vladimir Erofeev. 1938.

Giganty raportiruiut, seriia kino-khroniki k XVI-mu parts"ezdu. Directed by Nikolai Karmazinskii. 1931.

Granitsa. Directed and screenplay by Mikhail Dubson. Cinematography by V. Rapoport. Lenfil'm, 1935.

Granitsa na zamke. Directed by V. Zhuravlev. Screenplay by I. Bachelis and M. Dolgopolov. Cinematography by N. Prozorovskii. Soiuzdetfil'm, 1938.

Groza. Directed and screenplay by B. Petrov. Cinematography by V. Gardanov. Soiuzfil'm, 1933.

Istrebiteli. Directed by E. Pentslin. Screenplay by F. Knorre. Cinematography by N. Topchii. Kievskaia kinostudiia, 1939.

Iunost' Maksima. Directed and screenplay by Grigorii Kozintsev and Leonid Trauberg. Cinematography by Andrei Moskvin. Lenfil'm, 1935.

Ivan. Directed and screenplay by Aleksandr Dovzhenko. Cinematography by Daniil Demutskii, Iurii Ekel'chik, and Mikhail Glider. Ukrainfil'm, 1932.

K schastlivoi gavani. Directed by Vladimir Erofeev. 1930.

Kak zhivesh', tovarishch gorniak? Directed by Nikolai Karmazinskii. Kino-fabrika-poezd tresta Soiuzkinokhronika, 1932.

Karta kapital'nogo stroitel'stva. From 1929. Documentary film series.

Kat'ka—bumazhnyi ranet. Directed by Eduard Johanson and Friedrikh Ermler. Cinematography by E. Mikhailov and Andrei Moskvin. Sovkino, 1926.

Kinopravda 1. Directed by Dziga Vertov. 5 June 1922.

Kinopravda 7. Directed by Dziga Vertov. Titles by Aleksandr Rodchenko. Cinematography by Bystrov. Edited by Elizaveta Svilova. 25 July 1922.

Kinopravda 13 *(Vchera, sevodnia, zavtra).* Directed by Dziga Vertov. Edited (montage) by Elizaveta Svilova. Goskino, 1922.

Kinopravda 14. Directed by Dziga Vertov. Edited (montage) by Elizaveta Svilova. Titles by Aleksandr Rodchenko. Cinematography by Bystrov. Goskino, November 1922.

Kinopravda 15. Directed by Dziga Vertov, with Boris Frantsisson, Ivan Beliakov, and Mikhail Kaufman. Goskino, 1923.

Kinopravda 17. Directed by Dziga Vertov with Ivan Beliakov. Cinematography by Mikhail Kaufman. Edited (montage) by Elizaveta Svilova. Goskino, 1923.

Kinopravda 18. Directed by Dziga Vertov. General editor Anatoli Goldobin. Goskino, March 1924.

Kinopravda 19 *(Probeg kino-apparata Moskva-Ledovityi okean).* Cinematography by various contributors. General editor Anatoli Goldobin. Goskino, May 1924.

Kinopravda 20 *(Pionerskaia).* Directed by Dziga Vertov. Cinematography by Mikhail Kaufman. Goskino, 1924.

Kinopravda 21 *(Leninskaia)*. Directed by Dziga Vertov. Cinematography by Georgi Giver, Anatoli Livitskii, A. Lemberg, Petr Novitskii, Mikhail Kaufman, Eduard Tisse, and others. Goskino, 1924.

Kinopravda 23 *(Radio-pravda)*. Cinematography by Mikhail Kaufman, Ivan Beliakov, and Aleksandr Bushkin. Goskino, 1925.

Kolybel'naia. Directed by Dziga Vertov. Assisted by Elizaveta Svilova. Cinematography by Dmitri Surenskii. Soiuzkinokhronika, 1937.

Komsomol'sk. Directed by Sergei Gerasimov. Screenplay by Z. Markina, M. Vitukhnovskii, and Sergei Gerasimov. Cinematography by A. Gintsburg. Lenfil'm, 1938.

Konets Sankt Peterburga. Directed by Vsevolod Pudovkin. Screenplay by Natan Zarki. Cinematography by Anatolii Golognia. Mezhrabpom Rus', 1927.

Krest'iane. Directed by Friedrikh Ermler. Screenplay by Manuel' Bol'shintsov, Viktor Portnov, and Friedrikh Ermler. Cinematography by Aleksandr Gintsburg. Lenfil'm, 1934.

Krysha mira: ekspeditsiia na Pamir. Directed by Vladimir Erofeev. Cinematography by I. Beliakov. Soiuzkino, 1927.

Kubanskie Kazaki. Directed by Ivan Pyr'ev. Screenplay by Nikolai Pogodin. Cinematography by Valentin Pavlov. Mosfil'm, 1949.

La Belle Nivernaise. Directed by Jean Epstein. 1923.

La goutte de sang. Directed by Jean Epstein. 1924.

L'arrivée d'un train en gare de la Ciotat. Directed by Louis Lumière. 1895.

The Last Bolshevik. Directed and screenplay by Chris Marker. La Sept-ARTE/Channel Four/YLE, 1992.

Lesnye liudi: kraevedcheskii ocherk v 5 chast'iakh. Directed by A. Litvinov. 1928.

Letchiki. Directed by Iurii Raizman. Screenplay by Aleksandr Macheret. Cinematography by L. Kosmatov. Mosfil'm, 1935.

Letiat zhuravli. Directed by Mikhail Kalatozov. 1957.

Liudi moria. Directed by Vladimir Erofeev. 1939.

Luch smerti. Directed by Lev Kuleshov. Screenplay by Vsevolod Pudovkin. Cinematography by A. Levitskii. Goskino (First Factory), 1925.

Lunnyi kamen' (Pamir). Directed by A. Minkin and I. Sorokhtin. Screenplay by V. Nedobrovo. Cinematography by F. Zandberg and V. Livitin. Lenfil'm, 1935.

Mat'. Directed by Vsevolod Pudovkin. Screenplay by Natan Zarki. Cinematography by Anatolii Golovnia. Mezhrabpom-Rus', 1926.

Moskva. Directed by Il'ia Kopalin and Mikhail Kaufman. 1927.

Moskva. Directed by Boris Nebylitskii. 1930.

Moskva segodnia. Directed by Boris Nebylitskii. 1944.

Moskva v oktiabre. Directed by Boris Barnet. Screenplay by Valentin Chernykh. Cinematography by Igor' Slabnevich. Mezhrabpom-Rus', 1927.

Na Granitse. Directed and screenplay by A. Ivanov. Cinematography by V. Rapoport. Lenfil'm, 1938.

Na leninskom puti. 1932.

Nasha Moskva. Directed by Boris Nebylitskii. 1938.

Nashi dostizheniia 1. 1930.

Novaia Moskva. Directed and screenplay by Aleksandr Medvedkin. Cinematography by Igor Gelein. Mosfil'm (never released), 1938.

Novyi Vavilon. Directed and screenplay by Grigorii Kozintsev and Leonid Trauberg. Cinematography by Andrei Moskvin. Sovkino, 1929.

Neobychainye prichlyucheniia Mistera Vesta v strane bol'shevikov. Directed by Lev Kuleshov. Screenplay by Nikolai Aseiev. Cinematography by Anatolii Levitskii. Goskino, 1924.

Oblomok imperii. Directed by Friedrikh Ermler. Screenplay by Friedrikh Ermler and Katerina Vinogradskaia. Cinematography by Evgenii Shneider. Sovkino, 1929.

Odinnatsadyi. Directed and screenplay by Dziga Vertov. Assisted by Elizaveta Svilova. Cinematography by Mikhail Kaufman. VUFKU (Kiev), 1928.

Odna. Directed and screenplay by Grigorii Kozintsev and Leonid Trauberg. Cinematography by Andrei Moskvin. Soiuzkino, 1931.

Odnazhdy letom. Directed by Igor Il'inskii and Kh. Shmain. Screenplay by I. Il'f and E. Petrov. Cinematography by A. Lavrik. Ukrainfil'm, 1936.

Okraina. Directed by Boris Barnet. Screenplay by Konstantin Finn and Boris Barnet. Cinematography by Mikhail Kirillov and A. Spiridonov. Mezhrabpomfil'm, 1933.

Oktiabr'. Directed and screenplay by Sergei Eisenstein and Grigorii Aleksandrov. Cinematography by Eduard Tisse. Sovkino, 1927.

Olimpiada iskusstv. Directed by Vladimir Erofeev. Cinematography by Ivan Beliakov and Z. Zalkind. Soiuzkino, 1930.

Ona zashchishchaet rodinu. Directed by Friedrikh Ermler. Screenplay by Aleksei Kapler. Cinematography by Vladimir Rapoport. TSOKS, Alma-Ata, 1943.

Padenie Berlina. Directed by Mikhail Chiaureli. Gosfil'm, 1950.

Papirosnitsa ot Mossel'proma. Directed and cinematography by Iurii Zheliabuzhskii. Screenplay by Aleksandr Faiko. Mezhrabpom-Rus', 1924.

Parizhskii sapozhnik. Directed by Friedrikh Ermler. Screenplay by N. Nikitin and B. Leonidov. Cinematography by E. Mikhailov. Sovkino, 1927.

Pechora. 1936.

Persiia. Directed by Vladimir Erofeev. 1935.

Pervaia piatiletka v SSSR. 1929.

Pervomaiskii podarok trudiashchimsia strany. 1930.

Pis'mo kolkhoznikam. Cinematography by E. Lifshitz. Kino-fabrika-poezd tresta Soiuzkinokhronika, 1932.

Po sovetskim granitsam. Soyuzkinokhronika, 1931.

Po Uzbekistanu. Directed by Vladimir Shneiderov. 1925.

Po zakonu. Directed by Lev Kuleshov. Screenplay by Viktor Shklovskii. Cinematography by Konstantin Kuznetsov. Goskino (First Factory), 1926.

Pokhozhdeniia Oktiabriny. Directed and screenplay by Grigorii Kozintsev and Leonid Trauberg. Cinematography by F. Verigo-Darovskii and I. Frolov. Sevzapkino (FEKS-fil'm), 1924.

Port piati morei. Director by Aleksandr Lemberg. 1932–33.

Potomok Chingiz Khana. Directed by Vsevolod Pudovkin. Screenplay by Osip Brik. Cinematography by Anatolii Golovnia. Mezhrabpomfil'm, 1928.

Proryv. Kino-fabrika-poezd tresta soiuzkinokhronika, 1930.

Pusk Dneprostroia. Kino-fabrika-poezd tresta soiuzkinokhronika, 1932.

Put' entuziastov. Directed by Aleksandr Medvedkin. Kino-fabrika-poezd tresta soiuzkinokhronika, 1930.

Put' otkryt. Directed by Vladimir Erofeev. 1934.

Puteshestvie po SSSR., 1934–1937. Directed by S. Bubrik. Kino-fabrika-poezd imeni Voroshilova, 1937.

Putevka v zhizn'. Directed by Nikolai Ekk. Screenplay by Nikolai Ekk, R. Ianushkevich, and A. Stolper. Cinematography by V. Pronin. Mezhrabpomfil'm, 1931.

Rodina. Directed by N. Shengelaia. Screenplay by G. Mdiviani and N. Shengelaia. Cinematography by K. Kuznetsov, 1940.

Schast'e. Directed by and screenplay by Aleksandr Medvedkin. Cinematography by Gleb Troianskii. Mosfil'm, 1935.

Segodnia. Directed by Esfir Shub. Sovkino, 1930.

Sel'skoe khoziaistvo. From 1928. Documentary film series.

Semero smelykh. Directed by Sergei Gerasimov. Screenplay by Iurii German and Sergei Gerasimov. Cinematography by E. Velichko. Lenfil'm, 1935.

Serdtse Azii. Directed by Vladimir Erofeev. 1929.

Shagai, Sovet! Directed by Dziga Vertov. Assistant director Mikhail Kaufman. Cinematography by I. Beliakov. Kul'tkino, 1926.

Shakhmatnaia goriachka. Directed by Vsevolod Pudovkin. Screenplay by N. Shpikovskii. Cinematography by Anatoli I. Golovnia. Mezhrabpom-Rus', 1925.

Shestaia chast' mira. Directed by Dziga Vertov with E. Svilova, M. Kaufman (and three *kinorazvedchiki:* Aleksandr Kagarlitskii, Il'ia Kopalin, and Boris Kudinov). Kul'tkino, 1926.

Shinel'. Directed by Grigorii Kozintsev and Leonid Trauberg. Screenplay by Iurii Tynianov. Cinematography by Andrei Moskvin and Evgenii Mikhailov. Leningradkino, 1926.

Shturm na rel'sakh. 1931.

Shturm pustyni. 1935.

Shumi gorodok. Directed by N. Sadkovich. Screenplay by N. Shpikovskii. Cinematography by G. Khimchenko. Kievskaia kinostudiia, 1939.

Simfoniia Donbasa. Directed by Dziga Vertov. Screenplay by Dziga Vertov (assisted by Elizaveta Svilova). Cinematography by Boris Tseitlin. Ukrainfil'm, 1930.

Skazanie o zemle sibirskoi. Directed by Ivan Pyr'ev. Screenplay by Evgenii Pomeshchikov and Nikolai Rozhkov. Cinematography by Valentin Pavlov. Mosfil'm, 1947.

Soiuzkinozhurnal. Soiuz Kinokhroniki, June 1929–October 1941.

Sol' Svanetii (Shvante). Directed by Mikhail Kalatozov. 1930.

Stachka. Directed by Sergei Eisenstein. Screenplay by V. Pletnev, Sergei Eisenstein, Grigorii Aleksandrov, and Ilia Kravchunovskii. Cinematography by Eduard Tisse. Proletkul't, 1924.

Stalinskoe plemia. Directed by Vladimir Erofeev. 1937.

Strogii iunosha. Directed by Abram Room. Screenplay by Iurii Olesha. Cinematography by Iurii Ekel'chik. Ukrainfil'm, 1936.

Suvorov. Directed by Vsevolod Pudovkin. Screenplay by G. Grebner. Cinematography by A. Golovnia. Mosfil'm, 1940.

SVD (Soiuz velikogo dela). Directed by Grigorii Kozintsev and Leonid Trauberg. Screenplay by Iurii Tynianov and Iurii Oksman. Cinematography by Andrei Moskvin. Sovkino, 1927.

Svetlyi put'. Directed by Grigorii Aleksandrov. Screenplay by V. Ardov. Cinematography by B. Petrov. Mosfil'm, 1940.

Svinarka i pastukh. Directed by Ivan Pyr'ev. Screenplay by V. Gusev. Cinematography by V. Pavlov. Mosfil'm, 1940.

Tovarishch Prokuror: kino ocherk. Directed by S. Bubrik. Plan by N. Safronov. Kino-fabrika-poezd tresta Soiuzkinokhronika, 1933.

Traktoristy. Directed by Ivan Pyr'ev. Screenplay by E. Pomeshchikov. Cinematography by A. Gal'perin. Mosfil'm, 1939.

Tret'ia meshchanskaia. Directed by Abram Room. Screenplay by Viktor Shklovskii and Abram Room. Cinematography by G. Giber. Sovkino, 1927.

Tri pesni o Lenine. Directed and screenplay by Dziga Vertov. Assisted by Elizaveta Svilova and Ilia Kopalin. Cinematography by Mark Magidson, Bentsion Manastyrskii, and Dmitrii Surenskii. Mezhrabpomfil'm, 1934.

Tsirk. Directed and screenplay by Grigorii Aleksandrov. Cinematography by Vladimir Nil'sen and Boris Petrov. Mosfil'm, 1936.

Turksib. Directed by Ermolaev. Cinematography by Kozlov. 1930.

Turksib. Directed by Viktor Turin. Screenplay by Viktor Turin with Aleksandr Macheret, Viktor Shklovskii, and Iakov Aron. Vostokkino (five parts), 1930.

Turksib otkryt: kino-ocherk. Directed by G. Room. Vostokkino, 1930.

U samogo sinego moria. Directed by Boris Barnet. Screenplay by K. Mints. Cinematography by M. Kirillov. Mezhrabpomfil'm and Azerfil'm, 1935.

Uplotnenie. Directed by Anatolii Panteleev, Niolai Pashkovsky, and Anatolii Donilov. Screenplay by Anatolii Lunacharskii and Anatolii Panteleev. Cinematography by V. Lemke. Petrogradskii kinokomitet, 1918.

V strane Lenina. From 1929. Documentary series.

V ussuriiskoi taige. Directed by Vladimir Erofeev. 1938.

Valerii Chkalov. Directed by Mikhail Kalatozov. Screenplay by G. Baidunov. Cinematography by Aleksandr Gintsburg. Lenfil'm, 1941.

Vasha znakomaia. Directed by Lev Kuleshov. Screenplay by A. Kurs. Cinematography by K. Kuznetsov. Sovkino, 1927.

Veitlus: opyt luchshikh vsem kolkhozam. Kino-fabrika-poezd tresta Soyuzkinokhronika, 1932.

Velikii grazhdanin. Directed by Friedrikh Ermler. Screenplay by Mikhail Bleiman. Cinematography by Arkadii Kol'tsatyi. Lenfil'm, 1937–39.

Velikii perelet. Directed by Vladimir Shneiderov. 1925.

Velikii put'. Directed and screenplay by Esfir Shub. Sovkino, 1929.

Velikii uteshitel'. Directed by Lev Kuleshov. Screenplay by Lev Kuleshov and A. Kurs. Cinematography by K. Kuznetsov. Mezhrabpomfil'm, 1933.

Veselye rebiata. Directed by Grigorii Aleksandrov. Screenplay by Vladimir Mass, Nikolai Erdman, and Grigorii Aleksandrov. Cinematography by Vladimir Nilsen. Moskinokombinat, 1934.

Vesennii fel'eton. Directed by Nikolai Karmazinskii. Sovkino, 1929.

Volga-Volga. Directed by Grigorii Aleksandrov. Screenplay by Mikhail Vol'pin and Nikolai Erdman. Cinematography by Boris Petrov. Mosfil'm, 1938.

Vozdushnyi izvozchik. Directed by G. Rappaport. Screenplay by E. Petrov. Cinematography by A. Gal'perin. TSOKS, Alma-Ata, 1943.

Vozvrashchenie Maksima. Directed by Grigorii Kozintsev and Leonid Trauberg. Screenplay by Grigorii Kozintsev, Leonid Trauberg, and L. Slavin. Cinematography by Andrei Moskvin. Lenfil'm, 1938.

Vratar'. Directed by S. Timoshenko. Screenplay by L. Kassil' and M. Iudin. Cinematography by V. Danashevskii. Lenfil'm, 1936.

Vstrechnyi. Directed by Friedrikh Ermler and Sergei Iutkevich. Screenplay by L. Arnshtam, D. Del', Friedrikh Ermler, and Sergei Iutkevich. Cinematography by Aleksandr Gintsburg, Zh. Martov, and V. Rapoport. Rosfil'm, 1932.

Vyborgskaia storona. Directed and screenplay by Grigorii Kozintsev and Leonid Trauberg. Cinematography by Andrei Moskvin. Lenfil'm, 1939.

Za naivazhnyi . . . Kribassa (in Ukrainian). Directed by G. Piotrovskii. Kino-fabrika-poezd tresta soiuzkinokhronika, 1932.

Za poliarnym krugom. Directed by Vladimir Erofeev. 1927.

Za sotsialisticheskuiu derevniu 15–24. Soiuzkinozhurnal. 1931

Za zdorovyi transport. 1929.

Zakliuchennye. Directed by Evgenii Cherviakov. Sovkino, 1936.

Zemlia. Directed and screenplay by Aleksandr Dovzhenko. Cinematography by Daniil Demutskii. VUFKU (Kiev), 1930.

Zolotoe ozero. Directed by V. Shneiderov. Screenplay by A. Peregudov and V. Shneiderov. Cinematography by A. Shelenkov. Mezhrabpomfil'm, 1935.

Zvenigora. Directed by Aleksandr Dovzhenko. Screenplay by Mikhail Johansson and Iurii Tiutiunik. Cinematography by Boris Zaveliev. VUFKU (Kiev), 1928.

Zveno energetiki. Directed by Poselskii. Kino-fabrika-poezd tresta soiuzkinokhronika, 1931.

Zveno pobedy. Directed by S. Bubrik. Kino-fabrika-poezd tresta soiuzkinokhronika, 1933.

Bibliography

JOURNALS CONSULTED, 1924–32

ARK
Kino i zhizn'
Kinofot
Krasnaia panorama
Ogonek
Proletarskoe kino (PK)
Prozhektor
Sovetskoe kino: organ khudozhestvennogo soveta po delam kino (SK)
Sovremennaia arkhitektura (SA)
SSSR na stroike
Vokrug sveta
Zhizn' iskusstva

PRIMARY SOURCES

Antsiferov, N. P. *Kak izuchat' svoi gorod: v plane shkol'noi raboty.* Moscow, 1929.
Arkhitektura kanala Moskva-Volga. Moscow: Izdatel'stvo Akademii arkhitektury, 1939.
Babel', Isaak. *Neft'.* In *Sochineniia.* Vol. 2. Moscow: Khudozhestvennaia literatura, 1992.
Balázs, Béla. "Novye fil'my. Novoe zhizneoshchushchenie." *SK* 3–4 (1933): 19–24.

Baranskii, N. N. *Ekonomicheskaia geografiia SSSR: uchebnik dlia 8-go klassa srednei shkoly.* Moscow: Gosudarstvennoe uchebno-pedagogicheskoe izdatel'stvo, 1936.

"Beg paravoza." *Vokrug sveta* 26 (1928): 20.

Berdiaiev, Nikolai. *The Origin of Russian Communism.* Translated by R. M. French. Reprint, Ann Arbor: University of Michigan Press, 1969.

———. *Sud'ba Rossii.* 1918. Reprint, Moscow: Sovetskii pisatel', 1990.

Bergson, Henri. *Anri Bergson: Sobranie sochinenii.* Edited by M. I. Semenov. St. Petersburg, 1913–14.

———. *L'évolution créatrice.* Paris: Presses Universitaires de France, 1907.

Besserov, S. A. "Problema prostranstva v perspectivnom plane." *Planovoe Khoziastvo* 6 (1928): 63–90 and 7 (1928): 55–67.

Blok, Aleksandr. *Zapisnye knizhki.* 2 vols. Leningrad, 1930.

Bogdanov, Alexander (A. A. Malinovskii). *Filosofiia zhivogo opyta.* Moscow: Gosudarstvennoe izdanie, 1920.

Burliuk, David, Aleksandr Kruchenykh, Vladimir Maiakovskii, and Viktor Khlebnikov. "Poshchechina obshchestvennomu vkusu." Moscow, December 1912.

Chaianov, A. V. *Osnovnye idei i metody obshchestvennoi agronomii,* 1st ed. Moscow: Gosizdat', 1918.

———. *Puteshestvie moego brata Alekseia v stranu krest'ianskoi utopii.* Moscow: Gosizdat', 1928.

Chernia, I. "Na zemliu!" *Revoliutsiia i kul'tura* 7 (1930): 35–45.

Dvenadsat' udarnykh reisov. Moscow, 1934.

Deliuk, Lui. *Fotogeniia.* Translated by T. I. Sorokin. Moscow: Novye vekhi, 1924.

Delluc, Louis. *Ecrits cinématographiques.* Edited by Pierre Lherminier. 2 vols. Paris: Cinématèque française, 1985–86.

Eikhenbaum, Boris, ed. *Poetika kino.* Moscow: Kinopechat', 1927. Reprint, Berkeley, Calif.: Berkeley Slavic Specialties, 1984.

Eisenstein, Sergei. "October: Beyond the Played and the Non-played." In *An Eisenstein Reader.* Translated by Richard Taylor and William Powell. London: B. F. I., 1998.

"Elektricheskaia strana." *Vokrug sveta* 12 (1930): 10–12.

Epstein, Jean. *Cinéma.* Paris: Edition de la sirène, 1921.

———. "On Certain Characteristics of Photogénie." *After-Image* 10 (1981): 20–21.

———. "Photogénie and the Imponderable." In *French Film Theory and Criticism: A History/Anthology 1907–1939.* Edited by Richard Abel. Vol. 2. Princeton: Princeton University Press, 1998.

———. "The Senses 1 (b)." *After-Image* 10 (1981): 9–16.

Erenburg, Il'ia. *Materializatsiia fantastiki.* Moscow/Leningrad: Kinopechat', 1926.

Erofeev, Vladimir. "Iz dnevnika Pamirskoi ekspeditsii." *SK* 2–3 (1928): 19.

———. "Kino-industriia v Germanii." *SK* 4 (1927): 80–81.

———. *Po "krysha mira" s kino-apparatom (puteshestvie na Pamir).* Moscow: Molodaia Gvardiia, 1929.

"Etnografiia i kino." *SK* 4 (1927): 12–13.

Ezinger, M. *Pobezhdennoe more: ocherk karskikh ekspeditsii.* Moscow: Sovetskoe Aziia, 1932.

Finn, E. "Chuzhaia rodina." *Vokrug sveta* 13 (1931): 12.

Gan, Aleksei. *Da zdrastvuet demonstratsiia byta*. Moscow: Glavlit, 1923.

———. *Konstruktivizm*. Tver': Tverskoe izdatel'stvo, 1922.

———. "Kinopravda: trinadtsatyi opyt." *Kinofot* 5 (1922): 6–7.

Ginzburg, Moisei. "Konstruktivizm kak metod laboratornoi i pedagogicheskoi raboty." *SA* 6 (1927): 160–66.

———. *SA* 6 (1928): 170.

———. *Stil' i epokha*. Moscow: Gosizdat', 1924.

———. "Tselevaia ustanovka v sovremennoi arkhitekture." *SA* 1 (1927): 4–18.

"God sredi lesnogo naroda." *Vokrug sveta* 26 (1928): 2–3.

Gor'kii, Maksim, L. Averbakh, and S. Finn, eds. *Belomorsko-Baltiiskii kanal imeni Stalina: istoriia stroitelstva*. Moscow: Gosizdat' Istoriia fabrik i zavodov', 1934.

Grinevskii, M. "Kino i derevnia (kino-telega)." *SK* 5–6 (1927): 9–10.

Grossman-Roshchin, I. *Proletarskoe kino* 20 (1932): 21–22.

Il'in, M. *New Russia's Primer: The Story of the Five Year Plan*. Translated by George S. Counts and Nucia P. Lodge. Boston: Houghton Mifflin, 1931.

"Iz referirovannoi stenogrammy diskussii o planirovke sotsialisticheskogo goroda, sostaiav-sheisia v Komakademii, 20 i 21 maia 1930 g.." *Vestnik Komakademii* 42 (1930): 109–47.

Karmanyi atlas SSSR. Leningrad, 1939.

"Kartiny, kotorye nam pokazyvaiut." *Kino* (November 1925): 3.

Katsigras, Aleksandr. "Kino i derevnia: kino-obshchestvennost' i zadachi Sovkino v derevne." *SK* 3 (1927): 8.

Khersonskii, Kh. "Put' na Vostok: 'Velikii perelet.'" *ARK* 1 (1926).

Khlebnikov, Velimir. "My i doma." *Sobranie proizvedenii*. Vol. 4. Leningrad, 1928–30.

"Kino-ekspeditsii." *SK* 4 (1927): 22.

Kino i vremya: biulleten' Gosfil'mofonda. Vol. 4. Moscow: Gosfil'mofond, 1963.

Kliuchevskii, Vasilii. *Sochineniia v 8-i tomakh*. 8 vols. Moscow: Gospolitizdat, 1956.

Kostarev, Nikolai. *Granitsa na zamke*. Moscow: Molodaia gvardiia, 1930.

Kozintsev, Grigorii. *Ekstsentrizm*. Petrograd, 1922.

———. *Glubokii ekran: sobranie sochinenii v piati tomakh*. 5 vols. Leningrad: Iskusstvo, 1982.

Krasil'nikov, Nikolai. "Problemy sovremennoi arkhitektury." *SA* 6 (1928): 170–76.

Krasnaia panorama 8 (1928): 15.

Kravets, S. M. *Arkhitektura Moskovskogo metropolitena imeni L. M. Kaganovicha*. Moscow: Izdatel'stvo Akademii arkhitektura, 1939.

Kremnev, Ivan. [A. V. Chaianov]. *Puteshestvie moego brata Alekseia v stranu krestianskoi utopii*. Moscow: Gosizdat', 1920.

Krinitskii, A. I. "Ideologicheskie kino-direktivy." *SK* 2–3 (1928): 3–5.

Krupskaia, Nadezhda. "Goroda budushchego." In *Goroda sotsializma i sotsialisticheskaia rekonstruktsiia byta*. Edited by B. Lunin. Moscow: Rabotnik proveshcheniia, 1930. First published in *Pravda* (13 October 1929).

Krzhizhanovskii, G. M. *Desiat' let GOELRO: rech' na torzhestvennom plenume mosob-lispolkoma i mossoveta 25 Dek. 1930*. Moscow: OGIZ Moskovskii rabochii, 1931.

————. *Ob elektrofikatsii: rech' na 8-m S'ezde Sovetov.* Moscow: Gos. Izdat, 1921.

————. "Oblastnye elektricheskie stantsii na torfe i ikh znachenie dlia tsentral'nogo promyshlennogo raiona Rossii." *Trudy soveshchanii po podmoskovnou ugliu i torfu* 2 (1915).

Kuleshov, Lev. "Iskusstvo, sovremennaia zhizn' i kinomatograf." *Kinofot* 1 (1922): 2.

————. "Moi opyt." In *Sobranie sochinenii v trekh tomakh.* Edited by A. Khokhlova. 3 vols. Moscow: Iskusstvo, 1987–88.

Le Corbusier. "Spirit of Truth." *Mouvement* 1 (1933): 10–13.

Lebedev-Kumach, V. I. *Vpered k pobede! Pesni i stikhi.* Moscow: Voenmorizdat, 1943.

Lenin, V. I. *Polnoe sobranie sochinenii.* 5th ed. 40 vols. Moscow: Gosizdat', 1958–65.

Lesnovskii, I. "Kama-Pechora!" *Vokrug sveta* 4 (1931): 1.

"Litsom k litsu s rabochim zritel'em." *Kino i zhizn'* 4 (1929): 15–17.

"Magnitogor'e." *SA* 1–2 (1930): 38–56.

Maiakovskii, Vladimir. "Kino i kino." *Kinofot* 4 (1922): 5.

————. *Polnoe sobranie sochineniia.* 13 vols. Moscow: Khudozhestvennaia literatura, 1956.

Medvedkin, Aleksandr. "Chto takoe kinopoezd?" In *Iz istorii kino: dokumenty i materialy,* 27–60. Moscow: Iskusstvo, 1985.

————. "Positsii ne sdadim!" *PK* 10–11 (1931): 16–19.

————. "Pro belogo bychka." Reprint in *Iz istorii Kino,* 81–85. Moscow: Iskusstvo, 1974.

————. "294 dnia na kolesakh." Reprint in *Iz istorii Kino: dokumenty i materialy,* 27–62. Moscow: Isskustvo, 1977.

————. "Veselaia (Novaia) Moskva." *Stsenariia,* 1938.

"Model' mira." *Vokrug sveta* 11 (1931): 23.

Mur, Leo. "Fotogeniia." *Kino-zhurnal ARK* 6 (1925): 5–8.

"Na zabroshennoi stantsii." *Vokrug sveta* 13 (1931) 10.

"Nam nuzhno znat' svoiu stranu." *SK* 4 (1927): 1.

"O kinofikatsii derevni." *SK* 2–3 (1928): 6.

"Obzor pechati." *Voprosy kommunal'nogo khoziaistva* 6 (1930): 76–78.

"ODSK: kinofikatsiia derevni i obshchestvennost." *SK* 5–6 (1927): 24–25.

Okhitovich, Mikhail. "K probleme goroda." *SA* 4 (1929): 130–34.

————. "O sotsialisticheskoi planirovke rasseleniia." *SA* 6 (1930): 1.

————. "Sotsialisticheskoe rasselenie." *Vestnik Kommunisticheskoi Akademii* 35–36 (1929): 335–38.

————. "Zametki po teorii rasseleniia." *SA* 1–2 (1930): 7–16.

Olkhovyi, B. S., ed. *Puti kino: Vsesoiuznoe partiinoe soveshchanie po kinematografii.* Moscow: Tea Kino-pechat', 1929.

Ordzhonikidze, Sergo. "O razvitii chernoi metallurgii (Otchetnyi doklad narodnogo komissariata tiazheloi promyshlennosti, na plenume TsK VKP (b))." *Stat'i i rechi.* Moscow: Gosizdat', 1956.

Orleanskii, V. L. *Planirovka i rekonstrutsiia Mosvy.* Moscow: Izdatel'stvo Akademii arkhitektura, 1939.

Osinskii, N. [V. V. Obolenskii]. *Amerikanskii avtomobil' ili rossiiskaia telega: stat'i.* Moscow: Gosizdat', 1930.

————. *Avtomobilizatsiia SSSR.* Moscow: Gosizdat', 1930.

Pasternak, Aleksandr. "Urbanizm." *SA* 1 (1926): 1.

Petrov-Bytov, Pavel. "U nas net sovetskoi kinematografii." *Zhizn' iskusstva* 17 (1929): 8.

Piotrovskii, Adrian. "Platforma Petrova-Bytova i sovetskaia kinematografiia." *Zhizn' iskusstva* 19 (1929): 4.

"Pis'mo Korbus'e k Ginzburgu i otvet Ginzburga." *SA* 1–2 (1930): 61–62.

PK 4 (1931): 55.

PK 9 (1931): 4–15.

PK 10 (1931): 17–18.

Plan elektrifikatsii RSFSR: vvedenie k dokladu 8-my s'ezdu sovetov. Moscow: Nauchno Tekhnicheskii otdel vyschego soveta narodnogo khoziaistva, 1921.

"Po provintsii." *SK* 2 (1927): 24–25.

"Po taige—po porogam." *Vokrug sveta* 3 (1929): 17–22.

"Poiasnitel'naia zapiska k smete na ustroistvo tipovoi zhiloi iashcheiki po proektu Gosplana RSFSR." *SA* 6 (1930): 5–15.

Pozner, V. "Frantsuzkii kinomatograf v 1924 godu (pis'mo iz Parizha)." *Kino-zhurnal ARK* 2 (1925): 27–29.

Preobrazhenskii, N. F. "Predislovie." *Khronika* 1 (1918): 1.

"Prevrashchenie goroda." *Vokrug sveta* 17 (1931): 12.

Pudovkin, Vsevolod. "Fotogeniia." *Kino-zhurnal ARK* 4–5 (1925): 9–12.

"Puti na karte SSSR." *Vokrug sveta* 12 (1931): 13.

"Razvedchiki piatiletki." *Vokrug sveta* 15–16 (1931): 16.

S. A. *Proletarskoe kino* 4 (1931): 55.

"S kino-apparatom po Buriatii." *SK* 4 (1927): 13.

Sabsovich, Leonid. *Gorod budushchego i organizatsiia sotsialistichekogo byta.* Moscow: VAR-NITSO-Gostekhizdat, 1929.

———. *Sotsialisticheskie goroda.* Moscow: Moskovskii rabochii, 1930.

"Sem' soiuznykh sovetskikh stolits." *SSSR na stroike* 7–8 (1930): 5.

Semenov, Vladimir. *Blagoustroistvo gorodov.* Moscow: Sklad' Izdanie, 1912.

Shipulinskii, L. "Dusha kino." In *Kinomatograf: sbornik statei,* 8–20. Moscow: Gosizdat', 1919.

Shklovskii, Viktor. *Literatura i kinematograf.* Berlin: Russkoe universal'noe izdanie, 1923.

———. *O teorii prozy.* Moscow: Krug, 1925.

———. "Pogranichnaia liniia." (1923). In *Za 60 let,* 110–13. Moscow: Iskusstvo, 1985.

———. "Semantika Kino." In *Za 60 let,* 30–32. Moscow: Iskusstvo, 1985.

———. "'Velikii Perelet' i kinematografiia" (1925). In *Za 60 let: raboty o kino.* Moscow: Iskusstvo, 1985.

———. *Za 60 let: raboty o kino.* Edited by E. Levin. Moscow: Iskusstvo, 1985.

Shneiderov, Vladimir, and Georgii Blium. "Kak snimalsia 'Velikii perelet.'" *ARK* 1 (1926): 28–29.

Skvortsov-Stepanov, I. I. *Elektrifikatsiia R.S.F.S.R. v sviazi s perekhodnoi fazoi mirovogo khoziaistv.* Moscow: Gosizdat', 1923

Sovetskoe iskusstvo 3 (1925): 74–77.

SSSR na stroike 1 (1930): 3.

Stalin, I. V. "God velikogo pereloma." In *Sochineniia,* 118–31. Vol. 12. Moscow: Istitut Marksa-Engelsa-Lenina Stalina pri TsK KPSS, 1946–55.

———. "Golovokruzhenie ot uspekhov: k voprosam kolkhoznogo dvizheniia." In *Sochi-*

neniia, 191–200. Vol. 12. Moscow: Istitut Marksa-Engelsa-Lenina Stalina pri TsK KPSS, 1946–55.

———. *Sochineniia.* 13 vols. Moscow: Istitut Marksa-Engelsa-Lenina Stalina pri TsK KPSS, 1946–55.

———. "O dvukh osobennostiakh oktiabr'skoi revoliutsii, ili Oktiabr' i teorii permanentnoi revoliutsii Trotskogo." In *Sochineniia,* 862–80. Vol. 6. Moscow: Gosizdat', 1947.

———. "O proekte konstitutsii Soiuza SSSR." *Sobranie sochineniia.* Edited by Robert McNeal, 136–83. Vol. 1. Stanford, Calif.: Hoover Institute, 1967.

Sukharebskii, Leonid. *Nauchnoe kino.* Moscow: Gosizdat', 1926.

———. "Nauchnye kino-ekspeditsii i ikh zas"emka." *SK* 4 (1927): 13–14.

Sukhodrev, V. M. *Sostavlenie, oformlenie i podgotovka k izdaniiu uchebnykh kart.* Moscow, 1939.

Sverchkova, D. F., ed. *Ves' SSSR: spravochnik-putevoditel'.* Moscow: Izdanie transreklamy NKPS (Narodnyi komissariat prosveshcheniia), 1929.

"Tak rastut goroda." *Vokrug sveta* 2 (1928): 20–22.

Tekhnika, stroitel'stvo i promyshlennost' 3 (1922): 130–31.

Tret'iakov, Sergei. "Chem zhivo kino." *Novyi LEF* 3 (1928): 23–28.

———. "Skvoz neprotertye ochki." *Novyi LEF* 9 (1928): 20–24.

"Ul'tra-goloboi ugol': novyi istochnik energii." *Vokrug sveta* 3 (1928): 3–5.

Ushaov, A. V. "Nauchno-issledovatel'skaia rabota muzeev istoricheskogo profiliia 1917–1959 gg." *Muzeinoe delo* 19 (1989): 45–71.

"Vakhshkaia Dolina." *Vokrug sveta* 19–20 (1931): 19.

Veremienko, M. "O kul'turfil'me." *SK* 4 (1927): 14–15.

Vertov, Dziga. "Iz istorii kinokov." In *Stat'i, dnevniki, zamysly.* Edited by Sergei Drobashenko, 116–20. Moscow: Iskusstvo, 1966.

———. "Kinoglaz." In *Stat'i, dnevniki, zamysly.* Edited by Sergei Drobashenko, 989–93. Moscow: Iskusstvo, 1966.

———. "Kinoki. Perevorot." *Levyi front iskusstva (LEF)* 3 (1923): 141.

———. "My. Variant manifesta." *Stat'i, dnevniki, zamysly.* Edited by Sergei Drobashenko, 49. Moscow: Iskusstvo, 1966.

———. "O 'kinopravde.'" *Stat'i, dnevniki, zamysly.* Edited by Sergei Drobashenko, 75–79. Moscow: Iskusstvo, 1966.

———. "Ot 'kinoglaza' k 'radioglaza' (iz azbuki kinokov)." *Stat'i, dnevniki, zamysly.* Edited by Sergei Drobashenko, 109–16. Moscow: Iskusstvo, 1966.

———. "Pis'mo iz Berlina." *Stat'i, dnevniki, zamysly.* Edited by Sergei Drobashenko, 120–22. Moscow: Iskusstvo, 1966.

———. *Stat'i, dnevniki, zamysly.* Edited by Sergei Drobashenko. Moscow: Iskusstvo, 1966.

"Vtoroi v mire." *Vokrug sveta* 24 (1931): 1–4.

"Zadushevnoe slovo o puteshestvii vokrug sveta." *SK* 4 (1927): 18–19.

"Zelenyi gorod: sotsialisticheskaia rekonstruktsiia Moskvy." *SA* 1–2 (1930): 16–32.

SECONDARY SOURCES

Abel, Richard, ed. *French Film Theory and Criticism: A History/Anthology 1907–1939.* 2 vols. Princeton, N.J.: Princeton University Press, 1998.

Ades, Dawn, Tim Benton, David Elliott, and Iain Boyd Whyte, comps. *Art and Power: Europe under the Dictators.* Exhibition Catalogue. London: South Bank Centre, 1995.

Adler, Judith. "The Origins of Sight-seeing." *Annals of Tourism Research* 16 (1989): 7–29.

Afanasev, K. N., ed. *Iz istorii sovetskoi arkhitektury, 1917–1925 gg.* Moscow: Izdatel'stvo Akademii Nauk, 1963.

Afanasiev, A. N. *Russkie narodnie skazki.* Edited by A. Chach. St. Petersburg: Niva, 1994.

Albéra, François. *Eisenstein et le contructivisme russe.* Lausanne: L'âge d'homme, 1990.

Althusser, Louis. *Essays on Ideology.* London: Verso, 1984.

Andrew, Dudley. *Concepts in Film Theory.* Oxford: Oxford University Press, 1984.

———. *The Major Film Theories: An Introduction.* New York: Oxford University Press, 1976.

Antonova, Irina, and Jörn Merkert, eds. *Berlin-Moskva, Berlin-Moskau, 1900–1950.* Exhibition Catalogue. München: Prestel, 1995.

Antsiferov, N. P. *Antsferovskie chtenia: materialy i tezisy konferentsii (20–22 dekabria 1989 g.).* Edited by A. I. Dobkin and A.V. Kobak. Leningrad: Leningradskoe otdelenie sovetskogo fonda kul'tury, 1989.

Arapova, L. I., and L. N. Godunova, comps. *Muzeinoe delo v SSSR: Muzeinoe stroitel'stvo v SSSR, sbornik nauchnykh trudov* 19. Moscow: Ministerstvo kul'tury SSSR, 1989.

Arnheim, Rudolf. *Film as Art.* Berkeley: University of California Press, 1957.

Astaf'eva, Margarita I. "Razvitie teoreticheskoi mysli i printsipov sovetskogo gradostroitel'stva v pervye poslerevoliutsionnye gody, 1917–25." Diss., Research Institute in the Theory, History, and Problems of Soviet Architecture, Moscow, 1971.

Atwood, Lynn, ed. *Red Women on the Silver Screen: Soviet Women and Cinema from the Beginning to the End of the Communist Regime.* London: Pandora, 1993.

Aumont, Jaques. *Montage Eisenstein.* Paris: Albatros, 1979.

Babitsky, Paul, and John Rimberg. *The Soviet Film Industry.* New York: Praeger, 1955.

Bachelard, Gaston. *The Poetics of Space.* Translated by Maria Jolas. Boston: Beacon Press, 1994.

Bakhtin, Mikhail. *The Dialogic Imagination: Four Essays by Mikhail Bakhtin.* Edited by Michael Holquist. Translated by Michael Holquist and Caryl Emerson. Austin: University of Texas Press, 1981.

———. "K voprosam teorii romana, k voprosam teorii smekha, 'o Maiakovskom.'" *Sobranie sochinenii v semi tomakh.* Vol. 5. 1940–1960. Moscow: Russkie Slovari, 1996.

Bakhtin, Mikhail, and P. N. Medvedev. *The Formal Method in Literary Scholarship: A Critical Introduction to Sociological Poetics.* Translated by Albert Wehrle. Cambridge, Mass.: Harvard University Press, 1985.

Bálazs, Béla. *Character and Growth of a New Art.* New York: Dover, 1970.

———. "The Close-up." In *Film Theory and Criticism: Introductory Readings.* Edited by Gerald Mast, Marshall Cohen, and Leo Braudy. 4th ed. Oxford: Oxford University Press, 1992.

Bassin, Mark. "The Greening of Utopia." In *Architecture and Empire in Russia,* edited by James Cracraft and Dan Rowlands. Seattle: University of Washington Press, forthcoming.

———. "Russia between Europe and Asia: The Ideological Construction of Geographical Space." *Slavic Review* 50, no. 1 (1991): 1–17.

Baudelaire, Charles. "A une passante." *Les Fleurs du Mal et autres poèmes.* Paris: Flammarion, 1994.

Bazin, André. *What is Cinema?* Selected and translated by Hugh Gray. 2 vols. Berkeley: University of California Press, 1971.

Beer, Gillian. "The Island and the Aeroplane: The Case of Virginia Woolf." In *Nation and Narration,* edited by Homi K. Bhabha, 265–90. London: Routledge, 1990.

Benjamin, Walter. *Illuminations: Essays and Reflections.* Edited by Hannah Arendt. New York: Schocken, 1968.

———. *Reflections: Essays, Aphorisms, Autobiographical Writings.* Edited by Peter Demetz. New York: Schocken, 1978.

Bergson, Henri. *L'évolution créatrice.* Paris: F. Alcan, 1909.

———. *Matter and Memory.* Translated by N. M. Paul and W. S. Palmer. New York: Zone, 1991.

Bethea, David. *The Shape of Apocalypse in Modern Russian Fiction.* Princeton, N.J.: Princeton University Press, 1989.

Black, J. L. "Opening Up Siberia: Russia's 'Window on the East.'" In *The History of Siberia: From Russian Conquest to Revolution,* edited by Alan Wood. London: Routledge, 1991.

Bowlt, John E., ed. *Russian Art of the Avant Garde: Theory and Criticism.* London: Thames and Hudson, 1976.

Bowlt, John E., and Olga Matich, eds. *Laboratory of Dreams: The Russian Avant-Garde and Cultural Experiment.* Stanford, Calif.: Stanford University Press, 1996.

Boym, Svetlana. *Common Places: Mythologies of Everyday Life in Russia.* Cambridge, Mass.: Harvard University Press, 1994.

Brodsky, Joseph. *Less Than One: Selected Essays.* New York: Farrar, Straus & Giroux, 1986.

Brooks, Jeffrey. *Thank You, Comrade Stalin! Soviet Public Culture from Revolution to Cold War.* Princeton, N.J.: Princeton University Press, 2000.

———. *When Russia Learned to Read: Literacy and Popular Literature, 1861–1917.* Princeton, N.J.: Princeton University Press, 1985.

Brumfield, William Craft, and Blair Ruble, eds. *Russian Housing in the Modern Age: Design and Social History.* Cambridge, Mass.: Woodrow Wilson Center Press; Cambridge, Mass.: Cambridge University Press, 1993.

Bruno, Giuliana. *Streetwalking on a Ruined Map: Cultural Theory and the City Films of Elvira Notari.* Princeton, N.J.: Princeton University Press, 1993.

Buchli, Victor. *An Archeology of Socialism.* Oxford: Berg, 1999.

Buck-Morss, Susan. "The Cinema Screen as Prosthesis of Perception." In *The Senses Still: Perception and Memory as Material Culture in Modernity,* edited by Nadia Seremetakis, 45–62. Chicago: University of Chicago Press, 1996.

———. *Dialectics of Seeing.* Cambridge, Mass.: MIT Press, 1989.

———. *Dreamworld and Catastrophe: The Passing of Mass Utopia in East and West.* Cambridge, Mass.: MIT Press, 2000.

Bulgakowa, Oksana. "Sovetskoe kino v poiskakh 'obshchei modeli'." In *Sotsrealisticheskii kanon,* edited by Hans Günther and Evgenii Dobrenko. Moscow: Akadamicheskii proekt, 2000

Carr, E. H. *The Bolshevik Revolution.* 3 vols. London: Macmillan, 1950–53.

———. *The Interregnum 1923–24*. London: Macmillan, 1954.

———. *The Russian Revolution from Lenin to Stalin 1917–1929*. London: Macmillan, 1979.

Castillo, Greg. "Gorkii Street and the Design of the Stalin Revolution." In *Streets: Critical Perspectives on Public Space*, edited by Zeynip Çelik, Diane Favro, and Richard Ingersoll. Berkeley: University of California Press, 1994.

———. "Peoples at an Exhibition: Soviet Architecture and the National Question." *South Atlantic Quarterly* 3 (1995): 715–44.

———. "Socialist Realism: The Second 'International Style.'" In *Architecture and the Expression of Group Identity: The Russian Empire and the USSR*, edited by James Cracraft and Dan Rowland. Seattle: University of Washington Press, forthcoming.

Cavell, Stanley. *The World Viewed: Reflections on the Ontology of Film*. Cambridge, Mass.: Harvard University Press, 1979.

Charney, Leo, and Vanessa R. Schwartz. *Cinema and the Invention of Modern Life*. Berkeley: University of California Press, 1995.

Christie, Ian. "Myths of Total Cinema." *After-Image* 10 (1981): 10–15.

Clark, Katerina. *Petersburg: Crucible of a Cultural Revolution*. Cambridge, Mass.: Harvard University Press, 1995.

———. *The Soviet Novel: History as Ritual*. Chicago: University of Chicago Press, 1981.

Clifford, James. *The Predicament of Culture: Twentieth Century Ethnography, Literature, and Art*. Cambridge, Mass.: Harvard University Press, 1988.

Clifford, James, and George Marcus, eds. *Writing Culture: The Poetics and Politics of Ethnography*. Berkeley: University of California Press, 1986.

Collins, David N. "Subjections and Settlement in Seventeenth- and Eighteenth-Century Siberia." In *The History of Siberia: From Russian Conquest to Revolution*, edited by Alan Wood. London: Routledge, 1991.

Colomina, Beatriz, ed. *Sexuality and Space*. Princeton, N.J.: Princeton Architectural Press, 1992.

Colton, Timothy. *Moscow: Governing the Socialist Metropolis*. Cambridge, Mass.: Harvard University Press, 1995.

Cooke, Catherine. "'Form Is a Function X': The Development of the Constructivist Architect's Design Method." *Architectural Design* 53, nos. 5–6 (1983): 34–49.

———. "Nikolai Krasilnikov's Quantitative Approach to Architectural Design: An Early Example." *Environment and Planning B* 2, no. 1 (1975): 3–20.

———. *Russian Avant-Garde: Theories of Art, Architecture and the City*. London: Academy, 1995.

———. "The Town of Socialism." Diss., University of Cambridge, 1974.

Coopersmith, Jonathan. *The Electrification of Soviet Russia*. Ithaca, N.Y.: Cornell University Press, 1992.

Crary, Jonathan. *Techniques of the Observer: On Vision and Modernity in the 19th Century*. Cambridge, Mass.: MIT Press, 1990.

Curtis, James. "Bergson and Russian Formalism." *Comparative Literature* 28, no. 2 (1976): 109–21.

Dal', Vladimir. *Tolkovyi slovar' zhivogovelikorusskogo iazyka*. 3rd ed. St. Petersburg: Vol'f, 1905.

Davies, R. W. "Crisis and Progress in the Russian Economy, 1931–33." In *The Industrialization of Soviet Russia,* Vol. 4. Basingstoke: Macmillan, 1996.

———. "The Soviet Economy in Turmoil, 1929–30." In *The Industrialization of Soviet Russia.* Vol. 3. Basingstoke: Macmillan, 1989.

de Certeau, Michel. *The Practice of Everyday Life.* Translated by Steven Rendall. Berkeley: University of California Press, 1984.

Diment, Galya, and Yuri Slezkine, eds. *Between Heaven and Hell: The Myth of Siberia in Russian Culture.* New York: St. Martins Press, 1993.

Deleuze, Gilles. *Cinéma 1: The Movement-Image.* Translated by Hugh Tomlinson and Barbara Habberjam. Minneapolis: University of Minnesota Press, 1986.

———. *Cinéma 2: L'image-temps.* Paris: Editions de Minuit, 1985.

Deriabin, Aleksandr, ed. "Ves' Medvedkin: filmografiia." *Kinovedcheskie zapiski* 49 (2000): 86–146.

———. *Vladimir Alekseevich Erofeev (1898–1940): Materialy k 100-letiiu so dnia rozhdeniia.* Moscow: Muzei kino, 1998.

Doane, Mary-Anne. " ' . . . When the direction of the force acting on the body is changed': The Moving Image." *Wide Angle* 7 (1985): 42–58.

Dobrenko, Evgenii. "Do samykh do okrain." *Iskusstvo kino* 4 (1996): 97–102.

———. "Iazik prostranstva, szhatogo do tochki, ili estetika 'sotsial'noi klaustrofobii.'" *Iskusstvo kino* 11 (1996): 120–30.

———. "Seiatel' vetra 'tvorimoe prostranstvo' Aleksandr Dovzhenko." *Iskusstvo kino* 9 (1997): 59–73.

Drobashenko, Sergei, ed. *Dziga Vertov: stat'i, dnevniki, zamysly.* Moscow: Iskusstvo, 1966.

Dunham, Vera. *In Stalin's Time: Middle Class Values in Soviet Fiction.* Cambridge, Mass.: Cambridge University Press, 1976.

Dzhulai, Liudmila. *Dokumental'nyi illiuzion: otechestvennyi kinodokuentalism-opyty sotsial'nogo tvorchestva.* Moscow: Materk, 2001.

Efremov, Iu. K. "Local Studies and Geography." In *Soviet Geography: Accomplishments and Tasks,* edited by I. P. Gerasimov and G. M. Ignat'ev, 382–85. Translated by Lawrence Ecker. New York: American Geographical Society, 1962.

Elsaesser, Thomas, and Adam Barker. *Early Cinema: Space, Frame, Narrative.* London: B. F. I., 1990.

Engels, Friedrich. *The Condition of the Working Class in England.* Oxford: Blackwell, 1958.

Enzensberger, Masha. "'We were born to turn a fairytale into reality': Grigori Alexandrov's *The Radiant Path.*" In *Stalinism and Soviet Cinema,* edited by Richard Taylor and Derek Spring. London: Routledge, 1993.

Fanger, Donald. "The Peasant in Literature." In *The Peasant in Nineteenth Century Russia,* edited by Wayne Vucinich, 231–62. Stanford, Calif.: Stanford University Press, 1968.

Ferro, Marc. *Cinema and History.* Translated by Naomi Greene. Detroit, Mich.: Wayne State University Press, 1988.

Fielding, Raymond. "Hale's Tours: Ultra-realism in the Pre-1910 Motion Picture." In *Film before Griffith,* edited by John L. Fell, 116–30. Berkeley: University of California Press, 1983.

Fink, Hilary L. *Bergson and Russian Formalism 1900–1930.* Evanston, Ill.: Northwestern University Press, 1999.

Fitzpatrick, Sheila. *The Cultural Front: Power and Culture in Revolutionary Russia.* Ithaca, N.Y.: Cornell University Press, 1992.

———. *Everyday Stalinism: Ordinary Life in Extraordinary Times: Soviet Russia in the 1930s.* New York: Oxford University Press, 1999.

———. *Stalin's Peasants: Resistance and Survival in the Russian Village after Collectivization.* Oxford: Oxford University Press, 1994.

———, ed. *Cultural Revolution in Russia.* Bloomington: Indiana University Press, 1978.

Foucault, Michel. *Discipline and Punish: The Birth of the Prison.* Translated by Alan Sheridan. New York: Vintage, 1995.

———. "Of Other Spaces." *diacritics* 2 (1986): 22.

———. "Space, Knowledge, Power." In *The Foucault Reader: An Introduction to Foucault's Thought,* edited by Paul Rabinow, 239–57. Harmondsworth: Penguin, 1991.

Freud, Sigmund. "The Uncanny." In *Art and Literature: Jenson's Gravida, Leonardo da Vinci and Other Works.* The Penguin Freud Library, vol. 14. London: Penguin, 1985.

Friedberg, Anne. *Window Shopping: Cinema and the Postmodern.* Berkeley: University of California Press, 1993.

Frierson, Kathy. *Peasant Icons: Representations of Rural People in Late 19th Century Russia.* Oxford: Oxford University Press, 1993.

Galiushkin, A. Iu. "K istorii lichnykh i tvorcheskikh vzaimootnoshenii A. Platonova i V.B. Shklovskogo." In *Andrei Platonov: Vospominaniia sovremennikov, materialy k biografii,* edited by N. V. Kornienko and E. D. Shubinoi, 177. Moscow: Sovremennyi pisatel', 1994.

Garrard, John. *The Russian Novel from Pushkin to Pasternak.* New Haven, Conn.: Yale University Press, 1983.

Gerasimov, I. P., and G. M. Ignat'ev, *Soviet Geography: Accomplishments and Tasks,* translated by Lawrence Ecker. New York: American Geographical Society, 1962.

Giddens, Anthony. *The Constitution of Society: Outline of a Theory of Structuration.* Cambridge, England: Polity Press, 1984.

Gleason, Abbot, Peter Kenez, and Richard Stites, eds. *Bolshevik Culture: Experiment and Order in the Russian Revolution.* Bloomington: Indiana University Press, 1985.

Gogol', Nikolai. "Mertvye dushi: tom pervyi." *Sobranie sochinenii.* Vol. 5. Moscow: Miros, 1994.

Graffy, Julian. *Bed and Sofa.* London: I. B. Tauris, 2001.

———. "Moscow (Urban Legends: Ten Cities That Shook Cinema)." *Sight and Sound* (June 2000): 26–29.

Gregory, Derek. *Geographical Imaginations.* Oxford: Blackwell, 1994.

Groys, Boris. *The Total Art of Stalinism: Avant-Garde, Aesthetic Dictatorship, and Beyond.* Translated by Charles Rougle. Princeton, N.J.: Princeton University Press, 1992.

Gudkov, Lev, and Boris Dubin. *Literatura kak sotsialnyi institut: Stat'i po sotsiologii literatury.* Moscow: Novoe literaturnoe obozrenie, 1994.

Günther, Hans. *The Culture of the Stalin Period.* London: Macmillan, 1990.

———. "Zhiznestroenie." *Russian Literature* 20 (1986): 41–48.

Gutkin, Irina. *The Cultural Origins of the Socialist Aesthetic, 1890–1934.* Evanston, Ill.: Northwestern University Press, 1999.

Guseinov, Gasan. *Karta nashei rodiny: ideologema mezhdu slovomi telom.* Helsinki: Institute for Russian and East European Studies, 2000.

Hamm, Michael F., ed. *The City in Russian History.* Lexington: University of Kentucky, 1976.

Hansen, Miriam Bratu. *Babel and Babylon: Spectatorship in American Silent Film.* Cambridge, Mass.: Harvard University Press, 1981.

———. "The Mass Production of the Senses: Classical Cinema as Vernacular Modernism." In *Reinventing Film Studies,* edited by Christine Gledhill and Linda Williams. London: Arnold, 2000.

Hansen Löve, Katharina. *The Evolution of Space in Russian Literature: A Spatial Reading of 19th and 20th Century Narrative Literature.* Amsterdam: Rodopi, 1994.

Harvey, David. *The Condition of Post-Modernity: An Enquiry into the Origins of Social Change.* Oxford: Blackwell, 1989.

———. *Consciousness and the Urban Experience: Studies in the History and Theory of Capitalist Urbanization.* 2 vols. Oxford: Blackwell, 1985.

Heath, Stephen. *Questions of Cinema.* London: Macmillan, 1981.

Hellebust, Rolf. "Aleksei Gastev and the Metallization of the Revolutionary Body." *Slavic Review* 56, no. 3 (1997): 500–19.

Hindus, Maurice. *Red Bread.* London: Cape, 1931.

Hirsch, Francine. "The Soviet Union as a Work in Progress: Ethnographers and the Category *Nationality* in the 1926, 1937 and 1939 Censuses." *Slavic Review* 56, no. 2 (1997): 251–79.

Hobsbawm, Eric, and Terence Ranger. *The Invention of Tradition.* Cambridge: Cambridge University Press, 1983.

Hosking, Geoffrey. *A History of the Soviet Union.* London: Fontana, 1985.

Howard, Ebenezer. *Tomorrow: A Peaceful Path to Real Reform.* London: Swan Sonnenschein, 1898.

Iampol'skii, Mikhail. "'Smyslovaia veshch' v kinoteorii opoiaza." In *Tynianovskii sbornik: tret'i tynianovskie chteniia,* edited by M. O. Chudakova, 109–20. Riga: Zinatne, 1988.

———. *Vidimyi mir: ocherki rannei kinofenomenologii.* Moscow: Kinovedcheskie zapiski, 1993.

Iangirov, Rashit. "Iz istorii odnoi kinoutopii." *Kinovedcheskie zapiski* 8 (1990): 182–202.

Iurenev, R. *Aleksandr Medvedkin, satirik.* Moscow: Biuro propagandy sovetskogo kinoiskusstvo, 1981.

———. *Sovetskaia kinokomediia.* Moscow: Nauka, 1964.

———. "Tri Moskvy Il'i Kopalina." *Iskusstvo kino* 8 (1997): 69–74.

Iutkevich, S. I., and S. Ginzburg. *Kinoslovar' v dvukh tomakh.* Moscow: Sovetskaia entsyklopediia, 1996.

Iz istorii sovetskoi arkhitektury, 1917–1925 gg.: dokumenty i materialy. Moscow: Izdatel'stvo Akademii Nauk, 1963.

Izvolov, N. A. *Fenomen kino: istoriia i teoria.* Moscow: EGSI, 2000.

Jakobson, Roman. *Language in Literature.* Edited by Krystyna Pomorska and Stephen Rudy. London: Belknap Press, 1987.

Jameson, Frederic. "Cognitive Mapping" In *Marxism and the Interpretation of Culture,* edited by Gary Nelson and Laurence Grossberg, 347–60. Urbana: University of Illinois Press, 1988.

———. *The Geopolitical Aesthetic.* London: B. F. I., 1992.

Kardish, Laurence. *Junction and Journey: Trains and Film.* New York: Museum of Modern Art, 1991.

Kazus, Igor A. "The Competition for the Country's Supreme Building." In *Naum Gabo and the Competition for the Palace of Soviets, Moscow, 1931–1933.* Berlin: Berlinische Galerie, 1993.

Kenez, Peter. *Cinema and Soviet Society, 1917–1953.* Cambridge: Cambridge University Press, 1992.

Kepley, Vance. *In the Service of the State: The Cinema of Alexander Dovzhenko.* Madison: University of Wisconsin Press, 1986.

Kern, Stephen. *The Culture of Time and Space (1880–1915).* Cambridge, Mass.: Harvard University Press, 1983.

Khan-Magamedov, Selim O. *Arkhitektura sovetskogo avangarda.* Moscow: Stroiizdat, 1996.

———. *Pioneers of Soviet Archtitecture: The Search for New Solutions in the 1920s and 30s.* London: Thames and Hudson, 1983.

———. "Schöpferische Konzeptioned und soziale sowjetischen Avantgarde." In *Avantgarde II: Sowjetishche Architektur,* edited by Christian Schädlich and Dietrich W. Schmidt. Stuttgart: Verlag Gerd Hatje, 1993.

———. *U istokov formirovaniia ASNOVA i OSA: dve arkhitekturnye gruppy INKhUKHA.* Moscow: Arkhitektura, 1994.

Khazanova, V. I. *Sovetskaia arkhitektura pervoi piatiletki: problemy goroda budushchego.* Moscow: Nauka, 1980.

———. *Sovetskaia arkhitektura pervykh let Oktiabria.* Moscow: Nauka, 1970.

Kleiman, Naum. "Ekstsentricheskoe i tragicheskoe." *Kinovedcheskie zapiski* 7 (1990): 132–35.

Knight, Nathaniel. "Grigor'ev in Orenburg, 1851–1862: Russian Orientalism in the Service of Empire?" *Slavic Review* 59, no. 1 (spring 2000): 74–100.

———. "Science, Empire and Nationality: Ethnography and the Russian Geographical Society, 1845–1855. In *Imperial Russia: New Histories for the Empire,* edited by Jane Burbank and David L. Ransel. Bloomington: Indiana University Press, 1998.

Kopp, Anatole. *Ville et révolution (architecture et urbanisme soviétiques des années vingt).* Paris: Anthropos, 1967.

Kotkin, Stephen. *Magnetic Mountain: Stalinism as a Civilization.* Berkeley: University of California Press, 1995.

Kracauer, Siegfried. "Basic Concepts." In *Film Theory and Criticism: Introductory Readings,* edited by Gerald Mast, Marshall Cohen, and Leo Braudy, 9–20. 4th ed. Oxford: Oxford University Press, 1992.

———. "The Establishment of Physical Existence." In *Film Theory and Criticism: Introductory Readings,* edited by Gerald Mast, Marshall Cohen, and Leo Braudy, 249–460. 4th ed. Oxford: Oxford University Press, 1992.

———. *From Caligari to Hitler.* Princeton, N.J.: Dennis Dobson, 1957.

———. *Theory of Film: The Redemption of Physical Reality.* London: International Library of Theatre and Cinema, 1961.

Lacan, Jaques. "The Mirror Stage as Formative of the Function 'I.'" In *Ecrits. A Selection,* edited by Alan Sheridan. London: Tavistock, 1977.

Lefebvre, Henri. *The Production of Space.* Translated by Donald Nicholson-Smith. Oxford: Macmillan, 1994.

Lewin, Moshe. *The Making of the Soviet System: Essays in the Social History of Interwar Russia.* New York: New Press, 1985.

Leyda, Jay. *Kino: A History of the Russian and Soviet Film.* London: Allen and Unwin, 1960.

Ling, A. "Moving Buildings in the USSR." *Architects' Journal* 2 (1944): 155.

Listov, Viktor. *Istoriia smotrit v ob"ektiv.* Moscow: Iskusstvo, 1973.

———. *Lenin i kinematograf, 1917–24.* Moscow: Iskusstvo, 1986.

———. *Rossiia, revoliutsiia, kinematograf.* Moscow: Materik, 1995.

Listov, V. S., and G. A. Ambernadi, eds. *Oktiabr'skie stranitsy (1917–1941).* Moscow: Izvestiia, 1970.

Lotman, Iurii. "Simvolika Peterburga i problema semiotiki goroda." In *Vnutri mysliashchikh mirov: chelovek, tekst, semiosfera, istoriia,* 275–96. Moscow: Iazyki russkoi kul'tury, 1996.

———. *Universe of the Mind: A Semiotic Theory of Culture.* Translated by Ann Shukman. London: I. B. Tauris, 1990.

———. *Vnutri mysliashchikh mirov: chelovek, tekst, semiosfera, istoriia.* Moscow: Iaziki russkoi kul'tury, 1996.

Macheret, A. V., ed. *Sovetskie khudozhestvennye fil'my: annotirovannyi katalog.* 3 vols. Moscow: Iskusstvo, 1961.

Makhaev, Viktor. "Obraz puti v sovetskoi kul'ture i arkhitekture (arkhitektura obshchestvenno-transportnykh kompleksov 1930–50-x gg.)." Diss., Research Institute in the Theory of Architecture and Urban Planning, Moscow, 1994.

Maksimedov, Leonid. *Sumbur vmesto muzyki: stalinskaia kul'turnaia revoliutsia 1936–38.* Moscow: Iuridicheskaia kniga, 1997.

Mamatova, L. Kh. *Kino: Politika i liudi. 30-e gody.* Moscow: NIIK, 1995.

Margolit, Evgenii. "Perechitivaia istorii sovetskogo kino." In *'Close-up': isotiko teoricheskii seinar vo VGIKe.* Edited by A. S. Troshin. Moscow: Kinovedcheckie zapiski, VGIK, 1999.

Margolit, Evgenii, and Viacheslav Smyrov, eds. *Iz'iatnoe kino: katalog sovetskikh i grovyh kartin, ne vypushchenykh vo vsesoiuznyi prokat po sovershennii v proizvodstve ili ip'iatykh iz deistvuiushchego fil'nogonda v god vypuska na ekran 1924–1953.* Moscow: Gosfil'mofond/NIK, 1995.

Marx, Karl. "Critique of Hegel's Dialectic and General Philosophy (Economic and Philosophical Manuscripts of 1844)." In *Karl Marx: Selected Writings,* edited by David McClelland. 2nd ed. Oxford: Oxford University Press, 2000, 104–18. .

———. "Private Property and Communism (Economic and Philosophical Manuscripts of 1844)." In *Karl Marx: Selected Writings,* edited by David McClelland. 2nd ed. Oxford: Oxford University Press, 2000, 95–104.

———. *Economic and Philosophical Manuscripts of 1844.* Edited by Dirk Struik. London: Lawrence and Wishart, 1970.

Marx, Karl, and Friedrich Engels. *Communist Manifesto: Socialist Landmark,* edited by Harold J. Laski. Leicester: Blackfriars Press, 1948.

Mast, Gerald, Marshall Cohen, and Leo Braudy, eds. *Film Theory and Criticism: Introductory Readings.* 4th ed. Oxford: Oxford University Press, 1992.

Matich, Olga. "Remaking the Bed: Utopia in Daily Life." In *Laboratory of Dreams: The Avant-Garde and Cultural Experiment,* edited by John E. Bowlt and Olga Matich. Stanford, Calif.: Stanford University Press, 1996.

Merleau-Ponty, Maurice. *The Phenomenology of Perception.* Translated by Colin Smith. London: Routledge, 1994.

Michelson, Annette, ed. *Kino-eye: The Writings of Dziga Vertov.* Translated by Kevin O'Brien. London: Pluto, 1984.

Morson, Gary Saul, and Caryl Emerson, eds. *Mikhail Bakhtin: Creation of a Prosaics.* Stanford, Calif.: Stanford University Press, 1990.

Ol'shevskaia, G. K., and L. N. Godunova, comps. *Muzeinoe delo v SSSR: Istoriia XX veka v muzeinykh ekspozitsiiakh, sbornik nauchnykh trudov* 22. Moscow: Ministerstvo kul'tury SSSR, 1995.

Palmer, Scott W. "Aviation and Cinema in Stalin's Russia: Conformity, Collective, and the Cultural Revolution." Paper presented at the AAASS National Convention, Seattle, Washington, 1997.

Panofsky, Erwin. "Style and Medium in the Motion Pictures." In *Film Theory and Criticism: Introductory Readings,* edited by Gerald Mast, Marshall Cohen, and Leo Braudy, 233–48. 4th ed. Oxford: Oxford University Press, 1992.

Paperno, Irina, and Joan Delaney Grossman. *Creating Life: The Aesthetic Utopia of Russian Modernism.* Stanford, Calif.: Stanford University Press, 1994.

Papernyi, Vladimir. *Kul'tura Dva.* Ann Arbor: University of Michigan Press, 1985. Moscow: Novoe literaturnoe obozrenie, 1996.

Pethybridge, Roger. *The Social Origins of Stalinism.* London: Macmillan, 1974.

Petric, Vlada. *Constructivism in Film: The Man with the Movie Camera, a Cinematic Analysis.* Cambridge: Cambridge University Press, 1987.

———. "Vertov, Lenin and Perestroika: The Cinematic Transposition of Reality." *Historical Journal of Film, Radio and Television* 15, no. 1 (1995): 3–17.

Pipes, Richard. *The Formation of the Soviet Union: Communism and Nationalism, 1917–23.* Cambridge, Mass.: Harvard University Press, 1964.

———. *The Russian Revolution, 1899–1919.* London: Collins Harvell, 1990.

Platonov, Andrei. "Proletarskaia poeziia." *Sobranie sochinenii v trekh tomakh.* Vol. 3 Moscow: Sovetskaia Rossiia, 1985.

Poliakov, Iu. A., and S. V. Drobashenko, eds. *Sovetskaia kinokhronika, 1918–1925 gg. Annotirovnnyi katalog.* Moscow: TsGAKFD (now RGAKFD), 1965.

Propp, Vladimir. *Fol'klor i deistvitel'nost': izbrannye stat'i.* Edited by B. N. Putilova. Moscow: Nauka, 1976.

———. "Folklore and Reality." In *Theory and History of Folklore.* Edited by Anatoly Liberman. Translated by Ariadne Y. Martin and Richard P. Martin. Minneapolis: University of Minnesota Press, 1984.

———. *The Morphology of the Folktale.* American Folklore Society Bibliographical and Special Series 9. Austin: University of Texas Press, 1994.

Rassweiler, Anne D. *The Generation of Power: The History of Dneprostroi.* New York: Oxford University Press, 1988.

Roberts, Graham. *Forward Soviet!* London: I. B. Tauris, 1998.

Robin, Régine. *Socialist Realism: An Impossible Aesthetic.* Translated by Catherine Porter. Stanford, Calif.: Stanford University Press, 1992.

Roosa, Ruth. "The Association of Industry and Trade, 1906–1914." Ph.D. Diss., Columbia University, 1967.

———. "Russian Industrialists and State Socialism." *Soviet Studies* 23 (1972): 395–418.

Rosenberg, William, and Lewis Siegelbaum, eds. *Bolshevik Visions: First Phase of Cultural Revolution in Soviet Russia.* 2 vols. Ann Arbor: University of Michigan Press, 1990.

———, eds. *Social Dimensions of Soviet Industrialization.* Bloomington: Indiana University Press, 1993.

Said, Edward. *Orientalism.* London: Routledge, 1978.

Salishchev, K. A. "Cartography." In *Soviet Geography: Accomplishments and Tasks,* edited by I. P. Gerasimov and G. M. Ignat'ev, 45–52. Translated by Lawrence Ecker. New York: American Geographical Society, 1962.

Sazonova, L. I. "Ideia puti v drevnrusskoi literature." *Russian Literature* 29 (1991): 471–88.

Schivelbusch, Wolfgang. *The Railway Journey: The Industrialization of Time and Space in the Nineteenth Century.* Translated by Ansel Hollo. 2nd ed. Carl Hanser: Munich, 1977. Leamington Spa: Berg, 1986.

Sennett, Richard. *Flesh and Stone: The Body and the City in Western Civilization.* London: Faber and Faber, 1994.

Sepman, I. V., ed. *Friedrikh Ermler: dokumenty, stat'i, vospominaniia.* Leningrad: Iskusstvo, 1974.

Schlögel, Karl. "The Shadow of an Imaginary Tower." In *Naum Gabo and the Competition for the Palace of Soviets, Moscow, 1931–1933.* Berlin: Berlinische Galerie, 1993.

Simmel, Georg. "The Metropolis and Mental Life." In *Simmel on Culture,* edited by David Frisby and Mike Featherstone. London: Sage, 1997.

Sklar, Robert, and Charles Musser, eds. *Resisting Images: Essays on Cinema and History.* Philadelphia: Temple University Press, 1990.

Slezkine, Yuri. *Arctic Mirrors: Russia and the Small Peoples of the North.* Ithaca, N.Y.: Cornell University Press, 1994.

———. "The USSR as a Communal Apartment, or How a Socialist State Promoted Ethnic Particularism." *Slavic Review* 53, no. 2 (1994): 414–52.

Slovar' drevnerusskogo iazyka po pis'mennym pamiat'nikam. 4 vols. St. Petersburg, 1890–1906.

Slovar' sovremennogo russkogo literaturnogo iazyka. 17 vols. Moscow: Izdatel'stvo Akademii Nauk SSSR, 1956–64.

Smith, Anthony. *National Identity.* Harmondsworth: Penguin, 1991.

Soja, Edward. *Postmodern Geographies: The Reassertion of Space in Critical Social Theory.* London: Verso, 1989.

Soja, Edward, and Costis Hadjimichalis. "Between Geographical Materialism and Spatial Fetishim: Some Observations on the Development of Marxist Spatial Analysis." *Antipode: A Radical Journal of Geography* 11 (1979): 3–11.

Sovetskii entsiklopedicheskii slovar'. Moscow: Izdanie sovetskoi entsiklopedii, 1981.

Starr, S. Frederick. "Visionary Town Planning during the Cultural Revolution." In *Cultural Revolution in Russia 1928–31,* edited by Sheila Fitzpatrick, 207–40. Bloomington: Indiana University Press, 1978.

Stepanov, Iu. C. *Konstanty: slovar' russkoi kul'tury (opyt issledovaniia).* Moscow: Shkola iazyki russkoi kul'tury, 1997.

Stein, Gertrude. *Picasso.* London: Batsford, 1938.

Steklov, Vasilii. *V. I. Lenin i elektrifikatsiia.* Moscow: Nauka, 1975.

Stites, Richard. *Revolutionary Dreams: Utopian Vision and Experimental Life in the Russian Revolution.* New York: Oxford University Press, 1989.

———. *Russian Popular Culture: Entertainment and Society since 1900.* Cambridge: Cambridge University Press, 1992.

———, ed. *Culture and Entertainment in Wartime Russia.* Bloomington: Indiana University Press, 1995.

Tarkhanov, Alexei, and Sergei Kavtaradze, eds. *Architecture of the Stalin Era.* New York: Rizzoli, 1992.

Taylor, Richard. "'A Cinema for the Millions': Soviet Socialist Realism and the Problem of Film Comedy." *Journal of Contemporary History* 18, no. 3 (1983): 439–62.

———. *Film Propaganda: Soviet Russian and Nazi Germany.* London: Croom Helm, 1979.

———. *The Politics of the Soviet Cinema 1917–1929.* Cambridge: Cambridge University Press, 1979.

———, ed. *An Eisenstein Reader.* Translated by Richard Taylor and William Powell. London: B. F. I., 1998.

———, ed. *S. M. Eisenstein: Selected Works: Volume 1, Writings, 1922–34.* Translated by Richard Taylor. London: British Film Institute, 1988.

———, ed. *S. M. Eisenstein: Selected Works, Volume 3: Writings, 1934–47.* Translated by William Powell. London: British Film Institute, 1996.

Taylor, Richard, and Derek Spring, eds. *Stalinism and Soviet Cinema.* London: Routledge, 1993.

Taylor, Richard, and Ian Christie, eds. *Eisenstein Rediscovered.* London: Routledge, 1993.

———, eds. *The Film Factory: Russian and Soviet Cinema in Documents 1896–1939.* London: Routledge, 1988.

———, eds. *Inside the Film Factory: New Approaches to Russian and Soviet Cinema.* London: Routledge, 1991.

Taylor, Richard, and Michael Glenny, eds. *S. M. Eisenstein: Selected Works, Volume 2: Towards a Theory of Montage.* Translated by Michael Glenny. London: British Film Institute, 1991.

Toporov, Vladimir. *O mifopoeticheskom prostranstve.* Genova: ECIG, 1994.

———. "Prostranstvo." In *Mifi narodov mira v dvykh tomakh,* edited by S. A. Tokarev, 341. 2 vols. Moscow, 1980–82

Tsivian, Yuri. *Early Cinema in Russia and Its Cultural Reception.* Translated by Alan Bodger. London: Routledge, 1994.

———. *Immaterial Bodies: Cultural Anatomy of Early Russian Films.* University of Southern California Electronic Press, 2001. CD-ROM.

————. *Istoricheskaia retseptsiia kino: kinoatograf v Rossii 1896–1930.* Riga: Zinatne, 1991.

————. "K simvolike poezda v rannem kino." *Trudy po znakovym systemam* 21 (1987): 119–35.

————. *Silent Witnesses: Russian Films 1908–1919.* London: B. F. I., 1989.

Tsivian, Yuri, and Mikhail Iampol'skii. "La poétique d'un text hétérogène: 'Débris d'Empire' de Friedrikh Ermler." *La licorne* 7 (1990): 221–334.

Tucker, Robert. *Stalin as Revolutionary 1879–1929.* London: Chatto, 1974.

Turovskaia, Maia I. "I. A. Pyr'ev i ego musikal'nye komedii. K probleme zhanra." *Kinovedcheskie zapiski* 1 (1988): 111–46.

Ulam, Adam. *A History of Soviet Russia.* New York: Praeger, 1976.

————. *Stalin: The Man and His Era.* Boston: Beacon Press, 1989.

Urry, John. *The Tourist Gaze.* London: Sage, 1990.

Vaiskopf, Mikhail. "Morfologiia strakha." *Novoe literaturnoe obozrenie* 24 (1997): 53–59.

van Baak, Joost. "Continuity in Change: Some Remarks on World Pictures in Russian Literature." In *Signs of Friendship to Honour A. G. F. van Holk,* 365–76. Amsterdam: Rodopi, 1984.

————. "The House in Russian Avant-Garde Prose: Chronotope and Archetype." *Essays in Poetics* 15, no.1 (1990): 1–16.

————. *The Place of Space in Narration. With an Analysis of the Role of Space in I. Babel's 'Konarmia.'* Amsterdam: Rodopi, 1983.

————. "Visions of the North: Remarks on Russian Literary World Pictures." In *Dutch Contributions to the Tenth International Congress of Slavists,* 19–43. Amsterdam: Rodopi, 1988.

Van Den Abbeele, George. *Travel as Metaphor: From Montaigne to Rousseau.* Minneapolis: University of Minnesota Press, 1992.

van Geldern, James, and Richard Stites, eds. *Mass Culture in Soviet Russia: Tales, Songs, Movies, Plays and Folklore, 1917–53.* Bloomington: Indiana University Press, 1995.

Vasmer, Max. *Russisches etymologisches Wörterbuch.* 4 vols. Heidelberg: Indogermanische Bibliothek, 1950–58.

Viola, Lynn. *The Best Sons of the Fatherland: Workers in the Vanguard of Collectivization.* Oxford: Oxford University Press, 1987.

Virilio, Paul. *The Vision Machine.* Translated by Julie Rose. London: B. F. I., 1994.

————. *War and Cinema: The Logistics of Perception.* Translated by Patrick Camiller. London: Verso, 1989.

von Hagen, Mark. "Toward a Cultural and Intellectual History of Soviet Russia in the 1920s: Some Preliminary Directions for a Reevaluation of Politics and Culture." *Revue des études slaves* 68 (1996): 283–303.

Ward, Chris. *Stalin's Russia.* London: Edward Arnold, 1993.

Widdis, Emma. "Borders: The Aesthetic of Conquest in Soviet Cinema of the 1930s." *Journal of European Studies* 30, no. 4 (2000): 353–460.

Willemen, Paul. "On Reading Epstein on Photogénie." *After Image* 10 (1981): 40–47.

Williams, Raymond. *The Country and the City.* New York: Oxford University Press, 1973.

Youngblood, Denise. *Movies for the Masses: Popular Cinema and Soviet Society in the 1920s.* Cambridge: Cambridge University Press, 1992.

————. *Soviet Cinema in the Silent Era: 1919–1935.* Ann Arbor, Mich.: UMI Research, 1985.

Zamiatin, D. N., ed. *Prostranstva Rossii: khrestomatiia po geografii Rossii.* 8 vols. Moscow: Miros, 1994.

Zorkaia, Neia. *Na rubezhe stoletii: U istokov massovogo iskusstva v Rossii, 1900–1910 godov.* Moscow: Nauka, 1976.

Index

Page numbers in italic refer to illustrations.